RETHINKING HERITAGE LANGUAGE EDUCATION

Edited by **Peter Pericles Trifonas** and
Themistoklis Aravossitas

CAMBRIDGE
UNIVERSITY PRESS

CAMBRIDGE
UNIVERSITY PRESS

University Printing House, Cambridge CB2 8BS, United Kingdom

Cambridge University Press is part of the University of Cambridge.

It furthers the University's mission by disseminating knowledge in the pursuit of education, learning and research at the highest international levels of excellence.

Information on this title: education.cambridge.org

© Cambridge University Press 2014

First published 2014

Printed in the United Kingdom by Printondemand-worldwide, Peterborough

A catalogue record for this publication is available from the British Library

Library of Congress Cataloguing in Publication data

Includes bibliographical references and index
ISBN 13-9781107437623 Paperback

CONTENTS

Acknowledgements   v

Notes on contributors   vi

Series Editors' Preface   xi

Introduction *Peter Pericles Trifonas and Themistoklis Aravossitas*
(University of Toronto)   xiii

Chapter 1 Mainstreaming Plurilingualism: Restructuring Heritage Language
Provision in Schools
Jim Cummins (University of Toronto)   1

Chapter 2 Teaching Heritage Language Learners: A Study of Programme
Profiles, Practices and Needs
Maria Carreira (UCLA California State University)   20

Chapter 3 Rethinking Heritage Languages: Ideologies, Identities, Practices and
Priorities in Canada and China
Patricia A. Duff and Duanduan Li (University of British Columbia)   45

Chapter 4 The Place of Heritage Languages in Languages Education in Australia:
A Conceptual Challenge
Angela Scarino (University of South Australia)   66

Chapter 5 Courses in the Language and Culture of Origin and their Impact on
Youth Development in Cultural Transition: A Study Amongst
Immigrant and Dual-Heritage Youth in Switzerland
Elena Makarova (University of Bern)   89

Chapter 6 Language Policies in the Context of Australian Civic Pluralism
Eugenia Arvanitis (University of Patras), Mary Kalantzis and
Bill Cope (University of Illinois)   115

Chapter 7 Communities Taking the Lead: Mapping Heritage Language
Education Assets
Themistoklis Aravossitas (University of Toronto)   141

Chapter 8   Overcoming Challenges of Languages Choice in Heritage Language
Development Amongst Multilingual Immigrant Families
James C. Kigamwa (Indiana University – Purdue University Indianapolis)   167

Chapter 9   The Impact of the CEFR on Canada's Linguistic Plurality:
A Space for Heritage Languages?
Enrica Piccardo (University of Toronto)   183

Chapter 10   Strengthening our Teacher Community: Consolidating a 'Signature
Pedagogy' for the Teaching of Spanish as Heritage Language
María Luisa Parra (Harvard University)   213

Chapter 11   Canada's 'Other' Languages: The Role of Non-Official Languages
in Ethnic Persistence
Jack Jedwab (Association d'études Canadiennes)   237

Chapter 12   Rethinking Heritage Language in a Critical Pedagogy Framework
Panayota Gounari (University of Massachusets)   254

Index   270

ACKNOWLEDGEMENTS

This book is possible because of the support and inspiration of friends and colleagues dedicated to the right of linguistic and cultural diversity. We would like to thank the contributors whose scholarship has enriched our understanding and knowledge of the emerging field of heritage language education, pedagogy and research. This book rests on the work of pioneers who have embraced the challenge of rethinking the relationship between language, culture and identity beyond a simple teaching and learning of language as either 'native' or 'foreign'. By acknowledging the importance of heritage languages and honouring those who have dedicated their lives to preserving the linguistic rights of minority communities, Russell Campbell, Joshua Fishman, Tove Skutnabb-Kangas and Jim Cummins, among others, paved the way for an epistemological shift in language studies from an uncomplicated focus on the search for a 'best method' of teaching towards a recognition of diversity and the socio-political context of language pedagogy and learning in an increasingly multicultural, multilingual world.

We wish to recognise the lifelong scholarly achievement of Michalis Damanakis, founder of the Center of Intercultural and Migration Studies of The University of Crete's Department of Primary Education, for his significant contribution to the field through his exceptional work in the context of Greek Heritage Language Education in the Diaspora.

We would also like to thank Series Editor Michael Evans for his support of the concept for the book, and Paul Sloman and Emily Angus for taking care of the editorial details leading to its publication. Daphne Vlassis generously allowed us to use her artwork for the cover.

Lastly, we are grateful to our families and loved ones: Daphne, Andreas, Matoula, Peirce, Anthi and Yanni.

NOTES ON CONTRIBUTORS

Themistoklis Aravossitas teaches Modern Greek Language and Culture at the Centre for European, Russian and Eurasian Studies of the University of Toronto and at the Department of Languages, Literatures and Linguistics of York University. Currently he is completing a doctorate at the Department of Curriculum Teaching and Learning of the Ontario Institute for Studies in Education of the University of Toronto, where he is specialising in heritage language education (HLE) and Knowledge Media Design. Having served as an elementary school teacher in Europe, he is professionally involved with the International Language Programs (ILP) in Canada at the elementary, secondary and continuing education levels as teacher, administrator and researcher. He participates in several research projects in the field of HLE, mainly concerning teacher and curriculum development, as well as educational applications of new technologies. His research interests include: Language, Culture and Pedagogy; Multilingual Education; Networked Learning and Knowledge Media.

Eugenia Arvanitis is an elected lecturer at the Adult Education Postgraduate Programme at the Hellenic Open University. She has worked for a number of divisions in the Greek Ministry of Education and Religious Affairs and as the co-ordinator of the National Quality Assurance and Evaluation Office in the General Secretariat of Adult Education in Greece. Most recently, she has helped to establish the website www.neamathisi.com, a professional learning framework for school-based teachers' training trailing a set of interactive Web 2.0 tools. She is the author of several research papers and the editor of *Memories of Bonegilla: Recollections of an Insider* and author of *Greek Ethnic Schools in Australia in the late 1990s: Selected Case studies*.

Maria Carreira is Professor of Spanish at California State University, Long Beach, and Co-Director of the National Heritage Language Resource Center at UCLA. She is co-author of four Spanish textbooks including *Sí se Puede*, for Heritage speakers, and *Nexos*, recently adopted by Harvard. She is also Associate Editor of *Hispania* and Chair of the SAT Spanish committee. Her research focuses on Spanish in the US and Spanish as a heritage language. Her recent publications focus on differentiated teaching, assessment in heritage language teaching, community language programmes in Spanish, and the state of Spanish in the US in a capacity-opportunity-desire paradigm. Her forthcoming book *Voces: Growing up Latino in the US* is an annotated collection of writings by Latino youth on their experiences in school, home and their communities of residence.

Bill Cope is a Research Professor in the Department of Educational Policy Studies, University of Illinois, Urbana-Champaign, US, and an Adjunct Professor in the Globalism Institute at RMIT University, Melbourne. He is also a Director of Common Ground Publishing, developing and applying new publishing technologies. He is a former First Assistant Secretary in the Department of the Prime Minister and Cabinet and Director of the Office of Multicultural Affairs. His research interests include theories and practices of pedagogy, cultural and linguistic diversity, and new technologies of representation and communication. He was Research Director then Director of the Centre for Workplace Communication and Culture at the University of Technology, Sydney and RMIT University, Melbourne. He was also involved in a joint Common Ground/RMIT University research initiative, Creator to Consumer in a Digital Age, funded by the Australian Government's Department of Industry, Tourism and Resources. Amongst his recent publications are edited volumes on *The Future of the Book in the Digital Age* and *The Future of the Academic Journal.*

Jim Cummins is Professor in the Modern Languages Center at the Ontario Institute for Studies in Education at the University of Toronto. He has published extensively in the areas of heritage language, bilingualism, language rights and anti-racist pedagogy.

Duanduan Li is Co-Director of the Centre for Research in Chinese Language and Literacy Education and Associate Professor of Chinese Applied Linguistics at the University of British Columbia. Prior to becoming Director of the Chinese Language Program at UBC, a position she held for nine years, she taught in and directed the Chinese language programme in the Department of East Asian Languages and Cultures at Columbia University. Her textbooks, research and publications focus on issues in Heritage versus non-Heritage-Language instruction and learning, work that has been supported by two research grants from the Social Sciences and Humanities Research Council of Canada.

Patricia Duff is Co-Director of the Centre for Research in Chinese Language and Literacy Education and Professor of Applied Linguistics at the University of British Columbia. Her research interests include language socialisation across educational settings, qualitative research methods, and Heritage and international language education (particularly English and Mandarin, for the latter). She has published widely on these topics. Her work has been supported by a number of grants from the Social Sciences and Humanities Research Council of Canada.

Panayota Gounari is Associate Professor of Applied Linguistics at the University of Massachusetts, Boston, where she has taught since 2004. Her research focus is on the role of language in education, in human agency and in social transformation, and the implications for literacy and critical pedagogy. She has co-authored *The Hegemony of English* (2003), and co-edited the *Globalization of Racism* (2005) with Donaldo Macedo, both translated in many languages. More recently, she has co-edited *Critical Pedagogy: A Reader* (with George Grollios, 2010). She has authored numerous articles and book chapters.

Jack Jedwab is currently Executive Director of the Association for Canadian Studies (ACS). He has served as Director of the ACS since 1998, and previously served as Executive Director of the Quebec branch of the Canadian Jewish Congress (1994–8). He graduated with a BA in Canadian History and a minor in Economics, from McGill University, and went on to do an MA and PhD in Canadian History at Concordia University. Between 1983 and 2008, he lectured at McGill University in the Quebec Studies Program and in the Sociology and Political Science departments, as well as at the McGill Institute for the Study of Canada, where he taught courses on official language minorities in Canada and sports in Canada. He is the founding editor of the publications *Canadian Issues* and *Canadian Diversity*.

Mary Kalantzis is Dean of the College of Education at the University of Illinois, Urbana-Champaign, US. Before this, she was Dean of the Faculty of Education, Language and Community Services at RMIT University, Melbourne, Australia, and President of the Australian Council of Deans of Education. She has been a board member of Teaching Australia: The National Institute for Quality Teaching and School Leadership, a Commissioner of the Australian Human Rights and Equal Opportunity Commission, Chair of the Queensland Ethnic Affairs Ministerial Advisory Committee, Vice President of the National Languages and Literacy Institute of Australia and a member of the Australia Council's Community Cultural Development Board. With Bill Cope, she is co-author or editor of a number of books, including *The Powers of Literacy: Genre*

Approaches to Teaching Literacy, 1993; *Productive Diversity*, 1997; *A Place in the Sun: Re-Creating the Australian Way of Life*, 2000; *Multiliteracies: Literacy Learning and the Design of Social Futures*, 2000; *New Learning: Elements of a Science of Education*, 2008, and *Ubiquitous Learning*, 2009.

James Chamwada Kigamwa holds a PhD in Literacy, Culture, and Language Education from Indiana University Bloomington. He has taught courses on Language and Literacy; ESL Assessment, and Multicultural Education. James has research interests in heritage language maintenance, language and literacy practices of immigrant communities in the US, and bilingual education. James is currently a postdoctoral research fellow at the Great Lakes Equity Center in Indiana University-Purdue University Indianapolis (IUPUI).

Elena Makarova is a Senior Researcher and Lecturer at the University of Bern. She studied educational sciences at the National Pedagogical University of Kiev, Ukraine, and at the University of Bern, Switzerland, where she received her PhD in Philosophical and Human Sciences. Her main research interests are acculturation, ethnic identity development, intercultural relations and cultural diversity in education.

María Luisa Parra has a BA in Psychology and a PhD in Hispanic Linguistics. Her areas of expertise are Spanish language development, second language acquisition, Spanish as a heritage language and child bilingual development. She has taught Spanish Language and Culture for over fifteen years. She is currently Senior Preceptor and Course Head of the first-year Spanish programme and the advanced-level course 'Spanish in the Community' at the Department of Romance Languages and Literatures at Harvard. She also has broad experience working closely with immigrant families and children. She was coordinator of the Home-School Connection Programme at the Elliot-Pearson Department of Child Development at Tufts University, where she looked at the various ways in which parents and teachers supported transitions, school adaptation and academic success. In 2008 she continued and expanded her work as a postdoctoral fellow at Stanford University School of Education working with Mexican and African American children attending East Palo Alto public schools.

Enrica Piccardo is Assistant Professor at the Ontario Institute for Studies in Education at the University of Toronto. She has extensive international experience in language teaching and testing. Her publications in different languages (French, English, Italian and German) focus on three main domains of research: the role of creativity and of new technologies in second/foreign language learning, assessment and its role in the curriculum, and language teacher education. She is a specialist of the Common European Framework of Reference for Languages (CEFR) and its impact on language education and has coordinated a large international project of the European Centre for Modern Languages (ECML) funded by the Council of Europe, ECEP (Encouraging the Culture of Evaluation amongst Professionals). She has collaborated as consultant expert to the revision of the Canadian Language Benchmarks and the *Niveaux de compétence linguistique canadiens*. She is also Chief Editor of the scholarly journal *Synergies Europe*.

Angela Scarino is Associate Professor in Applied Linguistics and Director of the Research Centre for Languages and Cultures at the University of South Australia. Her research and publications are in the areas of language learning, language and culture in education, and language assessment. Her experience includes national work in Australia, as well as in Hong Kong, Singapore, Malaysia and New Zealand. She has led a number of research projects focused on intercultural language learning and the assessment of student achievement in learning languages. She is currently the lead writer of the *Shape Paper for Languages in the Australian Curriculum*. She has served as President of the Applied Linguistics Association of Australia and President of the Australian Federation of Modern Language Teachers Associations.

Peter Pericles Trifonas is a Professor at the Ontario Institute for Studies in Education/University of Toronto. His areas of interest include ethics, philosophy of education, cultural studies, literacy and technology. His publications include *Revolutionary Pedagogies: Cultural Politics, Instituting Education, and the Discourse of Theory*, *The Ethics of Writing: Derrida, Deconstruction, and Pedagogy*, *Ethics, Institutions and The Right to Philosophy* (with Jacques Derrida), *Roland Barthes and the Empire of Signs*, *Umberto Eco and Football*, *Pedagogies of Difference*, *Deconstructing the Machine* (with Jacques Derrida), *International Handbook of Semiotics* and *CounterTexts: Reading Culture*.

SERIES EDITORS' PREFACE

The manifold dimensions of the field of teacher education are increasingly attracting the attention of researchers, educators, classroom practitioners and policymakers, while awareness has also emerged of the blurred boundaries between these categories of stakeholders in the discipline. One notable feature of contemporary theory, research and practice in this field is consensus on the value of exploring the diversity of international experience for understanding the dynamics of educational development and the desired outcomes of teaching and learning. A second salient feature has been the view that theory and policy development in this field need to be evidence-driven and attentive to diversity of experience. Our aim in this series is to give space to in-depth examination and critical discussion of educational development in context with a particular focus on the role of the teacher and of teacher education. While significant, disparate studies have appeared in relation to specific areas of enquiry and activity, the *Cambridge Education Research Series* provides a platform for contributing to international debate by publishing within one overarching series monographs and edited collections by leading and emerging authors tackling innovative thinking, practice and research in education.

The series consists of three strands of publication representing three fundamental perspectives. The *Teacher Education* strand focuses on a range of issues and contexts and provides a re-examination of aspects of national and international teacher education systems or analysis of contextual examples of innovative practice in initial and continuing teacher education programmes in different national settings. The *International Education Reform* strand examines the global and country-specific moves to reform education and particularly teacher development, which is now widely acknowledged as central to educational systems development. Books published in the *Language Education* strand address the multilingual context of education in different national and international settings, critically examining among other phenomena the first, second and foreign language ambitions of different national settings and innovative classroom pedagogies and language teacher education approaches that take account of linguistic diversity.

Rethinking Heritage Language Education is a welcome addition to the *Language Education* strand in the series. The book not only articulates insightful rethinking of the theory and practice of heritage language education as a distinctive discipline, related but not identical to its sister disciplines within the second language education spectrum, but also raises important broader questions regarding the interplay of social, linguistic and cultural factors in the teaching and learning contexts of different national educational settings.

Michael Evans and Colleen McLaughlin

1 INTRODUCTION

Peter Pericles Trifonas (University of Toronto)
Themistoklis Aravossitas (University of Toronto)

Rethinking Heritage Language Education brings together emerging and established researchers to negotiate concepts and practices in the multi-dimensional field of heritage language education (HLE), and to investigate the correlation between culture and language from a pedagogic and cosmopolitical point of view. Education in heritage language (HL) is not just a new dimension in the areas of linguistic and/or pedagogic sciences; it is linked to the processes of identity negotiation and cultural inheritance, through language that passes from generation to generation as a tangible legacy of the past that looks forward to a future. Undoubtedly, HLE is a distinct pedagogical and curricular domain that cannot be confused or exhausted within the range of terms such as 'bilingualism' and 'second' or 'foreign language education'. A HL by definition is neither a second nor a foreign language. It is the vehicle whereby the cultural memory of entire peoples is transmitted over time from place to place, from community to community, and from generation to generation. In our contemporary educational reality of ever-expanding and compounding 'multies' ('multilingualism', 'multiculturalism', 'multimodality', 'multiliteracies', and so on), HLs have an important role to play to ensure the balance between coherence and pluralism in societies that have started to realise that diversity is not a disadvantage but an advantage, not exclusively for social and cultural but also for economic reasons.

The term 'heritage language' emerged from multilingual and second language research in Canada at a time when the country chose to integrate multiculturalism amongst its fundamental characteristics as a democracy. Today the heart of academic research and educational applications related to the theory and practice of HLE has begun to expand globally. In the US, it is mainly driven by the dynamics of the Spanish language and its large and diverse speaking and learning population. In Europe, however, the notion of 'plurilingualism' was conceptualised, and to some extent applied, using evaluative vehicles such as the Common European Framework of Reference for Languages (CEFR), to inform innovation in language education both for official and for unofficial or minority tongues. At the same time, in Australia

HLs are not only accepted and recognised for their importance, but through systematic steps are upgraded, entering mainstream education through a redesigning of the national curriculum. Meanwhile, in Asia and Africa, HLs are intergrated socially as cultures and traditions are embedded in voices that claim their own space and their own importance in a diverse language ecology.

In this edited collection, scholars who have contributed to the trajectory and growth of HLE as an autonomous discipline reconsider and enrich their discourse and findings as they draw new lines across the boundaries of research and practice. Both theory and practice in HLE are advanced through research grounded in topics that include: the use of new technologies blended in social and educational networks to advance teaching and learning in HLE; the application of internationally significant frameworks such as the CEFR in designing curricula and streamlining outcomes, competencies, methodologies and levels to reach commonly accepted understandings for HLE practitioners; the incorporation of action research initiatives by teachers who struggle for professional recognition, especially in community-based HLE settings where official support is absent.

The chapters in this book present each contributor's vision or interpretation of what an articulation of HLE entails in communal and global contexts in terms of its possibility as a ground for education. A rethinking of the dimensions of HLE and its pedagogical imperatives in communal and global contexts will enable new directions for a rethinking of the traditional interpretation of language education in relation to principles of educational equity and social justice. *Rethinking Heritage Language Education* addresses social, linguistic and cultural difference in educational contexts in a new way by taking up questions of globalisation, difference, community, identity, democracy, ethics, politics, technology, language rights and cultural politics through the evolving field of HLE. It directs stakeholders such as parents, community leaders, teachers and school administrators, as well as students and researchers, to the issues of linguistic and cultural diversity that have created a new ground for teaching and learning, and can serve as an excellent sourcebook for students and scholars to navigate the extensive literature on linguistic diversity, cultural difference and educational equity through the perspectives of leading theorists in the field of HLE. In doing so, it opens a much-needed new direction with respect to the question of difference, social justice and pedagogy in the new millennium.

In **Mainstreaming Plurilingualism: Restructuring Heritage Language Provision in Schools**, Jim Cummins explores how HL teaching of school-aged students is carried out both within public schools and in community-supported out-of-school programmes. Public school provision occurs in credit courses teaching second/foreign languages (e.g. high school Mandarin courses), bilingual/dual language programmes (e.g. Ukrainian/English programmes in Alberta), and in HL classes administered by school districts but generally taught outside of the normal school day (e.g. Ontario's International Languages Program). In all of these settings, the teaching of HLs is marginalised with respect to funding provision, the number of languages involved, and the number of students who participate. For example, only a handful of languages are taught in second/foreign language classes or in bilingual/dual-language programmes. Within the mainstream classroom, students' knowledge of additional languages has typically been viewed as either irrelevant or as an impediment to the learning of English and overall academic achievement. This situation of 'benign neglect' of students' language competencies within the mainstream classroom has resulted in a significant loss of HL skills in the early grades of school. This chapter articulates directions for challenging this loss of personal, community, and national linguistic and intellectual resources within the mainstream classroom, including the empirical basis and theoretical rationale for using bilingual instructional strategies to acknowledge, build upon and amplify students' linguistic competencies across the curriculum.

In **Teaching Heritage Language Learners: A Study of Programme Profiles, Practices and Needs**, Maria Carreira presents the results of a national survey of post-secondary language programmes that teach HL learners from 27 different languages. The survey identifies three different scenarios where HL learners study their home language: HL classes, mixed classes (classes with HL and Second Language learners), and customised instructional options such as independent studies, internships and tutoring arrangements. Common practices, perspectives and institutional conditions surrounding these scenarios are discussed, along with some innovative solutions to common problems.

In **Rethinking Heritage Languages: Ideologies, Identities, Practices and Priorities in Canada and China**, Patricia A. Duff and Duanduan Li analyse how for the past generation, the politics, ideologies and rhetoric surrounding HLE in Canada have vacillated considerably. If indigenous (i.e. non-immigrant) languages are included, the experiences of Canadians from minority-language backgrounds are all the more complicated and, in some cases, tragic. However, with respect to immigrant HLs, while the commitment of

Canadian parents and communities to the preservation of heritage cultures and languages has generally remained quite strong, particularly in the late 20th century, young children's and adolescents' investments in their ancestral languages have typically been much more ambivalent, conflicted and vulnerable to the pressures of peer (Anglo-) conformity, popular culture and monolingualism. These combined factors usually result in a language shift towards one of the country's dominant languages for first-, second- and third-generation immigrant communities (often leading to deep regret later). In the People's Republic of China, too, language shift from millennia-old indigenous languages is occurring at a fairly rapid rate towards regional and/or national *lingua francas* (major regional varieties of Chinese and/or Mandarin), often from the moment that children enter public school and now sometimes even earlier, within the home. Increasing internal migration, urbanisation, assimilationist policies, and the role of national media and language standardisation, coupled with campaigns supporting mass literacy, language reform and public education since the early 1990s, have accelerated this shift. The tremendous focus on English education as a national linguistic priority has also confounded attempts at the preservation and use of local languages. This chapter examines some of the factors affecting ideologies, identities and educational practices connected with heritage/ancestral languages in these two distinct contexts – and their consequences – based on our research in both countries over the past decade. In particular, the authors focus on examples from regions in Canada and China with large concentrations of minority-language communities, and especially with varieties of Chinese and other Asian languages: Yunnan Province, in southwestern China and British Columbia in western Canada. The chapter also considers some implications for language preservation, recognition and multilingualism.

In **The Place of Heritage Languages in Languages Education in Australia: A Conceptual Challenge**, Angela Scarino examines how the context of globalisation, with the unprecedented scale and speed of movement of people and ideas, languages and cultures, has altered the face of social, cultural and linguistic diversity in societies and in education. 'Super-diversity' is a term intended to capture a level of complexity surpassing anything that many migrant-receiving communities have previously experienced. Learning languages is a part of this complexity. In the field of language learning there is currently an allied reconceptualisation of multilinguality, including manifestations such as multi-competence, trans-languaging and considerations of identity theory. It is in this context that the Australian educational community is developing a new national curriculum, which includes a languages curriculum. Drawing on a brief history of HL learning in Australia and on her experience of contributing to the shaping of the new national curriculum for languages, in this chapter Scarino discusses the complexity of ensuring an adequate place for HLs in the languages education curriculum. It necessitates a process of working against the tendency towards generalisation and standardisation that normally characterises such curriculum developments. Scarino argues that providing for HL learning in contemporary education needs to be understood and addressed as a conceptual challenge.

In **Courses in the Language and Culture of Origin and their Impact on Youth Development in Cultural Transition: A Study Amongst Immigrant and Dual-Heritage Youth in Switzerland**, Elena Makarova traces how the concept of intercultural education in German-speaking European countries promotes the inclusion of courses in the Language and Culture of Origin (LCO) for immigrant youth in the school curriculum of host countries. Such courses are assumed to have positive effects on the development of immigrant youth in the host country. Particularly, it has been suggested that participation in LCO courses increases the self-esteem of immigrant youth, facilitates the development of their bicultural identity and improves their integration in the host society. However, there is a lack of empirical evidence on the nature of the effects of LCO course attendance on the acculturation of immigrant youth and their cultural identity. Accordingly, the aim of the study detailed in the chapter is to examine the impact of immigrant youth's attitudes towards LCO courses and of their attendance of such courses on their acculturation and cultural identity.

In **Language Policies in the Context of Australian Civic Pluralism**, Eugenia Arvanitis, Mary Kalantzis and Bill Cope explain how Australian public discourse on immigration has reflected a wide and changing spectrum of attitudes, from hostility and assimilationist practices to acceptance and encouragement of language and cultural maintenance. Similarly, the presence of multilingualism in Australia has triggered a direct and conscious political response in areas such as education, and has taken on different ideological complexions over time. Languages were seen as the clearest and most evident component of cultural diversity. This chapter partly presents the way in which Australian public discourse on community/migrant/heritage languages has been determined and implemented on the part of government bodies. It documents the changing understanding of language teaching within broader policy parameters. This includes references to broader policy implementation in regard to migrant issues, as language policy and programme development should be regarded as one of the most salient features of a modern post-industrial and highly liberal society and its concomitant plurality. The position of language within a multicultural society has to be interpreted and analysed in terms of power relations and self-determination. It is argued that minority languages have historically been viewed as tools of self-determination and access, pointing to the complex social framework in which communities operate. Language policy, however, cannot be understood only in terms of those vested interests as an important role is played by broader ideological considerations, such as the link between ethnicity and language and the evolution of ethnic relations. The perceived status of language and language policies as a surrogate for ethnicity and the politics of ethnicity on the basis of uniformity and ethnic unity deprives the official planning of a wider understanding of such issues.

In **Communities Taking the Lead: Mapping Heritage Language Education Assets**, Themistoklis Aravossitas details the research project of a community group in Canada that attempts to map its educational assets. Researchers, educators and community representatives collaborate in the study outlined in this chapter using models of ethnolinguistic vitality and language maintenance, blended with Community-Based Research (CBR) principles, to inform the theoretical basis and methodological approach of their quest. Data for the project is collected via an online survey, the archives of partner organisations and interviews with programme operators from HL schools across Canada. The practical phase of the project involves the development of a database to serve as a network hub for teachers, students, parents and programme administrators. The chapter begins with navigation in the field of HLE and looks at the status and challenges of community-based programmes. The discussion focuses on the lack of information around community language schools and the need for immigrant groups to generate support in order to develop their HL programmes. Instead of depending solely on external help, this chapter proposes that communities should locate their educational resources (assets), build networks and form partnerships with organisations interested in investing in the multilingual capital of HL learners. As we follow the path of this Greek CBR initiative in Canada, we visualise the potential for HL retention when stakeholders have a better understanding of the wealth and the capacity hidden within communities that form our multicultural and multilingual mosaic.

In **Overcoming Challenges of Language Choice in Heritage Language Development Amongst Multilingual Immigrant Families**, James Kigamwa clarifies why immigrant families are not generally able to sustain their HLs beyond the third generation (Portes and Schauffler, 1994). Different factors have been attributed to this loss of HLs and the predictable shift towards the use of dominant languages across generations. Amongst African immigrants, language practices that could be precursors of a language shift are observed in first generation immigrant families. This chapter highlights some of the challenges faced by speakers of minority languages in their quest to transmit and maintain their HLs and surfaces some issues that may need rethinking as immigrant families consider strategies for reinvigorating efforts at maintenance of minority languages. Observations from a case study of three families that includes parents, children and a grandparent are shared in this chapter. The observations depict some of the linguistic practices of immigrant families that influence HL development and expose a paradox associated with private and public use of HLs by parents and adult speakers of the HLs. Besides highlighting the language practices of the three families, this chapter also reviews some of the existent literature related to language and language shift. The discussion ends with some suggestions on how to reinvigorate HL development in the homes of language minorities by engaging stories, songs and dance in language learning.

In **The impact of the CEFR on Canada's Linguistic Plurality: A Space for Heritage Languages?** Enrica Piccardo considers why in the recent years Canada has shown a growing interest in the CEFR, published by the Council of Europe in 2001 and widely used all over the European continent and beyond. The interest in the CEFR has moved from academic discussion and feasibility studies to the publication of institutional documents informing language education policies (CMEC 2010). In spite of this, the CEFR seems so far to be implemented exclusively as a standard-setting tool, with a real risk of overlooking its conceptual density and its pedagogical value. In particular, the ground-breaking notion it presents, that of plurilingual competence where languages are interrelated and not just juxtaposed, appears to be completely undervalued. In fact, the particular linguistic landscape of Canada, with two official languages paired with a wealth of aboriginal and HLs, would be the ideal setting for implementation of effective plurilingualism and reconsideration of language education scope and practices. What is at stake is the linguistic capital of future Canadian generations. The adoption of the CEFR has a great potential for increasing real and effective plurilingualism, provided its implementation goes beyond paying lip service to the idea of plurality of languages and includes an awareness that (bio)diversity of languages needs to be nurtured and protected in order to avoid the risk of uniformity and language loss in the time span of a couple of generations. This contribution first presents the notion of plurilingualism in contrast with the myth of pureness of languages. It then analyses in what way the adoption of a plurilingual and pluricultural perspective may foster a paradigm shift in language education. Finally, it questions what specific role HLs can play to benefit from this paradigm shift and in turn enhance awareness of the value of language diversity.

In **Strengthening Our Teacher Community: Consolidating a 'Signature Pedagogy' for the Teaching of Spanish as Heritage Language**, María Luisa Parra looks at why HL courses and programmes for Spanish HL learners are on the rise in the US. However, the theoretical and pedagogical basis for building productive, creative and socially committed learning spaces, where Spanish HL learners can nurture and expand their linguistic and cultural repertoires, is far from being fully developed and established as a common practice in language departments. In this chapter Parra argues that, given the demographic changes brought by Latinos, this is a crucial moment to reflect critically on and rethink the goals of the profession of Spanish HL teachers. Such rethinking should be framed in terms of 1) the theoretical and pedagogical body of knowledge that still needs to be developed; 2) the limited and constrained circumstances for research under which faculty in the field of Spanish as HL can work to advance such knowledge; and 3) the steps still needed to take in order to become an effective community of practitioners and researchers. The ultimate goal is to develop more productive theoretical approaches and innovative curricula for teaching Spanish heritage speakers.

In **Canada's 'Other' Languages: The Role of Non-Official Languages in Ethnic Persistence**, Jack Jedwab maintains that analysts of immigrant integration in Canada have paid insufficient attention to the retention of languages other than English or French and the degree to which such languages are an important marker of identity. The condition of such languages has often been relegated to the study of ethnicity in Canada and, too frequently, the preservation of such languages is seen as an impediment to the adoption of an official language. Canada's 2011 census revealed that there is an ever-widening diversity of languages other than English or French. This chapter employs census data to give insight into the relationship between knowledge and use of official and non-official languages, providing a detailed statistical overview of Canada's non-official languages and tracing their evolution over the past four decades. On the basis of the statistical portrait, observations will be made about the retention prospects for the ten most widely known non-official languages.

In **Rethinking Heritage Language in a Critical Pedagogy Framework**, Panayota Gounari builds on a critical discussion of how HLs and HL speakers are discussed in the existing literature in North America. A brief review of the literature on HL points to a widespread concern for the nomenclature and for the ways in which it positions subjects, objects and processes in the educational arena. There is, however, much more in the name than the simple choice of words; these labels produce real or constructed subjectivities and inform material practices as well as pedagogies. In this context, there are two questions that critical researchers, educators, policymakers and other stakeholders must answer. First, how do we talk about students who negotiate more than one language in their lives in the current educational landscape? What are the referents and representations for the terms 'bilingual' and 'heritage' and how does language choice label the subjects of the educational process in particular ways? Second, how can we reconceptualise education for bilingual students through a critical pedagogy framework? Gounari explores this second question in the context of critical pedagogy as an emancipatory political theory of education. Critical educators need to take seriously the role of language in either enabling oppressed students to come to subjectivity and partake in the material resources and opportunities as the mainstream does or shut them out of these. This is not to suggest that English is automatically a vehicle for social mobility regardless of the larger socioeconomic structural changes. It rather means that engagement in rigorous analyses will unveil the intimate relationship between language, power, political economy and ideology, and the ensuing pedagogical and social consequences.

1 MAINSTREAMING PLURILINGUALISM: Restructuring Heritage Language Provision in Schools

Jim Cummins (University of Toronto)

This chapter argues that mainstream educators must share in the responsibility to support students who speak a heritage language (HL) to maintain and further develop their linguistic abilities. Typically, educators in Canada and elsewhere do not view the development of students' HL skills as part of their job mandate. They are responsible for teaching the official curriculum and, for the most part, HLs are not included in that curriculum aside from a small number of languages taught by specialist teachers for credit at high-school level. The argument that there is an *educational* responsibility to support the language development of students derives from the premise that schools should teach the 'whole child'. When educators choose to ignore the linguistic competencies that students bring to school, they are also choosing to be complicit with the societal power relations that devalue the linguistic and cultural capital of their students. In other words, they become part of a societal system that squanders the human capital represented by the plurilingual resources of students and communities. Simply put, a student who emerges from school fluent and literate in his or her home language in addition to English and/or French is more *educated* than a student who loses his or her home language competence in the process of acquiring English and/or French. Schools that fail to promote students' linguistic talents are also failing to fully educate them.

This argument is immediately confronted by the feasibility issue. Teachers may have students in their classrooms from multiple linguistic backgrounds – how can they possibly teach these languages, none of which they themselves speak, to their students? This issue is addressed in the sections that follow with specific reference to initiatives taking place across Canada, where educators and university researchers have collaborated to position students' home languages as a cognitive and social resource, thereby motivating students to view their linguistic talents in a positive, rather than a negative, way.

In the next section, I clarify the terms 'heritage language' and 'plurilingualism' and briefly sketch the context of HL provision in different Canadian provinces.

Terminology

Heritage language

As it has been used in the Canadian context, the term 'heritage language' usually refers to all languages other than the two official languages (English and French), the languages of First Nations (Native) and Inuit peoples, and the languages of the Deaf community (American Sign Language; ASL, and *langue des signes québécoise*; LSQ). However, a variety of other terms have also been used and these terms reflect broader struggles around status, identity, and rights of societal groups. The terms 'ancestral', 'ethnic', 'immigrant', 'international', 'minority', 'non-official', 'third' (after English and French), and 'world' have all been used at different times and in different contexts. The term used in Quebec is *langues d'origine* ('languages of origin'). In other countries the term 'community languages' has been used (e.g. Australia, New Zealand, the United Kingdom) and the term 'mother tongue' is also common in some contexts.

The term 'heritage language' came into widespread use in 1977 with the establishment of the Heritage Languages Program in the province of Ontario. Funded by the provincial government for the past 35 years, this programme provides support for the teaching of HL for up to two-and-a-half hours per week outside of the regular five-hour school day. All students can enrol in these programmes regardless of the specific language spoken at home. The term 'heritage language' was intended to acknowledge that these languages constitute important aspects of the heritage of individual children and communities and are worthy of financial support and recognition by the wider society. In the early 1990s, the term was changed to 'international languages' by the Ontario provincial government, reflecting misgivings amongst ethnocultural communities that the notion of 'heritage' entailed connotations of learning about past traditions rather than acquiring language skills that have significance for the overall educational and personal development of children. The term 'international languages' was intended to communicate that, in an era of globalisation, these languages were highly relevant to business and cultural exchanges and had economic as well as 'heritage' value.

Indigenous communities have resisted attempts to include their languages within the categories of 'heritage' or 'community' languages on the grounds that as 'First Nations,' the status of their languages is very different to the status of immigrant languages. Deaf communities also resisted having American Sign Language (ASL) taught as just another HL and argued successfully in the early 1990s for the institution of ASL as a language of instruction within a bilingual/bicultural programme in the provincial schools for the deaf. Thus, definitions of 'heritage language' remain dynamic rather than static, reflecting the contested cultural and political terrain to which the term refers.

Currently, HL teaching to school-aged students in Canada is carried out within three major educational contexts: public schools, private or independent schools, and in community-supported out-of-school programmes. Public school provision occurs in credit courses teaching second/foreign languages (e.g. high-school Mandarin courses), bilingual/dual-language programmes (e.g. Spanish/English programmes in Alberta), and in HL classes administered by school districts but generally taught outside of the normal school day (e.g. Ontario's International Languages Program).

Private or independent school provision is most obvious in the provinces of Alberta and Quebec where schools established by ethnocultural communities are funded by the province (typically around 80% of per-pupil costs) subject to these schools following provincial guidelines with respect to curricular content and language of instruction (typically the HL can be used for 40–50% of instructional time in these schools). In other provinces, private bilingual schools (e.g. Hebrew Day Schools) are not subsidised by the province.

Finally, community groups across Canada offer HL teaching to members of their linguistic and cultural communities. These programmes typically take place on weekends and are sometimes coordinated with provincially supported programmes (e.g. Ontario's International Languages Program). In the past, the federal government provided some funding to support these community-operated programmes but that support ended in the early 1990s.

Plurilingualism

The Council of Europe elaborated the construct of 'plurilingualism' to refer to the dynamically integrated and intersecting nature of bilingual and plurilingual individuals' linguistic repertoires, which include unevenly developed competencies in a variety of languages, dialects and registers (Beacco et al. 2010; Cenoz and Gorter 2013; Coste, Moore and Zarate 2009; Piccardo

2013). The Council of Europe distinguishes between 'plurilingualism' and 'multilingualism':

> Plurilingualism is the ability to use more than one language – and accordingly sees languages from the standpoint of speakers and learners. Multilingualism, on the other hand, refers to the presence of several languages in a given geographical area, regardless of those who speak them. (Beacco et al. 2010, 16)

This distinction is less common in other contexts (e.g. North America) where the term 'multilingualism' tends to be used inclusively to refer to both individual and societal linguistic diversity. For the purposes of this chapter, the Council of Europe's distinction between 'plurilingualism' and 'multilingualism' is retained.

Context

Four phases in relation to educational policies regarding children's home languages can be identified in the Canadian context:

1. Pre-1971: Social policy outside of Quebec was characterised by 'Anglo-conformity' and the active suppression of languages other than English and French in school. Minority francophone communities were also frequently denied access to French language instruction in school.

2. 1971–mid-1980s: The 1971 federal policy of multiculturalism within the framework of English and French as official languages gave rise to positive multicultural rhetoric, but was still accompanied by more subtle forms of language suppression (e.g. advising parents to switch to English in the home).

3. Mid-1980s–mid-2000s: This period was characterised by benign neglect of students' languages. Maintenance of home languages was seen as an issue for the parents rather than the school, and implicit 'English-only zone' policies continued to operate in schools.

4. Mid-2000s–current: There has been a small-scale shift towards pro-active support within schools to enable students to maintain and take pride in their languages (e.g. writing and publishing of bilingual books, projects carried out in both first language (L1) and English, and so on). Although still in its infancy, the principles underlying this shift have begun to gain

traction as a result of collaborations between university and school-based researchers/educators. The pedagogical principles underlying this development have been articulated by different researchers and concrete instructional strategies have been implemented in classrooms (e.g. Armand, Sirois and Ababou 2008; Chumak-Horbatsch 2012; Cummins and Early 2011; Marshall and Toohey 2010; Naqvi et al. 2012).

The Canadian context is complex because education is under provincial jurisdiction and thus different policies and provisions in relation to HL exists in different provinces. To illustrate the fact that provincial and school board policies currently span the range of the four phases sketched above, policies and provision in three provinces are briefly outlined.

In 1971, Alberta became the first province to legalise languages other than English or French as mediums of instruction in the public school system. Two years later, the Edmonton Public School Board introduced the English-Ukrainian and English-German bilingual programmes at the Kindergarten level (Cummins and Danesi 1990). Currently Edmonton has 50/50 English/HL bilingual programmes in American Sign Language, Arabic, Mandarin, German, Hebrew, Spanish and Ukrainian. Calgary operates similar bilingual programmes in Spanish, Mandarin and German. The Spanish programme has grown significantly in recent years and currently serves more than 3000 students.

In a document entitled *Language Education Policy for Alberta* (1988), the Alberta Government made explicit its orientation to the multilingual reality of the province:

> The government of Alberta . . . recognizes and supports a variety of languages other than English and French. These languages are used to fulfill a wide range of social, cultural, economic and educational purposes. They are vehicles of communication for many Albertans and the first language of many children in Alberta. The linguistic pluralism of Alberta is a valuable resource that enriches our cultural and intellectual lives and has potential for use in the international context. (Language Education Policy for Alberta 1988, 17)

Unlike Alberta, it is illegal in Ontario for public school boards to offer HL bilingual programmes except on a transitional basis to help students in the early stages of acquiring the language of mainstream instruction. The International Languages Program, instituted in 1977 (at that time as the Heritage Languages Program), serves approximately 100000 students usually in after-school or weekend contexts but its effectiveness in promoting HL development is considerably less than in the more intensive bilingual programmes operating in Alberta and elsewhere in western Canada (Cummins and Danesi 1990).

Ontario legislation permits the use of HL for short-term transitional purposes in order to help students acquire proficiency in the dominant language of instruction (i.e. English in most cases). Transitional bilingual programmes in Italian, Cantonese and Portuguese were offered in the Toronto area during the 1970s, and more recently an Arabic/English programme has been offered in the city of Windsor and a Mandarin/English programme in Hamilton. Both of these programmes have been evaluated as successfully meeting their objectives (Cummins et al. 2011a, 2011b). Despite spending about 50% of the instructional time through Arabic or Mandarin, which enabled students to develop literacy in those languages, students' English literacy skills developed at least as well as those of comparison groups.

Despite occasional pressure from community groups, the Ontario government has shown little interest in changing the legislation to permit 'enrichment' bilingual programmes (which aim to promote bilingualism and biliteracy) in addition to transitional programmes. The issue was briefly considered in the *Report of the Royal Commission on Learning* (1994), which was established by a left-of-centre provincial government in the early 1990s to review all aspects of educational provision. The report acknowledged the range of submissions they received supporting an amendment to the Education Act to permit HLs to be used as mediums of instruction and they also acknowledged that enrichment bilingual programmes were in operation in British Columbia, Alberta, Saskatchewan and Manitoba. However, they went on to note:

> We do not recommend a change in Ontario's legislation with respect to languages of instruction at this time. We strongly support the use of other languages as a transitional strategy, which is already permitted . . . We also support a learning system that places more value on languages as subjects, and we hope that many more students will learn third (and fourth) languages, and take courses in them at secondary and post-secondary levels . . . But we are very concerned that all students in Ontario be truly literate in one of the official languages. In our view, the school system is obliged to help students function at a high level in English or French, and to gain a reasonable knowledge of the other official language. We appreciate the value of the existing, optional International (formerly Heritage) Language programme, elementary, but we are not prepared to go well beyond that by suggesting that students be educated in an immersion or bilingual

programme in any one of a vast number of non-official languages. (Report of the Royal Commission on Learning 1994, 106–7)

The commissioners' failure to engage with the research evidence on this issue is, unfortunately, very obvious. They imply that students who enrol in a bilingual programme involving English and a HL (such as the Alberta programmes outlined above) will fail to become 'truly literate' in English or French despite the fact that there is not a shred of evidence from the Alberta programmes or any other bilingual programme for minority group students to support this assumption (Cummins and Danesi 1990). They raise the spectre of demands for bilingual programmes from speakers of a 'vast number of non-official languages' despite the fact that the demand for HL bilingual programmes both in the Prairie provinces and in Ontario has been modest.

In Quebec, the government provides funding for the Programme d'enseignement des langues d'origine (PELO), which was originally introduced in 1977. The website of the Commission Scolaire de Montréal (CSDM) expresses the rationale for this programme as follows:

> *Le Programme d'enseignement des langues d'origine (PELO) améliore les conditions d'apprentissage du français et la réussite éducative des élèves en utilisant les langues d'origine. Le PELO permet aux élèves de faire des transferts d'une langue à l'autre, d'une culture à l'autre.*
>
> ('The Heritage Language Instruction Programme uses students' home languages as a means of supporting them in learning French and succeeding academically. This programme enables students to transfer knowledge and skills from one language to the other and from one culture to the other.')

It is worth noting that this rationale focuses on the home language as a resource for learning French and overall academic success. Historically, as in most other provinces, Quebec schools have provided little encouragement to students to use their home languages within the school. However, in recent years, some school boards have imposed formal prohibitions against the use of any language other than French in school corridors and playgrounds. For example, in November 2011, the CSDM, whose school population includes 47% of students whose home language is neither English nor French, mandated that all students use only French throughout the school. As reported in an article in the Quebec newspaper *Le Devoir*, this policy was opposed by Françoise Armand, a professor at the University of Montreal:

*L'exclusion des autres langues est mise en lien avec l'apprentissage du français.
C'est plutôt inquiétant', soutient-elle. 'D'autant que la recherche menée au cours
des 50 dernières années indique tout le contraire.* (Gervais 2012)

('The exclusion of other languages is linked to the learning of French. It is rather
disturbing', she suggested. 'Especially since research conducted during the past
50 years demonstrates the opposite reality.')

The article went on to document Professor Armand's view that in an era of
globalisation this policy reflects a simplistic and outdated view of language
learning. It also reported that the CSDM justified the policy on the grounds
that, in a survey of parents it conducted (two-thirds of whom were from diverse origins), 70% were in agreement that students should be required to
speak French throughout the school.

The 86 comments on this article were predominantly in favour of the
CSDM's policy to restrict the use of any languages other than French in
schools. This ambivalence and insecurity in relation to the perceived threat
that linguistic and cultural diversity poses to the integrity of the province
is also reflected in the Quebec government's proposed Charter of Quebec
Values of 2013 that would prohibit the wearing of overt and conspicuous
religious symbols (e.g. Muslim head scarves) by those offering or receiving
public services (including education). Initial polls showed 57% support for
the Charter amongst Quebeckers.

In short, across Canada, the only province that has made any attempt to
develop and seriously implement a coherent and evidence-based set of policies in relation to HL is Alberta. This fact is surprising to many people because Alberta is also widely regarded as the most conservative of Canadian
provinces (see Cummins and Danesi 1990, for discussion of the origins and
motivations behind Alberta's HL bilingual programmes). The federal government has opted out of any involvement in relation to HL since the early
1990s (partly because education is not within the jurisdiction of the federal
government). Thus, contrary to the image it projects globally as a leader in
language education, Canadian policies and educational practices in relation
to HLs are largely incoherent, with minimal political will (except in Alberta
and, to a lesser extent, the other Prairie provinces) to pursue imaginative
initiatives except when they serve the interests of the English and French
dominant groups. Obviously, the lack of political will to engage with this
sphere of public policy reflects the lack of sustained political pressure from
the general public and ethnocultural groups to implement effective policies.

The absence of leadership and vision in the political arena in relation to HL does not make these languages disappear. In major urban centres across Canada (e.g. Toronto, Vancouver, Montreal, Calgary), close to 50% of students speak a HL at home, reflecting more than 20 years of high levels of immigration (approximately 250000 newcomers have arrived annually during this period). During the past decade, educators and university-based researchers have collaborated in contexts across Canada to explore and document ways in which students' home languages might be incorporated into mainstream educational provision. The next section reviews some of this research (organised by province) that has attempted to position HLs as a linguistic, cognitive and cultural resource for individual students, their families and the society as a whole.

Quebec

The ÉLODiL project (*Éveil au Langage et Ouverture à la Diversité Linguistique* – Awakening to Language and Opening up to Linguistic Diversity)[1] has developed a variety of classroom activities to develop students' awareness of language and appreciation of linguistic diversity. This project has been undertaken both in Montreal, by Dr Françoise Armand, Université de Montréal, and in Vancouver, by Dr Diane Dagenais, Simon Fraser University (Armand and Dagenais 2005, 2012; Armand, Sirois and Ababou 2008). The overall goal of the project is to contribute to the development of inclusive multilingual and multicultural societies by raising awareness about languages and the diversity of people who speak those languages. The specific activities are designed to stimulate students' interest in linguistic diversity, to develop their auditory discrimination abilities and to acknowledge and legitimise the linguistic knowledge of allophone students.

Armand and Dagenais (2012) describe one illustrative activity as follows:

> Dans l'activité 'À la découverte de mon quartier', des élèves de Montréal découvrent leur quartier et les langues qui y sont présentes, ainsi que le quartier d'élèves d'une classe située dans un autre contexte linguistique et géographique, à Vancouver. Chaque classe découvre, au moyen d'une vidéo ou d'une affiche, le quartier de l'autre classe. Les élèves identifient les différences et ressemblances entre les deux environnements, ce qui les amène à réfléchir sur les origines de la présence de la diversité culturelle et linguistique dans les deux contextes (présence autochtone, flux migratoires, etc.). (Armand and Dagenais 2012)

('In the activity "Discovering my neighborhood", students in Montreal explore their neighborhood and the languages that are present in it, together with the neighborhood of students from a class situated in another linguistic and geographic context, namely Vancouver. Each class discovers by means of a video or a poster the neighborhood of the other class. Students identify similarities and differences between the two environments, which leads them to reflect on the origins of the linguistic and cultural diversity present in the two contexts (indigenous presence, migratory waves, etc.).')

Other activities incorporated in ÉLODiL include:

- In the 'animal communication' activity, students become conscious of the fact that different languages reproduce animal sounds in different ways. The activity invites allophone students to demonstrate how different animal sounds (e.g. cocks, frogs, dogs, cats, etc.) are reproduced in their languages.
- The 'languages in contact' activity explores the linguistic consequences of the contact amongst speakers of different languages over the course of history. These contacts have been brought about through trade, colonialism, slavery etc.). Languages represented in the class are categorised according to their language families and then students research why and how these languages evolved and the relationships that emerged between different languages.

Armand and Dagenais (2012) conclude on the basis of their research that the incorporation of students' languages into mainstream curriculum promotes positive orientations amongst both students and teachers in regard to linguistic diversity and also enhances students' metalinguistic awareness and appreciation of their own linguistic talents.

Ontario

Several projects carried out in the Greater Toronto Area (GTA) over the past decade have demonstrated the feasibility of incorporating students' home languages into mainstream instruction in productive ways. We focus on three of these projects.

The Dual-Language Showcase

This initiative emerged in the context of a collaboration between two elementary schools in the Peel District Board of Education and researchers at York University and University of Toronto (Schecter and Cummins 2003).

The Dual-Language Showcase was created by educators at Thornwood Public School in the Peel District School Board to demonstrate the feasibility of enabling elementary grades students who were learning English as an additional language to write stories in both English and their home languages (Chow and Cummins 2003). In some cases, students wrote the stories initially in English in the context of classroom instruction and then worked with their parents to translate the stories into the home language. In other cases, students who were newcomers or very much dominant in L1 wrote the stories initially in L1 and then worked with teachers and/or parents to translate the story into English. These dual-language texts in 20 languages have been published on the school's website.[2]

The Multiliteracies Project

The Multiliteracies project involved a series of collaborations between educators and researchers Dr Margaret Early at the University of British Columbia in Vancouver and Dr Jim Cummins at the University of Toronto.[3] Drawing on the construct of 'multiliteracies' (New London Group 1996), the projects focused on broadening conceptions of literacy within schools with respect both to modality and language. According to the New London Group, if literacy pedagogy is to be effective, it must take into account, and build upon, the multilingual competencies that students bring to school and also expand the traditional definitions of literacy beyond the linear text-based reading and writing of western schooling. The projects carried out in the Greater Toronto Area focused on enabling bilingual and newcomer students to use their home languages as cognitive and academic resources within the classroom. This focus continues with ongoing collaborative projects involving educators and university researchers (e.g. Stille and Cummins 2013).

The potential of teaching for transfer across languages can be illustrated in the instructional practice of teacher Lisa Leoni who encouraged her Grades 6–8 English Language Learners (ELL) to carry out projects and write stories using both English and their home languages. In one example, three students from Pakistan wrote a 20-page book entitled *The New Country* in both English and Urdu, which was based on their own experiences of immigrating from Pakistan to Canada.[4] Two of the Grade 7 students (Kanta and Sulmana) had been in Canada since Grade 4 and were reasonably fluent in both English and Urdu. The third, Madiha, had arrived only six weeks before the writing project started and had minimal knowledge of English (see Cummins and Early 2011). Writing the dual-language book enabled Madiha to participate fully in a cognitively challenging project that was organised in such a way that she could build on her prior knowledge and use her L1 as a cognitive tool. The three students planned the narrative initially in Urdu and decided on the content and illustrations of each page. Then they wrote the initial version in English and discussed it with their teacher. After making changes based on their teacher's feedback, they proceeded to translate the story into Urdu. We focus here on comments from the students that illustrate how the validation of their home language within the mainstream classroom made them more conscious of language itself and increased their motivation to continue to develop that language:

> *Kanta:* It helped me a lot to be able to write it in two languages and especially for Madiha who was just beginning to learn English because the structure of the two languages is so different. So if you want to say something in Urdu it might take just three words but in English to say the same thing you'd have to use more words. So for Madiha it helped the differences between the two languages become clear . . .

> The roles came automatically when we were deciding on what to do. Sulmana really knew how to write well in English and Urdu but she didn't really know how to translate back and forth, so I did that pretty easily, and then there was Madiha who had a really good Urdu vocabulary since she was new, so she started telling us how to say different things that we were writing more accurately, and we started telling each other our experiences and I started translating. Sulmana started writing, and Madiha started helping us with the vocabulary and the order of the grammar.

> *Sulmana:* When we were working on *The New Country* I felt really good and I wanted to write more stories afterward. When I was doing it I was really happy. It was fun to be able to write in both languages and to work on a project with my friends, and I really liked having the chance to write in both languages and to improve my Urdu. It was my first experience translating English to Urdu so we worked together because I had forgotten many of the words in the last three years, so my vocabulary improved a lot too. I had to ask my Mom a lot of words when we were writing it in Urdu but also before that, when I realised that we were going to be writing it in both languages, I went home from that day and started reading more books in Urdu at home because I hadn't been doing that so much. I had forgotten some words and I wanted my writing to make sense.

These comments illustrate how two-way transfer across languages is stimulated by dual-language writing projects in which students invest their identities. For Sulmana, her L1 became relevant again as a language of schooling and a language of creativity and, as a consequence, her desire to continue to develop that language increased significantly.

Linguistically Appropriate Practice (LAP)

LAP is an approach to working with preschool and primary-grade immigrant-background children pioneered by Dr Roma Chumak-Horbatsch (2012) at Ryerson University in Toronto. LAP consists of both an educational philosophy and a set of concrete instructional activities that builds upon children's home language and literacy experiences to encourage them to use the language in the classroom, take pride in their bilingualism, and continue to develop it as they are acquiring fluency and literacy in the dominant language of instruction. Chumak-Horbatsch articulates how the basic assumptions of LAP are different from the predominant 'benign neglect' orientation to children's plurilingual realities:

> LAP is an inclusive approach to working with immigrant children. It looks at them differently – not simply as learners of the classroom language but as bilinguals in the making. The starting point for LAP is that immigrant children have two language environments – the home and the classroom. As a result, they have dual language and literacy needs. (Chumak-Horbatsch 2012, 51)

Chumak-Horbatsch describes almost 50 different LAP activities, two of which are summarised here for illustrative purposes.

Activity 2.18: Home Language Websites
Many home language websites and video clips especially created for children are available on the Internet. Invite parents to spend classroom time visiting these websites with children who share the same home languages. Prepare a schedule for parental visits and computer use. (Chumak-Horbatsch 2012, 123)

Activity 5.2: Story Time
The language centre is a good place for story time. As you read books in the classroom language, invite children to provide home language translations for single words and phrases. (e.g. Azin, how do you say 'water' in your language?). Initially, children may hesitate, but when they understand that their home languages have a place in the classroom, they will eagerly contribute and participate. Invite parents and community members to come to the language centre to share stories and provide translations. (Ibid., 131)

LAP activities were piloted in a number of Toronto area preschool settings and, in the 2013/14 school year, it is being implemented in a variety of kindergarten classes in the Toronto District School Board.

Alberta

The Dual-Language Reading Project

Research conducted by Dr Rahat Naqvi of the University of Calgary and colleagues on the Calgary Board of Education has documented the impact of teachers and community members reading dual-language books to students in both linguistically diverse schools and in the Calgary Board of Education's Spanish-English bilingual programme.[5] The goal of these projects was to explore how the presence of multiple languages in a class could serve as a bridge, rather than a barrier, between different cultures and ethnicities. The dual-language books typically have English on one page and the other language on the facing page. The teacher reads the English text to the students and a guest reader proficient in the other language then reads the same page in the second language. Guest readers can be parents, grandparents, community volunteers, older students or graduate students.

The project demonstrated how teachers and volunteer readers who speak different languages can build on the linguistic and cultural resources of learners in the early grades to help them gain metalinguistic awareness and pride in their cultural background, as well as develop identities as confident and capable learners. The use of dual-language books positioned multilingualism as a normal and positive reality within the school and challenged the implicit 'English-only zone' assumptions of students, parents and teachers. Additionally, the quantitative research outcomes indicated that the use of dual-language books facilitated the language and literacy development of students who speak the languages targeted in these books while not in any way hindering the literacy development of students who speak only English (Naqvi et al. 2012).

The project also established 'The Dual-language Book Database' to provide educators, parents and others easy access to available dual-language resources. The database has more than 2300 book titles in over 40 languages.[6]

British Colombia

At Simon Fraser University in British Columbia, Dr Diane Dagenais and Dr Kelleen Toohey have collaborated for many years with educators in the implementation of projects focused on developing students' awareness of language and promoting their multilingual and multiliteracy skills. This work has resulted in the website www.scribjab.com, which is described as follows: 'ScribJab is a website and iPad application for children (aged 10–13) to read and create digital stories (text, illustrations and audio recordings) in multiple languages (English, French and other non-official languages). *ScribJab* creates a space for children to communicate about their stories, and come to an enhanced appreciation of their own multilingual resources.'

Marshall and Toohey (2011) document an intergenerational literacy project that involved Grades 4 and 5 students from Punjabi, Hindi and Malay linguistic home backgrounds who interviewed and audio-recorded their grandparents telling stories about some aspect of their childhoods. They describe the project as follows:

> The stories varied. Some elders told narratives about particular incidents in their young lives; others provided reminiscences that were not so easily translatable into a normative school notion of 'story,' which included setting, characters, and plot. Initially, Suzanne [the teacher] asked the children to take some *part* of their grandparents' recording and translate that into English and then turn that part into a *story*, with plot, setting, characters, and so on. Some of the children found it easy to select an incident from the raw recordings that translated into the kind of story Suzanne envisioned, but others found it difficult, as their grandparents' narratives were more in the form of memories than a linear life story. (Marshall and Toohey, 225–6)

The students typed up the stories on the computer and then illustrated them. They then translated the stories back into their grandparents' L1. Some students were literate in the L1 and so could carry out this task independently. Those who were not literate in the L1 got handwritten translations from their parents or grandparents, or from a research assistant working on the project. Finally, students recorded themselves reading their stories in both English and their L1 and made these available on CDs that were included with the hardcopy story.

Marshall and Toohey highlight both the successes of the project and also the difficult questions it raises about the nature of the curriculum and the lack of critical literacy practices in most school contexts:

> While modest, this dual-language project, designed to draw on the funds of knowledge in a community, was successful on many levels. The children produced new hybrid semiotic resources for the school – dual-language books in a resolutely monolingual school – and they provided representations of the usually invisible and seldom talked about issues at school such as historical events in India and religious conflict. The project stimulated discussions amongst the children about why Punjabi was not taught in a school where 73% of the children came to school speaking the language and why there were not more dual-language resources

in the school. These results are important and challenge dominant schooling practices. The books the children created also challenged normative ideas about public schooling by telling violent stories and talking explicitly about religious difference as well as creating and using multilingual texts not 'approved' by curricular goals or a district committee for content. (Ibid., 238)

However, they note that the project was seen by teachers, parents and students as 'not really school' and the pedagogical potential of the stories to promote critical literacy was not actively pursued in the classroom:

Bringing this critical consciousness into dialogue with others who might feel or think differently is what education is supposed to be about. It is important to try to create some kinds of critical pedagogies around these funds of knowledge projects. Otherwise, we run the risk of keeping the institutional violence of schooling in place through literacy and language practices that pay only lip service to the lives and experiences of children and their families. (Ibid., 238)

Conclusion

This sampling of illustrative projects that are being carried out in mainstream classrooms across Canada demonstrate the feasibility of enabling students from HL backgrounds to use their L1 as a cognitive and academic resource. They also show how parental and community engagement with the school can be fostered when the pedagogical space is expanded to include students' plurilingual realities.

The projects also illustrate the fact that mainstream educational goals are being addressed when students use their L1 as a tool for intellectual enquiry. For example, it is generally acknowledged that instruction for Second Language (L2) learners must 'scaffold meaning' to facilitate L2 comprehension and production. In Madiha's case, the 20-page dual-language story she wrote with her friends, *The New Country*, could not have been accomplished without the mediation of her L1. Paradoxically, before she wrote the story, she could not have read the English version, but after she had written it, she could also read and understand it.

Most educators also acknowledge the importance of activating students' background knowledge and connecting instruction both to their lives and the funds of knowledge in their communities. Much of students' experience outside the school is encoded in their L1 and thus it makes sense to acknowledge the L1 as a powerful tool for learning, as demonstrated in the Marshall and Toohey (2011) study.

All of the projects described expand students' awareness of language by bringing the two languages into productive contact with each other, either through reading dual-language books, writing dual-language books, or activities focused directly on building metalinguistic awareness (e.g. the ÉLODiL project in Montreal and the LAP project in Toronto).

Finally, identity emerges as a fundamental component of all of these projects. A major reason why so many students from HL backgrounds choose not to pursue the learning of that language is that they internalise the (usually implicit) negative messages they receive in the school and wider society in relation to their plurilingualism. When schools treat the cultural knowledge and linguistic talents of plurilingual students with benign neglect, essentially asking students to leave this knowledge at the schoolhouse door, they are complicit with a wider societal discourse that views 'literacy' only as literacy in English (or French) and devalues other languages and forms of cultural knowledge. By contrast, when educators implement pedagogical approaches that explicitly affirm students' plurilingualism as a cognitive and academic resource, they are sending a message of validation that is likely to motivate students to continue to develop their home language (as articulated by Sulmana in discussing her writing of *The New Country*).

Clearly, HL bilingual programmes such as those in operation in Alberta for more than 40 years provide the greatest opportunities for students to develop bilingual and biliteracy skills. However, only a small number of HL speakers are likely to have access to such programmes either in Canada or elsewhere. In the absence of access to bilingual education, students will become motivated to continue to develop their HL when it is positioned accurately in the mainstream classroom and school as an intellectual, cultural and economic asset. Under these circumstances, HL teaching in contexts outside the mainstream school is likely to be more successful than is currently the case where the HL is implicitly or explicitly devalued in the school and wider society.

REFERENCES

Alberta Government (1988). *Language Education Policy for Alberta.* Edmonton: Alberta Government.

Armand, F. and **Dagenais, D.** (2005). 'Langues en contexte d'immigration: éveiller au langage et à la diversité linguistique en milieu scolaire. Thèmes canadiens'. *Revue de l'Association des études Canadiennes,* numéro spécial printemps, 110–13. www.elodil.com/files/articlePRIMAIRE%20fr.pdf.

Armand, F. and **Dagenais, D.** (2012). 'S'ouvrir à la langue de l'Autre et à la diversité linguistique'. *Education Canada* 52 (2). www.cea-ace.ca/fr/education-canada/.

Armand, F., Sirois, F. and **Ababou, F.** (2008). 'Entrée dans l'écrit en contexte plurilingue et défavorisé: Développer les capacités métaphonologiques et sensibiliser à la diversité linguistique'. *Canadian Modern Language Review* 65 (1), 61–87.

Beacco, J-C., Byram, M., Cavalli, M., Coste, D., Cuenat, M.E., Goullier, F. and **Panthier, J.** (2010). *Guide for the Development and Implementation of Curricula for Plurilingual and Intercultural Education.* Strasbourg: Council of Europe.

Cenoz, J. and **Gorter, D.** (2013). 'Towards a Plurilingual Approach in English Language Teaching: Softening the Boundaries between Languages'. *TESOL Quarterly,* doi: 10.1002/tesq.121.

Chow, P. and **Cummins, J.** (2003). 'Valuing Multilingual and Multicultural Approaches to Learning'. In S.R. Schecter and J. Cummins, eds, *Multilingual Education in Practice: Using Diversity as a Resource.* Portsmouth, NH: Heinemann.

Chumak-Horbatsch, R. (2012). *Linguistically Appropriate Practice: A Guide for Working with Young Immigrant Children.* Toronto: University of Toronto Press.

Coste, D., Moore, D. and **Zarate, G.** (2009). *Plurilingual and Pluricultural Competence. Studies towards a Common European Framework of Reference for Language Learning and Teaching.* Strasbourg: Council of Europe.

Cummins, J., Chen-Bumgardner, B.X., Al-Alawi, M., El-fiki, H., Pasquarella, A., Luo, Y. and **Li, J.** (2011a, January). *Evaluation of the Greater Essex County District School Board English/Arabic Bilingual Language Transition Program at Begley Public School.* Final Report submitted to the Greater Essex County District School Board.

Cummins, J., Chen-Bumgardner, B.X., Li, J., Luo, Y. and **Pasquarella, A.** (2011b, April). *Evaluation of the Hamilton-Wentworth District School Board English/Mandarin Bilingual Language Transition Program at Prince Philip Public School.* Final Report submitted to the Hamilton Wentworth District School Board.

Cummins, J. and **Danesi, M.** (1990). *Heritage Languages: The Development and Denial of Canada's Linguistic Resources.* Toronto: Our Schools/Our Selves and Garamond Press.

Cummins, J. and **Early, M.** (2011). *Identity Texts: The Collaborative Creation of Power in Multilingual Schools.* Stoke-on-Trent: Trentham Books.

Gervais, L-M. (2012, 4 January). 'L'école 100% Francophone, un Raccourci Dangereux?' *Le Devoir.* www.ledevoir.com/societe/education/339523/l-ecole-100-francophone-un-raccourci-dangereux.

Marshall, E. and **Toohey, K.** (2010). 'Representing Family: Community Funds of Knowledge, Bilingualism, and Multimodality'. *Harvard Educational Review* 80 (2), 221–41.

Naqvi, R., Thorne, K., Pfitscher, C., Nordstokke, D. and McKeough, A. (2012). 'Reading Dual-language Books: Improving Early Literacy Skills in Linguistically Diverse Classrooms'. *Journal of Early Childhood Research*. Published online 12 October 2012, doi:0.1177/1476718X12449453.

Piccardo, E. (2013). 'Plurilingualism and Curriculum Design: Towards a Synergic Vision'. *TESOL Quarterly* 47 (3), 600–14.

Royal Commission on Learning. (1994). *For the Love of Learning. Volume II. Learning: Our Vision for Schools*. Toronto: Queen's Printer for Ontario.

Schecter, S. and Cummins, J. eds (2003). *Multilingual Education in Practice: Using Diversity as a Resource*. Portsmouth, NH: Heinemann.

Stille, S. and Cummins, J. (2013). 'Foundation for Learning: Engaging Plurilingual Students' Linguistic Repertoires in the Elementary Classroom'. *TESOL Quarterly* 47, 630–38.

NOTES

1 www.elodil.com/.
2 www.thornwoodps.ca/dual/index.htm.
3 www.multiliteracies.ca.
4 www.multiliteracies.ca/index.php/folio/viewGalleryBook/8/42.
5 www.rahatnaqvi.ca.
6 www.rahatnaqvi.ca/wordpress/dual-languages-database/Books.

2 TEACHING HERITAGE LANGUAGE LEARNERS: A Study of Programme Profiles, Practices and Needs

Maria Carreira (UCLA California State University)

Introduction

Recent research has greatly expanded our understanding of a wide range of issues surrounding heritage languages. Cross-linguistic studies of grammatical systems pinpoint key factors in heritage language (HL) acquisition, in particular, the age of acquisition of English, the relative order of acquisition of English and the HL, and the amount and type of HL input available to learners (Montrul 2008; Montrul, Foote and Perpiñán 2008; Polinsky 2007). Research on immigrant languages in society identify factors that bear on language shift and maintenance, including demographics, market forces, language resilience, and societal attitudes towards bilingualism and particular immigrant populations (Fishman 2001; Lo Bianco 2008; Villa 2000; Villa and Rivera-Mills 2009). Profiles of HL learners shed light on key linguistic practices, attitudes and experiences of these individuals and their pedagogical significance (Carreira and Kagan 2010; Beaudrie 2009; Valdés 2001). Studies of institutional practices identify a variety of factors that impact the quality and availability of HL courses (Beaudrie 2009, 2011, 2012; Ingold et al. 2002; Valdés et al. 2003; Wherritt and Cleary 1990).

This chapter aims to contribute to the latter line of enquiry, namely institutional practices surrounding HL teaching. To that end, it presents the findings of an ongoing national survey of post-secondary foreign language programmes that teach HL learners. For the purposes of this study, a 'heritage language' is a language that 'was first in the order of acquisition but was not completely acquired because of the individual's switch to another dominant language,' (Valdés 2000, 369), and HL learners are individuals who are engaged in studying their HL.

A key objective of this chapter is to examine how the practices of some post-secondary language programmes that teach HL learners measure up against recent research in the field of HLs. Another objective is to identify trends, strengths and needs, with a view towards improving HL education at the post-secondary levels.

Overview of the research on institutional practices

Relative to other strands of research in the field of HLs, institutional practices have received modest attention. This is particularly true as it applies to the post-secondary levels of instruction, where Spanish is the sole language with a body of research. The study that constitutes the focus of this chapter was designed to address the language gap in post-secondary studies, along with other objectives, as will be discussed later.

Wherritt and Cleary (1990) conducted a nationwide survey of college-level Spanish HL programmes to seek information on testing for placement and outcomes assessment. Of the 126 institutions that responded to the survey, 18% offered specialised instruction for HL speakers. More than a decade later, Ingold et al. (2002) obtained strikingly similar results in their nationwide survey: 17.8% of the 146 Spanish programmes that participated in the survey offered separate courses for HL learners. This study also pinpointed a number of challenges surrounding HL teaching. Amongst these, programmes with HL courses cited a lack of student interest and inadequate course-placement procedures, while programmes with no such courses identified low enrolments, insufficient funding, lack of trained instructors, and lack of interest from the administration, students and faculty as impediments to offering such courses.

Two regional studies shed light on the relationship between demographics and the availability of HL courses. Focusing on California, the state with the largest population of Latinos in the country (Ennis, Ríos-Vargas and Albert 2011) Valdés et al. (2006) found strikingly higher rates (62%) of HL course availability in post-secondary programmes than reported in nationwide surveys.

Focusing on the Southwest, the US region with the largest concentration of Latinos, Beaudrie's comprehensive 2011 study of 173 universities found that 38% of programmes offered HL courses. This study also found a direct positive relationship between the availability of Spanish HL programmes and the size of the Latino population in particular universities. She cautions however, that the existence of more HL classes does not necessarily translate into more well-crafted pedagogical experiences that are likely to lead to successful learning on the part of HL learners.

Other findings of these studies are also noteworthy. Valdés et al. (2006) found room for improvement in the areas of placement, teacher education and curriculum design. With the majority of institutions lacking placement tools for HL learners, students were left to self-select into a course or rely on the advice of counselors, who may not be knowledgeable of the pertinent issues. Having limited knowledge of language variation, HL instructors were found to place too much emphasis on the teaching of the standard language, to the neglect and detriment of the Spanish varieties represented in class and local communities. With little emphasis on language maintenance or using the HL language outside the classroom, many curricula failed to address some of the main goals of Spanish HL instruction (Valdés 2001).

Beaudrie (2011) found similar areas of deficiencies, as well as others. In the area of curriculum design, literacy skills (particularly writing) were over-emphasised in many HL courses, to the neglect of other language skills and students' heritage cultures. Terms such as 'beginning', 'intermediate', and 'advanced' were used differently from one programme to another, making articulation between programmes and placement difficult. Also, HL curricula were targeted largely at students around the midpoint of the bilingual continuum (Valdés 2001), to the neglect of those at the two ends of this continuum.

Beaudrie (2012) reports on a comprehensive nationwide survey of Spanish programmes in four-year universities with a Latino student population of 5% and more. Of 422 such institutions, 40% (169) were found to offer specialised Spanish HL courses. For the most part, programmes with an HL track offer one or two HL courses. As was the case with earlier studies, programmes without an HL track cited low student numbers, limited resources and a lack of trained faculty as primary obstacles. Comparing her finding of 40% availability of HL courses to those of earlier studies, Sara Beaudrie concludes: 'This finding provides ample evidence that the call for special courses for heritage language learners has received an overwhelming response from post-secondary institutions with sizable populations of Hispanic students' (Beaudrie 2012, 207).

Benmamoun and Kagan (forthcoming) examine institutional issues surrounding the teaching of HLs. Following a question and answer format, they address common challenges faced by programmes with HL learners. Chief amongst these is the question of whether to have separate tracks for Heritage and non-Heritage students. As they explain, amongst practitioners there is a sense that HL learners are different enough from Second Language (L2) learners to warrant specialised courses. This assessment is believed to be particularly valid as it concerns the lower levels of instruction where, the reasoning goes, HL learners' linguistic abilities, no matter how limited, are likely to exceed those of non-HL learners.

However, as Benmamoun explains, for some languages this rationale may not always hold. For example, Heritage Arabic speakers with no knowledge of the standard language and no literacy skills may not necessarily have an edge over their non-Heritage peers in classes where these topics constitute the focus of instruction. On the other hand, if the focus is on developing basic communicative and cultural competence, the rationale for separate sections may hold.

Be that as it may, for many language programmes the question of whether to offer specialised or mixed courses is moot. With limited resources, low numbers of HL learners and a lack of trained instructors, many programmes simply cannot support separate instruction for HL learners. The critical question facing these programmes is how to optimise learning for HL and non-HL learners in mixed classes.

The authors underscore the importance of faculty interests and initiative to the vitality of HL programmes, offering the anecdote below by way of example. Importantly, this anecdote also offers an example of a department doing well by excelling in the area of HL teaching.

> At UCLA we noticed an increase in the heritage speakers of Russian in the mid-90s . . . All of these students, including the lowest proficiency group, were so different from our traditional foreign language or L2 students that the department felt they needed their own curriculum. This was an educationally motivated decision, but in a sense that decision was also motivated by what can be called financial considerations. If we could offer these students the kind of instruction they would benefit from they would continue taking Russian, thus increasing the numbers of students in the department. A new course, *Literacy in Russian*, was launched that enrolled 10 students in the first year. This course has now been offered for 10 years. The enrolments have grown and the student population changed. (Benmamoun and Kagan, forthcoming)

In the present study, the role of faculty also emerges as an essential factor in the success of particular programmes that lack one or more conditions associated with vibrant HL programmes, e.g. a critical mass of HL learners, institutional resources and support, trained instructors and faculty initiative.

Before turning to this study, it is important to acknowledge the existence of research on institutional practices at the lower levels of instruction, particularly community schools. In contrast with the situation in higher education, this research spans a wide range of languages, such as, for example, Turkish (Otcu 2010), Korean (Sook Lee and Shin 2008; Wiley 2007; Zhou and Kim 2006), Chinese (Hsu Chao 1997, Wang 1996, Zhou and Kim 2006), and Japanese (Chinen and Tucker 2005; Shibata 2000).

The present study itself is part of a larger project on institutional practices, which is inclusive of pre-kindergarten to Grade K-12. The Heritage Language Programs Database aims to document the state of HL education in the US across languages and educational levels (community-based, K-12 and university settings) and to form a network to exchange ideas and resources.[1]

Survey methodology and overview

The online survey of higher education programmes is a project of the National Heritage Language Resource Center (NHLRC) at UCLA. Created by a team of HL specialists from Arabic, Spanish and Vietnamese, the survey was designed to build on the existing research and address gaps of knowledge.[2] Accordingly, in keeping with previous research, the survey seeks information on curricula, placement procedures, the size of the HL learner population and areas of concerns for programmes. In addition, addressing gaps in previous surveys, the survey seeks in-depth information in other areas: teacher training/professional development, proficiency levels of HL courses, the adequacy of pedagogical materials, and the background and status of instructors who teach HL learners.

The NHLRC piloted the online survey with a number of instructors during the design stage. The team analysed the responses and modified the survey as needed. The final product consists of 21 content questions, including discrete-point questions as well as open-ended ones.

The survey was launched in October 2010. Respondents were recruited through a variety of methods, including through 'listserv' announcements, general advertising of the survey on the NHLRC website, announcements and booths at national conferences, and through personal contacts. Given these recruitment methods, it is impossible to tabulate a response rate for the survey.

To be included in the survey, programmes must meet three conditions: 1) be at the post secondary level of instruction, 2) be involved in teaching the language for which they are answering the survey, and 3) have HL learners of that language. As of the writing of this paper, there are 296 programmes in the database, representing a range of geographic locations, institution types, and languages.

In terms of location, 34 states with different immigrant population profiles are represented in the survey. All states with immigrant populations that exceed the national average of 12.9% are represented (Arizona, California, Colorado, Connecticut, Florida, Hawaii, Illinois, Massachusetts, Maryland, Nevada, New Jersey and New York, as well as the District of Columbia). Also included are 5 out of the 10 states with the highest growth rates in their immigrant population (Alabama, Georgia, Indiana, Kentucky and South Carolina). In addition, a number of states that do not meet the above conditions are included as well (e.g. Washington, Ohio, Wisconsin, Michigan) (Kandel 2011).

In terms of institution type, roughly two thirds (202/296) of the institutions represented are public and the rest are private. One third (99) are PhD-granting institutions, 21.9% (65) are terminal MA-granting institutions, 16.2% (48) are terminal BA-granting institutions, and 11% (34) are community colleges.[3]

A total of 27 languages are represented in the database. Listed by number of respondents, they are as follows: Spanish (76), Chinese (50), Arabic (44), Russian (36), Hindi/Urdu (32), Korean (13), Farsi (11), Vietnamese (5), Japanese (4), Tagalog (3), Hebrew (2), Portuguese (2), Punjabi (2), Serbo-Croatian (2), Yoruba (2), Armenian (1), Bulgarian (1), French (1), Greek (1), Hmong (1), Hungarian (1), Indonesian (2), Italian (1), Polish (1), Tamil (1), Thai (1), and Yiddish (1).

Three points are in order about the information collected. First, the responses are not confidential. This is because one of the objectives of the Heritage Language Programs Database is to create a network of professionals who are interested in sharing information and pooling resources. Second, the goal of the survey is not to gather information on every programme in the US teaching HL learners, but rather to collect representative information on the practices of programmes surrounding these learners. Since this is an ongoing survey, the findings and the conclusions reported here are subject to modification as more responses are collected, particularly in the less represented languages. Third, noted inaccuracies or discrepancies in the information entered by some respondents were corrected in consultation with programme representatives. Several follow-up interviews were also conducted with selected respondents to assess further information on particular issues.

The next section offers an overview of the findings. Because of space limitations, this presentation is not exhaustive, but focuses on three issues: 1) HL course availability, 2) over-performing programmes, 3) the proficiency levels of HL courses, and 4) programme concerns. The particular findings to be presented have been selected on the basis of the insights they bring into issues raised by previous surveys, as well as for what they reveal about how current practices address the needs of HL learners.

Overview of the findings

HL course availability

Close to half of the programmes in the database (47.6%; 141/296) offer specialised instruction, with notable differences between languages, as shown below (only languages with 10 or more programmes are included).

Table 1: Percentage of programmes offering HL classes, by language

Language	Programmes offering one or more specialised HL courses
Spanish	80.2% (61/76)
Korean	69% (9/13)
Chinese	54.9% (28/51)
Russian	47.2% (17/36)
Farsi	33.6% (4/11)
Hindi/Urdu	25% (8/32)
Arabic	6.8% (3/44)

For the most part, the above numbers are significantly higher than would be expected by the nationwide surveys discussed earlier. Though such surveys were only for Spanish, it makes sense to consider them as benchmarks, albeit limited ones. This is particularly true for Beaudrie (2012), which overlaps in time with the present study and which has a very large dataset (422).

What could account for the discrepancy between that study, which puts the number of programmes with an HL track at 40%, and the present one? It will be recalled that Beaudrie (2012) was a comprehensive nationwide survey of all Spanish programmes in four-year colleges. By comparison, the present survey includes only programmes that accepted the invitation to participate in the survey. As such, a self-selecting bias in the present study may overstate the frequency of programmes with specialised HL courses. Be that as it may, there are important insights to be gained from the information collected.

In particular, the fact that the present results compare favourably to those of other nationwide surveys that also involved self-selection (i.e. Wherritt and Cleary 1990; Ingold et al. 2002) supports Beaudrie's (2012) observation that post-secondary institutions have responded favorably to the call for more HL courses. Furthermore, additional findings indicate that this response has not been limited to special courses, but also includes a variety of other instructional options for HL learners such as independent studies, tutoring, seminars and internships. Widely attested across languages and programme types, these are some of the most common ways in which departments attend to the needs of HL learners. It is particularly noteworthy that roughly half of programmes (48%) without HL courses offer one or more of these options.

At 6.8%, the availability of HL courses in Arabic falls strikingly below the other languages and begs for an explanation. One possible explanation is suggested by a previously noted comment by Abbas Benmamoun that for languages such as Arabic (characterised by diglossia and great dialectal variation) mixed classes may be appropriate when the goal of instruction is to teach the standard language. On the other hand, when the focus is on communication, separating HL and non-HL learners may be more appropriate because HL learners can progress faster than L2 learners.

A review of the description of the mixed Arabic classes and their pedagogical materials in the survey does not support that account. Running counter to Benmamoun's recommendations, all but two of the mixed courses appear to have a communicative focus. This raises questions about how well the needs of Arabic HL learners are met in mixed courses, as currently configured.

Similar questions arise across other languages. In many cases, it appears that mixed classes may be effectively no different from traditional L2 classes. For one, many of the descriptions of such courses note that the textbook and other materials are not appropriate for HL learners. Remarkably, this was true even in mixed classes where HL learners make up 50% or more of the student population. For another, a number of comments in the survey pertaining to mixed classes with very small numbers of HL learners express outright disregard for the needs of these learners.[4] The comments below illustrate this issue:

1. I did not give particular consideration to HL – they are usually a very small segment of the class.

2. In the past five-and-a-half years of our programme, we only had two heritage speakers. So we focus on true beginners, and we don't address the needs of the HL learners.

3. [Name of book] does not address the needs of HL but it does a good job at the beginning level where the majority of our students take the [name of language] as a general language requirement and where we have less HL (15%) than at more advanced levels.

The above comments warrant concern, given the ubiquity of mixed language classes with few HL learners. As shown in Table 2, in programmes without an HL track, roughly one third of language classes have HL learner populations of 10% or less and another third have HL learner population between 10 and 25%.[5] In light of this, it is important to understand how widespread the above sentiments might be and how the practices that flow from them impact HL learners.

Table 2: Programmes without an HL track, by percent of HL learner population

Percentage of HL learners in mixed language classes	Number of programmes
<10%	47 (30.7%)
10–25%	47 (30.7%)
25–50%	29 (19.07%)
50–75%	14 (9.2%)
>75%	15 (9.9%)

Mixed classes with roughly similar proportions of HL and L2 learners, and classes where HL learners are in the majority, are also fairly common. Amongst the latter, super-majority HL-learner classes (>75%) raise important questions: Do they function as de facto HL classes or are they more like L2 classes? What general approaches, teaching practices, curricula and materials are best suited to these types of classes? And, given the high presence of HL learners, why not have HL classes?

Examining the last question, there is a positive relationship between the representation of HL students at the programme level and the availability of HL courses. As shown in Table 3, the likelihood of having HL courses goes up with the percentage of HL learners in a programme. The converse is also true. However, there are significant numbers of programmes that go against this generalisation. In particular, 17 programmes with an HL learner population of 10% or less have HL courses, and 13 programmes with populations of 75% and above, do not. The former programmes raise questions such as: How can they? What about them enables the existence of HL courses? On the other hand, the latter programmes raise questions such as: How can they not? What about them prevents the existence of such courses? The next section takes up these issues.

Table 3: Percentage of HL learners and HL learner class size, by programme type

Percentage of HL learners in programme	*Total programmes N=294	Programmes that offer HL courses N= 140	Programmes that do not offer HL courses N= 154
<10	69	24.6% (17)	75.3% (52)
10–25	77	42.8% (33)	57.1% (44)
25–50	68	55.9% (38)	44.1% (30)
50–75	41	63.4% (26)	36.5% (15)
>75	39	66.6% (26)	33.3% (13)

* Two programmes did not respond to this question

To summarise, the survey results point to three different instructional configurations where HL learners study their home language: HL classes, mixed classes, and a variety of customised options (e.g. internships, independent studies, tutoring, and so on). With regard to HL courses, the survey indicates that there is a positive relationship between the size of the HL population at the programme level and the availability of HL courses. Regarding mixed classes, survey results raise awareness of three types, with potentially different pedagogical needs: minority HL learner mixed classes, roughly balanced HL-L2 learner mixed classes and majority HL learner classes. Finally, survey results identify customised options such as independent studies and internships as significant purveyors of HL instruction across all languages and programmes.

Overperforming HL programmes: A window to HL programme vitality

This section examines two groups of HL programmes that excel with regard to their course offerings. One such group consists of programmes that offer four or more HL courses. The other consists of programmes that offer HL courses, despite having very few HL learners. A review of these programmes sheds light on the factors that contribute to HL programme vitality.

Mirroring the findings of Beaudrie (2012), the present survey found that most HL programmes (65.2%; 92/142) offer one or two levels of instruction. Programmes with four or more levels are significantly less common. As shown in Table 4, the present survey registers only 20 such programmes. Significantly, the large majority of these have healthy enrolments in their HL courses: 15 have enrolments of 20 or more and 3 have between 11 and 20. Many also have a proportionally large HL learner student population, as shown in column 4. Crucially, most programmes with four or more HL courses have a critical mass of HL learners, as defined in terms of enrolments in HL classes and overall programme representation.

Table 4: Selected characteristics of programmes with four or more HL courses

Language	Programmes with four or more HL courses/ programmes with HL courses	Typical HL class size (number of programmes)	Percent of HL learners in the programme (number of programmes)
Chinese	14/28	20+ (13)	10–25% (2)
		*11–20 (1)	25–50% (4)
			*50–75% (4)
			> 75% (2)
Korean	1/9	20+	25–50%
Russian	1/17	11– 20	25–50%
Spanish	3/61	20+ (all)	10–25% (1)
			25–50% (1)
			>75% (1)
Vietnamese	1/3	5–10	50–75%

* In the programme with an average class size of 11–20 students, HL learners comprise 50–75% of the total student population.

Numbers alone, however, do not account for the curricular richness of these programmes. After all, many other programmes in the survey with similar demographic profiles have far more modest course offerings. What distinguishes many of the programmes in Table 4 is their special access to institutional resources and faculty with initiative and expertise. For example, the

Vietnamese and Spanish programmes are connected with leading researchers in the field of HLs. The Russian programme is at UCLA, which is home to the NHLRC. Directed by Olga Kagan, a Russian professor at UCLA and also leader in the field of HLs, the NHLRC offers many professional development opportunities and sponsors research and conferences in the area of HLs. UCLA is also home to two other language programmes in this table, namely the Korean programme and one of the Chinese programmes. In short, many of the programmes in Table 4 do not just have a critical mass of HL students; they also have institutional support and human capital.

Another category of programmes further underscores this point. Only 5 programmes in the survey offer HL courses with average enrolments of 5 or fewer students. One of these is the Indonesian programme at the University of Wisconsin at Madison, Wisconsin. This programme not only has very low HL course enrolments, but it also has a proportionally small HL student population of 10–25%. Tellingly, this programme's home institution, the University of Wisconsin at Madison, is a national leader in South and Southeast Asia studies, hosting the annual South Asia Summer Language Institute (SASLI; www.sasli.wisc.edu), outreach K-12 programmes, and other projects that promote the study and teaching of the languages of this region (www.southasia.wisc.edu).

Another such programme, the Japanese programme at LaGuardia Community College of the City University of New York, is the product of remarkable faculty initiative, as explained in a follow-up interview:

> Our college administrators are probably the primary reason why we were able to run HL courses with low enrolment. As for Japanese, I tried to convince our president and provost that LaGuardia could serve as a hub of HL instruction in NY because no other colleges in the area offer HL Japanese courses. They were persuaded by my argument and decided to make HL one of the college's goals this year. The idea of HL seemed intriguing to our school, where the majority of students are immigrants or the second generation of immigrant families. We also actively sought external grants. With both internal/external funding, we tried to offer professional development events on HL frequently so that we could reach out to our college community. Finally, HL worked quite well as a common theme amongst our colleagues' research interests. Our department is a multi-disciplinary department which offers ESL, Education, Linguistics and Modern Languages. We figured that HL would be an interesting theme that everyone in different disciplines could contribute their expertise. Our colleagues have been very supportive in our initiative in HL for this reason.

In summary, the programmes highlighted in this section underscore the critical role that institutional support and faculty initiative and expertise play in the success of HL programmes. Having a critical mass of learners, in absolute numbers at the course level, as well as proportionally at the department level, is also of the essence.

Proficiency levels in the HL track

In 2004, the Modern Language Association (MLA) set out to develop an agenda that would respond to the nation's language needs and drive new initiatives in language education. The report 'Foreign Languages and Higher Education: New Structures for a Changed World', released in 2007, identified HL teaching as a priority, and called for adopting and promoting best HL teaching practices, increasing the range of languages offered, and producing students with advanced competencies (MLA Ad Hoc Committee on Foreign Languages 2007).

Where do HL programmes stand with regard to proficiency? What proficiency levels are targeted by HL courses? How well do these levels match HL learners' actual proficiency in their HL? These are the issues taken up in this section.

The survey asked respondents to mark the proficiency levels targeted by their HL courses, using the ACTFL (American Council on the Teaching of Foreign Languages) proficiency levels and their equivalents on the ILR (Interagency Language Roundtable), as shown in Table 5. The descriptions were provided in an effort to avoid the kinds of terminological inconsistencies that Beaudrie (2012) encountered.

The responses indicate that HL courses are largely geared towards students at the intermediate–high levels and above. Courses for novice learners are considerably less common.

Table 5: HL courses by proficiency levels

ACTFL Scale (ILR Scale)	Definition	Number of responses
Superior (3 – 3+)	Able to speak the language with sufficient structural accuracy and vocabulary to participate effectively in most formal and informal conversations	49
Advanced Plus (2+)	Able to satisfy most work requirements and show some ability to communicate on concrete topics	70
Advanced (2)	Able to satisfy routine social demands and limited work requirements	72
Intermediate – High (1+)	Able to satisfy most survival needs and limited social demands	75
Intermediate – Mid/Low (1)	Able to satisfy some survival needs and some limited social demands	46
Novice – High (0+)	Able to satisfy immediate needs with learned utterances	27
Novice – Mid/Low (0)	Able to operate in only a very limited capacity	21

From the above, it appears that HL programmes are following the MLA's proficiency recommendations, in so far as they are targeting the higher levels of the ACTFL scale. But how well do these target levels correspond to HL learners' actual proficiency levels?

Carreira and Kagan (2010) report on a national survey of some 1800 college HL learners from 22 different languages. The survey (henceforth the 'HL learner survey') sought information on the linguistic profiles, goals, and attitudes of HL learners with a view towards informing the design of curricula, materials and professional development projects in the area of HL teaching.

Amongst other questions, HL learners were asked to assess their own HL abilities in listening, speaking, reading and writing, using a five-point scale: 'none', 'low', 'intermediate', 'advanced' and 'native-like'. Their responses are represented in Figure 1. As shown, for the most part, aural skills were in the range of advanced and above, with listening rating higher than speaking. In the area of literacy, the majority of learners rated their reading skills in the range of intermediate and above, and their writing skills slightly lower than that.

Figure 1: HL learners' self assessment of their proficiency in the four modalities

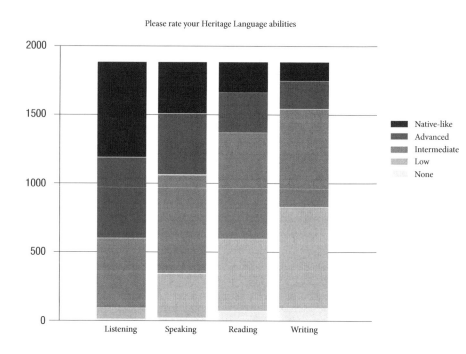

Please rate your Heritage Language abilities

Comparing the two surveys, there is a fair amount of correspondence between HL learners' self assessments and the proficiency levels of HL courses, in the sense that the bulk of the responses in both surveys fall in the higher ranges of their respective scales. This would suggest that HL programmes are generally aiming instruction at the right proficiency levels.

Another comparison also supports this point. The HL learner survey found significant differences in proficiency by language. Table 6 represents the relative aural proficiency of HL learners in different languages. Following that, Table 7 shows their literacy skills.

Table 6: HL learners' self-assessed aural skills (average of listening and speaking scores), by language

Native-like	Advanced	Intermediate	Low
	Spanish, Russian	Persian, Korean	
		Vietnamese	
		Mandarin and Cantonese	
		Tagalog	

Table 7: HL learners' self-assessed literacy skills (average of reading and writing scores), by language

Native-like	Advanced	Intermediate	Low
	Spanish	Russian	Korean
			Vietnamese
			Mandarin and Cantonese
			Tagalog

For the most part, HL course offerings in the programmes survey parallel the above rankings. In particular, Spanish and Russian programmes report having more HL courses in the advanced-superior category than the other languages while Korean, Persian and Vietnamese have more courses in the lower ranges of proficiency (with the exception of Chinese, discussed below).[6] Once again, these findings suggest that HL programmes are largely attuned to the linguistic abilities of their HL learners and offer instruction that is calibrated accordingly. However, a few qualifications are in order.

First, research indicates that HL learners tend to over-assess their proficiency. In their study of the oral proficiency of Spanish and Russian heritage speakers, Matin, Swendler and Rivera-Martínez (forthcoming) found that:

> . . . (H)eritage speakers in both groups had a general tendency to over-assess their proficiency level. In the Spanish group, half of those who were officially rated Intermediate self-assessed at Advanced; half (52%) of those who were rated Advanced self-assessed as Superior. In light of this, the question of whether HL courses are generally aiming instruction at the right proficiency levels should be questioned. (Rivera-Martínez, forthcoming)

Another consideration is that the intermediate-high, advanced and superior levels of proficiency require good control of higher-order skills such as the ability to discuss topics at an abstract level, support an idea, or hypothesise in the target language. Given their academic nature, these types of skills require significant formal instruction and exposure to the formal registers. However, such levels of instructions and exposure are not commonly attested amongst HL learners. According to the HL learner survey, the large majority of college HL learners have little or no formal instruction in their HL and little exposure to the written language, let alone the academic registers. In light of this, self-assessments of Intermediate-High and above by HL learners should be questioned and, by extension, the contention that HL courses are well calibrated to HL learners' proficiency.[7]

Chinese programmes are noteworthy in this regard because they cast a wider proficiency net than other programmes, offering HL curricula that respond to learners across all proficiency levels, including the often-neglected novice levels. What, if anything, should be made of these findings?

Chinese programmes have benefitted tremendously from the rise of China and the concomitant growing professional currency of Chinese. Between 2006 and 2009, Chinese enrolments at the post-secondary levels grew by 18.2%, outpacing those of the five most commonly studied languages in the US: Spanish (5.1%), French (4.8%), German (2.2%), ASL (16.4%), and Italian (3.0%) (Furman, Goldberg, and Lusin 2010). Survey findings suggest that Chinese educators have responded to the fortuitous climate in which they found themselves by investing in HL education at all levels of instruction.

To complete this discussion, two points are in order about the ends of the proficiency scale. Regarding the advanced levels of instruction, it is important to understand that coursework alone is limited in what it can do in the way of producing speakers with the highest levels of proficiency. Out-of-classroom experiences such as intensive summer language institutes, internships and the kinds of overseas experiences such as those supported by the National Flagship programmes, are also very important (Carreira (2013); Malone, Rifkin, Christian and Johnson 2005). Other options identified in the survey, such as tutorials and independent studies, may also prove valuable.

As for the lower levels of instruction, survey results underscore the need to strengthen the options available to HL learners. In programmes with only one or two HL courses – the most common scenario in programmes with an HL track – courses targeting the novice range are fairly rare: only 12.8% of programmes have them. These results mirror Beaudrie's (2012) findings and circle back to the previous discussion surrounding HL teaching in mixed classes. With these classes being the primary provider of instruction for novice HL learners, it is important to prioritise the development of HL principles and practices that are fine-tuned to this context.

A survey of first-year college language learners by Reynolds, Howard and Deák (2009) underscores the importance of this task. This study found that lower proficiency HL students are often mistakenly placed in beginning or intermediate level L2 classes. Beaudrie (2009) argues that this situation hurts HL learners by keeping them developing their full linguistic potential and, in some cases, exacerbating their linguistic insecurities.

Overall, the results presented in this section indicate that HL programmes privilege the higher levels of proficiency. How closely HL courses align with learners' actual competency remains unclear and merits further research.

Areas of need

There is a great deal of consensus across programme types and languages surrounding the needs of HL teaching. This was somewhat unexpected, given the range of languages and programme types represented in the survey. Respondents were asked to rank seven areas of need identified in the research literature. The results are listed below, from most pressing to least.

1. Inadequate or lacking course options for HL learners
2. HL teaching and research are not on the path to tenure
3. Inadequate professional training opportunities
4. Inadequate or lacking placement tools
5. Inadequate or lacking pedagogical materials
6. Low enrolments
7. Low retention

The issues surrounding 'inadequate or lacking course options for HL learners' have already been discussed at length. Suffice it to say that their presence at the top of the hierarchy underscores the need to attend to the various issues surrounding this topic.

Regarding the second most pressing concern – 'HL teaching and research are not on the path to tenure' – survey results indicate that HL teaching is largely in the hands of non-tenure track faculty (mostly lecturers, graduate students and visiting fellows). The significance of this finding does not reside in what it says about the quality of HL teaching. Indeed, there is no evidence that contingent faculty are less effective HL teachers than tenure track faculty. Rather, the importance of this finding resides in what it indicates about institutional commitment to HL teaching and how the absence of tenur track faculty undercuts the vitality of HL teaching.

One of the main reasons why tenure track faculty are so important to the vitality of HL teaching (and their absence so detrimental) is because they are available for long-term institutional and curricular planning, for hiring and mentoring new faculty, and other functions that support HL teaching in language programmes. Another reason is that they can marshal resources that are out of the reach of most contingent faculty. The comment below by an Arabic professor who participated in the survey illustrates this point. His knowledge of institutional issues and resourcefulness enable him to clear institutional obstacles that stand in the way of offering instructional options for HL learners.

In the end, I think that the success of this programme is based on a lot of reasons. First, I built the programme methodically and realistically (not over-anticipating enrolments, as is often the case). Second, I have spread out expenditures by, say, offering certain courses through the evening programme, which is another budget. Or, I open sections of courses (languages or content courses) specifically through the Honors Programmes, which attracts a highly motivated and high achieving group of students. I also frequently take on students in independent studies, usually graduate students or upper class students, to accommodate the need for advanced language, literature, and culture courses.

Regarding 'inadequate professional training opportunities', a sizable majority (60%) of the programmes surveyed do not offer any training in HL teaching. However, considerable numbers of programmes have special speakers, workshops, and courses focusing wholly or in part on HL issues. In addition, many survey respondents reported taking advantage of external sources of training and information, such as professional conferences, summer workshops and online resources.

Given the variety of training options identified, it would be important to understand what types of professional development opportunities and how much training or instruction enable good HL teaching and promote faculty initiative. In this regard, it is important to remember that questions about the adequacy of professional training opportunities do not just bear on the current state of teaching, but also on the long-term vitality of HL teaching. If today's graduate students are not instructed on the principles of HL teaching and learning, they will not have the knowledge or see the need to push forward an HL agenda when they enter the profession as faculty members, administrators, textbook editors, and so on.

The next concern, placement, is an area where considerable process has been made in the recent past. Notably, the NHLRC has created a webpage offering a collection of references, proficiency assessments, background questionnaires, and other research tools that may be utilised for assessing HL learners (www.nhlrc.ucla.edu/data/). Another major contribution is the special issue of the *Heritage Language Journal* on Spanish assessment (HLJ, Spring 2012, 9:1). What is not clear is whether practitioners are able to put the existing tools to use to meet their particular needs – that is, whether they can articulate the findings of existing placement tests and their courses. This may be particularly difficult to do with mixed courses, since HL learners' competencies in different areas of grammar may span various course levels. For example, it is not unusual for HL learners to have fairly well developed listening skills but limited to no reading and writing skills.

Concerns over 'Inadequate or lacking pedagogical materials' were previously discussed with reference to mixed classes. Survey results indicate that there is also a need for more textbooks and materials for HL courses across all languages, including Spanish, Chinese and Russian, which already have a variety of HL textbooks.

As for 'low enrolments', in keeping with the findings of previous studies, this was more of a concern for programmes without an HL track than for those with an HL track. This follows on from the earlier observation that programmes need a critical mass of students to support HL courses. Thus, low enrolments and not having an HL track are interconnected factors.

Enrolments and the other areas of needs are also interconnected. The same goes for retention rates. In particular, deficiencies in the areas of instructional options, assessment tools, teaching approaches and materials may undermine programmes' ability to respond to the goals and needs of HL learners. In turn, this may diminish the value of language learning for HL learners, leading to low enrolments and retention rates.

This means that in order to maximise its value to HL learners, HL teaching must address all areas of concern at once. Looping back to the top of the needs list, an increase in instructional options must be accompanied by efforts to improve teacher training, placement tools and pedagogical materials, as well as efforts to hire tenure track faculty that will serve as stewards of HL issues.

The situation of a Hindi/Urdu programme in the survey illustrates how missing just one of these links undercuts the ability of programmes to serve HL learners. With large numbers of HL learners, a working placement test, and a director with initiative and expertise, this programme is nevertheless unable to offer the HL courses in its course catalogue (including a fully developed online tutorial for HL learners designed to be used in a variety of instructional contexts) due to the lack of trained faculty.

With the presentation of the selected findings now complete, it is now possible to consider the implications of these findings.

Directions for future research and conclusions

Survey results present a mixed picture of the state of HL teaching. On the one hand, there is evidence that significant progress has been made in the availability of HL courses and customised options that cater for the needs of HL learners. At the same time, there are considerable challenges to contend with.

In the latter category, the situation of mixed classes is especially pressing because institutional restrictions and other factors often render HL courses beyond the realm of possibility. As such, it is important to square practice with the stated goals and philosophy of HL teaching and to develop protocols for addressing the needs of HL learners in mixed classes and other instructional options.

To that end, there is a need for more studies along the line of Bowles (2011 a, b) to shed light on general approaches for dealing with mixed classes, including teaching strategies, placement tools, and materials and syllabus design. There is also a need for research that sheds light on the particularities of each type of mixed classes, i.e. minority HL learner classes, balanced HL-L2 learner classes and majority HL learner classes.

Another reason to focus on mixed classes is because they are the main purveyors of instruction for HL learners at the lowest levels of the proficiency scales. Arguably the most neglected category of HL learners, these students have the potential to enrich the field of HL teaching by virtue of their strong personal attachment to their HL and the reservoir of cultural and linguistic knowledge that they bring to the classroom (Au 2002; Beaudrie 2009; Beaudrie and Ducar 2005).

The so-called 'customised options' offer a promising pathway forward for HL teaching. What makes them so valuable is their potential ability to serve the needs of HL learners in the absence of other options or where available options may not be appropriate. Internships, summer institutes and study abroad programmes are particularly valuable by virtue of the role they play in facilitating the development of the higher levels of proficiency.

None of this is to say that HL specialists and practitioners should stop advocating for more HL classes, but, rather, that their efforts on this front should be accompanied by equally persistent efforts to provide the best possible education for HL learners under all current instructional configurations. Both courses of action necessarily involve addressing the areas of needs discussed in the previous section. As explained, these must be attended to in tandem because they are interdependent.

Arguably, more than any other factor, the vitality of HL teaching and learning hinges on the existence of faculty and administrators with the knowhow and authority to push forward an HL agenda and surmount organisational impediments. Case studies of the contributions and strategies employed by leaders in this area would be very beneficial. In this vein, increasing the number of tenure track faculty with expertise in HLs, and shoring up teacher training, are critically important to the future of the field.

There is much to be learned from studying successful programmes such as those featured here, which exceed expectations for their profile, as well as programmes with innovative coursework and approaches to HL teaching. In this regard, it is important to note that the existence of HL classes using HL appropriate materials is an indication, but not a guarantee, that the needs of HL learners are being effectively met. Conversely, the absence of specialised HL courses in any given programme does not necessarily mean that student needs are going unmet. Assessing this issue requires an in-depth evaluation of each programme that is beyond the scope of a survey, but that the profession would do well to pursue.

Besides limitations of scope, the present survey has other limitations. For some programme types and languages, the number of responses is too small to draw conclusions. Some of the information collected may already be out of date. Indeed, a number of survey respondents commented on impending changes to their programmes, both negative and positive. Finally, as mentioned earlier, some of the responses entered did not turn out to be accurate upon close inspection. It is possible that more undetected incorrect answers remain. Moving forward, increasing the number of responses in key languages and programme types, and updating existing ones, is a priority.

REFERENCES

Au, T. K-F., Knightly, L.M. Jun, S-A. and Oh, J.S. (2002). 'Overhearing a Language during Childhood'. *Psychological Science* 13 (3), 238–43.

Beaudrie, S. (2012). 'Research on University-Based Spanish Heritage Language Programmes in the United States: The Current State of Affairs'. In S. Beaudrie and M. Fairclough, eds, *Spanish as a Heritage Language in the United States: State of the field*, 203–21. Washington, DC: Georgetown University Press.

Beaudrie, S. (2011). 'Spanish Heritage Language Programs: A Snapshot of Current Programs in the Southwestern United States'. *Foreign Language Annals* 44 (2), 321–37.

Beaudrie, S. (2009). 'Receptive Bilinguals' Language Development in the Classroom: The Differential Effects of Heritage versus Foreign Language Curriculum.' In M. Lacorte and J. Leeman, eds, *Español en Estados Unidos y otros contextos de contacto: Sociolingüística, ideología y pedagogía*, 325–46. Madrid: Iberoamericana / Vervuert Verlag.

Beaudrie, S. and Ducar, C. (2005). 'Beginning Level University Heritage Programs: Creating a Space for All Heritage Language Learners'. *Heritage Language Journal* 3, 1–26.

Bowles, M. (2011a). 'Measuring Implicit and Explicit Linguistic Knowledge: What Can HLLs contribute?' *Studies in Second Language Acquisition*, 33, 247–72.

Bowles, M. (2011b). 'Exploring The Role of Modality: L2-Heritage Learner Interactions in the Spanish Language Classroom'. *Heritage Language Journal* 8 (1). www.international. ucla.edu/languages/heritagelanguages/journal/.

Carreira, M. (2013). 'The Advanced Speaker: An Overview of the Issues in Heritage Language Teaching'. Position paper. www.nhlrc.ucla.edu/.

Carreira, M. and Kagan, O. (2011). 'The Results of the National Heritage Language Survey: Implications for Teaching, Curriculum Design, and Professional Development'. *Foreign Language Annals* 43 (3), 40–64.

Chinen, K. and Tucker., G.R. (2005). 'In Heritage Language Development: Understanding the Roles of Ethnic Identity and Saturday School Participation'. *Heritage Language Journal* 3 (11), 27–59.

Ennis, S.R., Ríos-Vargas, M. and Albert, N. (2011). 'The Hispanic Population: 2010'. *2010 Census Briefs*. www.census.gov/2010census/.

Fishman, J.A., ed. (2001). *Can Threatened Languages be Saved? Reversing Language Shift, Revisited*. Clevedon, UK: Multilingual Matters.

Furmin, N., Goldberg, D. and Lusin, N. (2010). 'Enrolments in Languages other than English in United States Institutions of Higher Education, Fall 2009'. *Modern Language Association Web Publication*. www.mla.org/pdf/2009_enrolment_survey.pdf.

Hsu Chao, T. (1997). 'Chinese Heritage Community Language Schools in the United States'. Center for Applied Linguistics.

Ingold, C. W., Rivers, W., Chavez Tesser, C. and Ashby, E. (2002). 'Report on the NFLC/ AATSP Survey of Spanish Language Programs for Native Speakers'. *Hispania* 85 (2), 324–9.

Kandel, W.A. (2011). 'The U.S. Foreign Born Population: Trends and Selected Characteristics'. *CRS Report for Congress*. www.fas.org/sgp/crs/misc/R41592.pdf.

Lo Bianco, J. (2008). 'Organizing for Multilingualism: Ecological and Sociological Perspectives, Keeping Language Diversity Alive'. *A TESOL Symposium*. Alexandria, VA: Teachers of English to Speakers of Other Languages.

Malone, M.E., Rifkin, B., Christian and Johnson, D. (2005). 'Attaining High Levels of Proficiency: Challenges for Foreign Language Education in the United States'. Center for Applied Linguistics. www.cal.org/resources/digest/attain.html.

MLA Ad Hoc Committee on Foreign Languages (2007). 'Foreign Languages and Higher Education: New Structures for a Changed World'. Modern Language Association. www.mla.org/pdf/forlang_news_pdf.pdf.

Montrul, S. (2008). *Incomplete Acquisition in Bilingualism. Re-examining the Age Factor*. Amsterdam: John Benjamins.

Montrul, S. and Potowski, K. (2007). 'Command of Gender Agreement in School-Age Spanish Bilingual Children'. *International Journal of Bilingualism* 11, 301–28.

Montrul, S., Foote, R. and Perpiñán, S. (2008). 'Gender Agreement in Adult Second Language Learners and Spanish Heritage Speakers: The Effects of Age and Context of Acquisition'. *Language Learning* 58, 3–53.

Polinsky, M. (2007). 'Incomplete Acquisition: American Russian'. *Journal of Slavic Linguistics* 14, 191–262.

Otcu, B. (2010). 'Language Maintenance and Cultural Identity Construction: A Linguistic Ethnography of Discourses in a Complementary School in the US'. VDM Verlag Dr. Mueller.

Reynolds, R.R., Howard, K.M. and Deák, J. (2009). 'Heritage Language Learners in First-Year Foreign Language Courses: A Report of General Data Across Learner Subtypes'. *Foreign Language Annals* 42 (2), 250–69.

Shibata, S. (2000). 'Opening a Japanese Saturday School in a Small Town in the United States: Community Collaboration to Teach Japanese as a Heritage Language'. *Bilingual Research Journal* 24 (4), 465–74.

Sook Lee, J. and Shin, S. (2008). 'Korean Heritage Language Education in the United States: The Current State, Opportunities, and Possibilities'. *Heritage Language Journal* 6 (2), 1–20.

Swendler, E. (2012). 'ACTFL Proficiency Levels in the Workworld'. http://nble.org/wp-content/uploads/2012/03/ACTFLWorkplaceProficiencyAssess.pdf.

Valdés, G. (2000). 'The Teaching of Heritage Languages: An Introduction for Slavic-Teaching Professionals'. In O. Kagan and B. Rifkin, eds, *The learning and teaching of Slavic languages and cultures*, 375–403. Bloomington, IN: Slavica.

— (2001). 'Heritage Language Students: Profiles and Possibilities'. In J. Peyton, D. Ranard, and S. McGinnis, eds, *Heritage languages in America: Preserving a national resource*, 37–77. Washington, DC: Center for Applied Linguistics and Delta Systems.

Valdés, G., González, S., López García, D. and Márquez, P. (2003). 'Language Ideology: The Case of Spanish in Departments of Foreign Languages'. *Anthropology and Education Quarterly* 34 (1), 3–26.

Valdés, G., Fishman, J.A., Chávez, R. and Pérez, W. (2006). *Developing Minority Language Resources: The Case of Spanish in California*. Buffalo, NY: Multilingual Matters.

Villa, D.J. (2000). 'Languages have Armies, and Economies, Too: The Presence of U.S. Spanish in the Spanish-Speaking World'. *Southwest Journal of Linguistics* 19, 143–54.

Villa, D.J. and Rivera-Mills, S. V. (2009). 'An Integrated Multi-Generational Model for Language Maintenance and Shift: The Case of Spanish in the Southwest'. *Spanish In Context* 6 (1), 26–42.

Wang, X., ed. (1996). *A view from within: A case study of Chinese Heritage Community Language Schools in the United States*. Washington, DC: National Foreign Language Center.

Wiley, T. (2007). 'Immigrant Language Minorities in the United States'. In M. Hellinger and A. Pauwels, eds, *Handbook of Language and Communication: Diversity and Change*, 53–85. New York: Mouton de Gruyter.

Zhou, M. and Kim, S. (2006). 'Community Forces, Social Capital, and Educational Achievement: The Case of Supplementary Education in the Chinese and Korean Immigrant Communities'. *Harvard Educational Review* 76 (1), 1–29.

NOTES

1   Information on this project and a collection of profiles of community-based and K-12 HL programmes can be found at www.cal.org/heritage/profiles/index.html.
2   Team members are: Afaf Nash (UCLA), Tri Tran (UC Irvine), and this author (Maria Carreira, UCLA and California State University, Long Beach).
3   A number of respondents indicated that they were uncertain as to the answer, the remaining others failed to answer this question.
4   These quotes have been modified to remove all identifying information.
5   Three programmes without an HL track did not answer this question
6   None of the Tagalog programmes in the survey have HL courses, hence their exclusion from this discussion.
7   It is also possible that survey respondents overestimated the level of proficiency of their courses, which could mean that courses and learners are relatively well matched, although at a lower level than indicated by the two studies. This remains to be studied.

RETHINKING HERITAGE LANGUAGES: Ideologies, Identities, Practices and Priorities in Canada and China[1]

Patricia A. Duff (University of British Columbia)
Duanduan Li (University of British Columbia)

Introduction

For the past generation, the politics, ideologies, rhetoric and provision for heritage languages (HLs) and HL education in Canada and many other countries have vacillated considerably (Duff 2008; Duff and Li 2009, 2013; Li and Duff 2008; see reviews in Ashworth 1988; Beynon and Toohey 1991; Brinton, Kagan and Bauckus 2008; Cummins 1983, 1991, 1992, 1993; Cummins and Danesi 1990; Danesi et al. 1993). Attitudes toward HL maintenance and education have ranged from hostile, to ambivalent, to genuinely (or in some cases just superficially) celebratory. Some critics of governments' and language-majority citizens' orientation toward others' (minority) languages consider the exclusive focus on official languages and cultures to be hegemonic. When indigenous (i.e. non-immigrant) languages are included in these discussions, other discourses connected with colonisation, decolonisation, discrimination, linguistic and cultural homogenisation, and even genocide, are invoked (e.g. McCarty 2003). Nevertheless, international (i.e. foreign governments') national, regional, provincial/state, municipal, philanthropic and other private sources of support have often sponsored the transmission and retention of minority languages in response to HL community demands, desires and advocacy. Yet language policies and their underlying ideologies are often completely misaligned with those just a generation earlier, for better or worse.

In this chapter, we examine some of the factors affecting ideologies, identities and educational practices connected with heritage/ancestral languages in Canada and China, as well as some of their consequences. To narrow the focus and scope of our discussion, we consider regions in each country with large minority-language communities (often numbering in the hundreds of thousands, or even millions), and especially those using varieties of Chinese and other Asian languages spoken in China. The regions examined are British Columbia in southwestern Canada and Yunnan Province in southwestern China. We close by considering some implications of this work for language preservation, recognition and multilingualism.

Rethinking heritage languages in Canada: The case of Chinese

With respect to immigrant HLs in Canada, the commitment of parents and communities to the preservation of their familial languages and cultures has remained reasonably strong in the late 20th and early 21st centuries, although that does not necessarily result in HL retention by younger generations (Duff 2007, 2008), programmatic funding, or supportive language education policies. In addition, Canada's political and economic relationship with other countries, wars and other factors often change the status of (or stigma associated with) the HL language and its speakers within Canada. Regardless of their background and the political status of their home language, many immigrant parents are nevertheless deeply committed to facilitating their children's mastery of dominant or official languages and may believe strongly that focusing on the first language (L1)/HL will impede that goal, despite research to the contrary (Duff 2007).

Children and adolescents are often even more ambivalent and conflicted in terms of interests and investments in their ancestral/familial languages – or *any* languages other than those dominant in society. They are particularly vulnerable to social pressures from peers to conform linguistically and culturally (Duff 2007). These factors usually trigger and expedite language shift toward one of the country's dominant languages for first- and second-generation immigrants, an outcome they and their descendants often regret later (He and Xiao 2008; Brinton et al. 2008; Kouritzen 1999).

However, some ethnolinguistic groups and individuals who have not had or seized upon opportunities to retain and pass their HLs onto the next generation express no particular remorse about that situation. They may view language shift not simply as inevitable but perhaps advantageous as well, and interpret their choices as a form of agency rather than acquiescence (Mizuta, forthcoming).

G. Li's 2006 ethnographic Chinese HL socialisation research in the Metro Vancouver area, for example, provides detailed case studies of three immigrant Chinese-speaking families' attitudes and home-literacy practices chiefly fostering either 1) Chinese, 2) English, or 3) Chinese-English bilingualism and biliteracy, and the many sociological and economic factors affecting their choices related to HL maintenance. These factors might include prioritising success in English mainstream schools or ensuring possibilities of repatriation (for transnational families) to seek better employment opportunities and social status in their (original) home countries (e.g. Hong Kong or China). Whereas the former case (focusing on English schooling) often contributes to language shift, the latter (transnationalism) entails socialising children into Chinese language and literacy practices to support families' future mobility and children's social, cultural and educational integration in English-speaking as well as Chinese-speaking countries.

Chinese ranks third in Canada (after the official languages English and French) in terms of number of self-identified home-language speakers (Statistics Canada 2011). This demographic fact helps account for the growing interest in language programmes for Chinese HL children. Furthermore, families with non-Chinese-background parents attempting to construct an ethnolinguistic heritage for their adopted children from China also seek Chinese HL opportunities for the children, despite the fact that the parents themselves may have little or no familiarity with Chinese language or culture (Duff, forthcoming; Louie 2009). In addition, the growing number of non-Chinese Canadian families who have opted to live, work and study in China, given the growing economy, often seek out opportunities for their children to retain their Chinese upon their return to Canada.

Of course, the linguistic shorthand label 'Chinese' represents more than one language and ethnolinguistic identity (Duff et al. 2013; Duff and Li 2008; Li and Duff, forthcoming 2014). Indeed, the multiplicity of languages and dialects subsumed under that deceptively simple and singular label constitutes part of the challenge facing advocates of Chinese HL retention and education. To make matters more complicated, different varieties of Chinese have been privileged over time both in regions in Greater China and in diaspora contexts, as a consequence of immigration patterns, economics and politics (Jiang 2010). In the analysis of the 20th and early 21st century in British Columbia in Table 1, for example, the language variety (dialect) on the left was at the time more prestigious than the one on the right with which it is paired (e.g. Taishanese vs. Cantonese). However, these pairings, relationships and relative status reveal contestation and change over time as well. Currently, there is some tension between the status of Taiwanese oral/written Chinese and oral/written Mandarin (Putonghua) of mainland China, but given the growing power of the latter, in China, in the world and in diasporas, there is little doubt where this trend is heading.

Table 1: Relative status of certain varieties of Chinese in 20th and 21st century British Columbia and shifts

Early 20th century	→	→	→	Early 21st century
Taishanese → Cantonese				
	Cantonese → Mandarin			
		Mandarin → Cantonese		
				Taiwan Mandarin → Putonghua

→ indicates shift in status from left-in-pair (earlier dominant) to right-in-pair.

Research on Chinese populations and the development and use of their HLs has received increased attention and visibility in the past decade in Canada and beyond (e.g. Duff and Li 2013; He and Xiao 2008; Lo Bianco 2007; Tao 2006; Tsung and Cruickshank 2011). This trend in Chinese language education stems from a number of inter-related demographic, sociopolitical and economic factors. First is the dramatically changing status and visibility of Chinese language(s) internationally, particularly Mandarin, in both diaspora and non-diaspora contexts (Duff et al. 2013; McDonald 2011; Tsung and Cruickshank 2011). Recent waves of immigrants to North America from 'Greater China' – from Hong Kong, Mainland China and Taiwan especially – have higher levels of education and bilingual proficiency in Chinese and English, higher socio-economic status and a greater sense of cosmopolitanism. They therefore have different social, cultural and economic capital, aspirations and global social networks than their predecessors in the 19th- and 20th-century diaspora (P. Li 1998). As a result, the newer immigrants are often very proactive in establishing language schools and community centres and local, regional and national teaching associations, while still actively maintaining their transnational ties and travel to Chinese-speaking regions.

A prominent theme in HL research worldwide concerns not just ethnicity and proficiency but also *identity* in language learning, use and loss (Blackledge and Creese 2008; Duff 2012; He 2008, 2010; Hornberger and Wang 2008; Leung et al. 1997; Liu and Lo Bianco 2007; Pavlenko and Lantolf 2000; Norton and Toohey 2011). In the Chinese-related research specifically, discourses of 'Chineseness' or Sinophone identity are very pronounced (Curdt-Christiansen and Hancock, forthcoming 2014; Louie 2004, 2009). This theme surfaces in discussions regarding Chinese-background learners who embrace being or 'becoming' Chinese, and non-Chinese learners with repertoires and experiences similar to those of HL learners (e.g. Anglophone or ethnically mixed Canadian families who have lived in China or Taiwan, raising children there who also attended Chinese public schools), who seek integration and validation within Chinese communities based on their own histories (Duff et al. 2013). For both populations, the assumed conflation of Chinese heritage, linguistic proficiency/expertise, 'Chineseness,' and an affinity to or affiliation with Chinese language/culture, poses numerous dilemmas (cf. Leung et al. 1997). For example, those who do *not* seek or have access to (traditional) Chinese identities, despite having reached high levels of cultural and linguistic proficiency and possibly significant engagements with Chinese-speaking communities, may feel marginalised by both Chinese communities and the Anglophone interlocutors who make assumptions about what 'Chineseness' should entail (i.e. knowledge of Chinese and heritage). Chinese HL-background students, in turn, may feel burdened and unfairly judged by those with traditional expectations of Chinese maintenance that they do not fulfil, for whatever reason (e.g. Ang 2001).

Chinese language-education programmes either established within the public education sector or, more commonly, run privately through community schools, have long been an option for Chinese-background learners in major global cities, and Canada is no exception (Chen 2006; Jiang 2010). From the turn of the last century, many children of Chinese immigrants in British Columbia started to receive Chinese language education at Chinese public schools in Victoria and Vancouver (Jiang 2010). The schools used pedagogical materials, teaching methods and ideologies heavily influenced by traditions as well as dramatic political movements in China; therefore Chinese HL teaching experienced some major upheavals in the 20th century (Jiang 2010).

In British Columbia today, beyond the 200 or so private Chinese HL schools that exist, Chinese HL students also have some (limited) opportunities to enroll in credit-bearing Chinese courses in (mainstream) public schools and post-secondary institutions, reflecting a number of demographic and educational changes (Li and Duff 2008; Liu and Lo Bianco 2007). However, discourses and policies supporting the linguistic 'duality' of Canada, privileging English and French almost exclusively (and thus French language education in western Canada at the expense of other languages), mitigate against greater provision for formal, credit-bearing Chinese language learning, especially in K-12 schooling. The 'Canadianness' of those aiming to hone their Chinese language(s) and embrace and cultivate their Sinophone identities sometimes comes under attack in response to fears that Chinese language retention and education will somehow undermine Canada's bilingual Anglophone-Francophone history and national 'brand' or distinctiveness (e.g. from the US) as an officially bilingual country.

In the Chinese (K-12) public school language courses that exist, Chinese HL learners' classmates often include 1) those with no prior experience with Chinese language(s) or culture(s); 2) new immigrants to Canada with considerable prior history of Chinese-medium education; or 3) Chinese international students who, similarly, have received almost all their prior formal education in Mandarin (T. Lim, personal communication, September 2013). Somewhere in between these two proficiency and experiential extremes are the majority of the vaguely defined 'HL students' who themselves represent an enormous range of backgrounds – geographical, political, generational, linguistic and cultural – as well as home-dialect knowledge (from none to expert) and preferences.

Li and Duff (forthcoming) provide profiles of Chinese HL learners in Canada taking university Chinese HL courses in Vancouver. One was born in Vancouver, one in Hong Kong, and one each in Beijing and Indonesia. The four illustrate the vastly different backgrounds, trajectories, multilingual repertoires, abilities, preferences and identities of Chinese HL learners. The students had different proficiency levels and most mentioned challenges they had encountered developing and maintaining high levels of literacy in Chinese. Most acknowledged, however, that their personal goal for learning Chinese was also connected to their quest for 'authenticity' as Chinese people. A male Indonesian-Chinese student who had been denied the opportunity to learn Chinese during his youth in Indonesia for political reasons recounted in an interview with us the following experience that he had found troubling, precisely because it called into question his 'Chineseness':

> I'm a Chinese. I remember a person asked me where was I from. I said 'Indonesia.' But he said 'You don't look like a person from Indonesia, you look like a Chinese.' I said 'yeah, I'm a Chinese born in Indonesia.' And he said 'then you could speak Chinese?' I said 'I can't' and I'm very embarrassed. So I want to speak Chinese then I can be recognised as a Chinese.

The 'politics of recognition' that Canadian philosopher Charles Taylor (1994) discussed two decades ago – recognition of one's heritage, affiliation, language and rights – is a major concern for many HL learners at the community (group) level and also in a deeply personal way. They report wanting to know and be able to use Chinese for a variety of purposes, but also long to be seen as proficient, legitimate, 'authentic' Chinese and valid Chinese language learners who are accorded recognition and access to appropriate instruction as well (Wiley 2008).

This kind of desired recognition is evident in the account of a much more proficient student in our study than the Indonesian-Chinese student in the previous example. Born and raised in Taiwan, where he had completed elementary and junior high school, he had arrived in Canada with his family at age 15. At the time of our first interview he was taking a third-year Chinese (HL-orientated) literature course, and working at a local Chinese radio station in Canada as a (Chinese) news anchor and journalist. He described to us very enthusiastically how proud he was to be a Chinese news reporter because of how that positioned him in relation to other Chinese speakers (as he imagined them):

> I thought, it's really cool if you talk to people [in Chinese on the radio] and all of a sudden you can say something really meaningful, something that people rarely know, and you can show that 'oh my God, that guy is so smart', or you know, 'he knows so much'.

Thus, advanced language proficiency, Chinese literacy and cultural knowledge constituted significant symbolic and cultural capital for him. Knowing and being able to communicate effectively appealed to him. Even more powerful a motivator, perhaps, was that he wanted to impress his listeners and readers, stating: 'I am proud that I can write and speak Chinese because for other people, it looks really complicated.'

Younger Chinese HL students, conversely, often resist going to weekend Chinese HL programmes or being taught in the home, and they shift from Chinese to English upon entering public schools, if not before. Peer pressure in childhood and early adolescence in an Anglo-dominant environment involves participating in recreational and discursive activities mediated by English and developing identities as English speakers with deep roots in contemporary local Anglophone culture (He 2006, 2008, 2010). One student in our study whose family had immigrated to Canada from Beijing when she was five mentioned in her interview that learning Chinese had seemed pointless at that time, despite the efforts her parents made in order to help her develop her proficiency further:

> So, to me it was still like being forced to learn a language that has no real use. It is not like a child learning English because they have to live in an environment where everyone speaks English. Because no one spoke Chinese here, I felt it was really difficult, annoying and bothersome at that time. But I guess as I grew up and went to high school, more and more Chinese came to Vancouver, and at that point I realized, you know, my heritage is not something to be annoyed about or shamed about. So you know, I want to embrace it. And, yes, that's why I developed the interest in learning Chinese.

This sense of 'embracing' one's HL culture is often mentioned by students who choose to enrol in Chinese HL courses at university. There is significant emotional investment amongst many who identify as Chinese in Canada to the wider educational community now, to the preservation, use, value and teaching of Standard Modern Chinese (Putonghua), not only for personal cultural reasons, but for future employment opportunities as well (Li and Duff, forthcoming). Naturally, those who have *not* chosen to engage in Chinese HL education often feel quite differently (e.g. Ang 2001).

From these very few excerpts from Chinese HL learners in BC we gain a sense of the identity positions that students negotiate as young adults. The diverse Chinese HL population at schools and universities poses myriad challenges for curriculum, pedagogy and assessment. It also raises issues and resistance because of their perceived (il)legitimacy and their entitlement to high quality formal Chinese education, possibly in the language variety they most identify with (Duff and Li 2013; Kelleher 2008 2010; Li and Duff 2008), which may or may not be Mandarin. In addition to different dialects of Chinese spoken, learned, taught and used locally, nationally and internationally, the different writing (script) systems, and perceptions and sensibilities regarding the economic significance and (soft) power of Mandarin-speaking Greater China, are also factors. Indeed, the active engagement of Mainland Chinese and Taiwanese governments in promoting Chinese language education by supplying teachers and textbooks for Chinese HL teaching and providing other instructional opportunities also illustrate this (Duff et al. 2013; Duff and Li 2013; Li and Duff 2008). Many of these ideological, contextual and practical matters are now being investigated in Canadian Sinophone contexts (e.g. Duff et al. 2013; Duff and Lester 2008; Mizuta, forthcoming).

For example, the textbooks used in Chinese HL education in British Columbia and across Canada have received scrutiny and critique because of the reified and narrowly limited Chinese subject positions they offer to students (Chiu 2011; Curdt-Christiansen 2008; Jiang 2010). These include filial piety and familism ingrained in the Taiwanese learning materials and grand notions of the Chinese motherland in the Mainland Chinese ones – reflecting an imagined community (Anderson 1981) portrayed in Chinese media and curricula, replete with celebrated thinkers and iconic monuments and landmarks that students are expected to embrace and from which they are expected to gain inspiration, together with the language itself. However, the students themselves may not find such discourses and cultural reference points motivating or primary in their own learning trajectories.

To summarise, Chinese HL education in the western Canadian context has, as elsewhere, needed to wrestle with tensions regarding which Chinese dialects/varieties, orthographies, narratives and values are fostered and privileged, and the impact of those choices on learners from different home-dialects. Furthermore, students and their families and teachers (particularly in Chinese HL programmes) are often conflicted as they try to bridge cultures, languages, pedagogies and identities (e.g. more 'Chinese' versus more 'Canadian') that children may identify with to varying degrees at different stages of their formative years, often having identities and practices imposed on them that they no longer align or affiliate with. The quality of Chinese language education for heritage (and non-heritage) learners must also be examined and rethought. In mainstream schooling/education contexts (K-16) it is often assumed that teaching methods, materials and objectives developed for 'foreign language' (truly novice) learners of Chinese are appropriate for learners from Chinese backgrounds (Li 2008), denying who they are, in terms of their lived experiences and linguistic/cultural repertoires. In stark contrast, in private community Chinese HL programmes, the methods, materials and objectives are often comparable to those developed for native speakers of Mandarin in Chinese-speaking countries, again showing little recognition of their lives and cultures in Canada and thus proving of limited relevance to them. These tendencies often drive students away from Chinese rather than towards it, with only the most resilient, determined and highly motivated students remaining in Chinese HL courses (Comanaru and Noels 2009).

Rethinking heritage languages in China

Canada is certainly not alone in having enacted contradictory and often quite detrimental policies affecting non-official language learning and use over the past century. Nor is Canada unique in being home to a very large number of minority languages. When conducting research in China in the late 2000s, we encountered similar sorts of issues surrounding the status of heritage (and indigenous) languages, and education in those languages in communities and schools, and codified in policies. Unlike Canada, however, China has traditionally not received large numbers of immigrant settlers who have sought to retain and cultivate their own languages. Instead, as China's territory and control expanded historically and came to encompass a vast number of millennia-old local languages and dialects, not all of which are Sinitic, increased language contact and internal migration ensued. The result was, predictably, language shift, language loss and attrition, and the hegemony of the northern variety of Standard Mandarin (Putonghua), which is transmitted through educational and other means. Practically speaking, having an official language serve as the country's *lingua franca*, and the language of education and media, provided a means of unifying the country, creating more opportunities for social and physical mobility that was otherwise constrained by mutually incomprehensible languages. The downside of such a *lingua franca* as the official standard language, however, is that the recognition, survival, and thus retention of many minority languages is severely compromised.

Increasing levels and types of Chinese migration, urbanisation, public education, information and communication technologies and mass media since the early 1990s, building on earlier campaigns throughout the 20th century supporting literacy, language reform and language standardisation, have accelerated this shift toward Mandarin and, by extension, Beijing-centric education. The tremendous focus on English education as a national linguistic priority has also confounded attempts at promoting the learning and use of local languages (e.g. Bai) or those of non-anglophone neighbouring countries (e.g. Burmese).

In a recent special issue of the *International Journal of the Sociology of Education*, Zhou (2012) and his contributors illustrate some of the tensions, policies, contexts and outcomes of language contact in China for individuals, communities and languages. In our own research in southwest China, we observed the proverbial 'push and pull' of minority (HL) language maintenance and (at least nominal) Chinese-English bilingualism involving

Putonghua. For our project, we explored the multilingual repertoires and language ideologies of a group of local English teachers and their students in one minority high school that attracted speakers from different minority-language backgrounds. As in Canada, tensions between home/HL maintenance and bilingual Standard Chinese (*lingua franca*), and English development became evident. Here we reflect mainly on issues connected to the participants' home or ancestral languages as 'Heritage' languages which, in general, the students have little possibility to learn or maintain through either community or public schools (with just a few exceptions; e.g. Hui is taught in some weekend community-run Muslim schools).

Yunnan Province is home to 25 official minority groups, also known as 'nationalities', or nearly half the total number (55) of official minority groups across China. According to 2010 national census data (Ma 2011), Han Chinese, the majority ethnic group, constituted roughly 91.5% of the national population. Yunnan is one of the 31 provinces, autonomous regions and municipalities in China (i.e. Mainland China), with a reported population of 46 million in 2010,[2] of whom 34% are counted as minorities. Although some of the province's languages are considered regional or local dialects of Han Chinese, others are quite distinct (non-Chinese) languages associated with particular ethnolinguistic minority groups (e.g. Hui, Naxi, Yi, Lisu, Dai, Tibetan, Bai),[3] each with its own traditions. Because Yunnan borders on Laos, Myanmar (Burma), and Vietnam, has a substantial Dai (Thai) population, and is adjacent to the Tibetan Autonomous Region, it naturally has many speakers of these languages. The local cultural, linguistic, political and physical geography has, over the past two millennia, ensured that many languages indigenous to the area co-exist. Sinification efforts, in the post-World War II era especially, spread Mandarin throughout the province. Thus, Yunnan, like British Columbia, boasts a rich variety and number of minority and indigenous languages.

However, despite a provision in the Chinese Constitution entitling minority groups ('nationalities') to develop and use their HLs (Zhou 2000), public educational institutions (as in Canada) do little of this. In part this is due to the weighty pressure to ensure that children attain high levels of performance in Mandarin, English and academic subjects. Only by doing so can students compete favourably on the high-stakes college entrance examinations at the end of high school and achieve upward social mobility and integration within mainstream society (i.e. ideally large, modern cities from the perspective of those who have endured hardships in isolated rural subsistence farming communities, particularly in the mountains). Also, schools that attract students from minority-language backgrounds use Mandarin as a *lingua franca* because students typically come from many different parts of the province or country and thus ethnolinguistic backgrounds. As a result, few schools manage to successfully leverage, encourage and assess students' bilingual proficiency in minority languages and the national standard language. However, some successful cases have been reported in Yunnan (e.g. Dai (Thai) in Xishuangbana and Bai language in Dali) (Cobbey 2007). The fact that not all of the minority languages have writing systems poses another obstacle to HL education and development, and those that do often use completely different scripts (Roman and non-Roman, Sinographic and otherwise). Even the same minority language can use multiple script systems, as in the case of Dai.

Putonghua and English are rigorously promoted nationwide and thus in Yunnan also through public, private and higher education, language contact and mass media. However, the other languages competing for recognition, validation – and survival – particularly in minority and borderland regions, are being examined by a growing number of scholars (Beckett and MacPherson 2005; Blachford 1999; Feng 2007; L. Li 2011; Lo Bianco et al. 2009; Zhou 2012). By survival we mean not just the vitality of the language itself but also its continuing role, presence and status in people's lives in education and in communities.

Cobbey (2007), who has worked for years in Yunnanese minority regions dealing with issues connected with bilingualism, biliteracy and education, notes several encouraging trends in support of HLs in schools and also local and systemic constraints related to costs, the preparation of teachers and bilingual/biliterate materials, and the issue of scripts mentioned earlier. Those languages (e.g. Dai (Thai)) widely used in a region outside of China (e.g. in Thailand) as well as within Yunnan (in the south) typically are better resourced for literacy education. To date, although many minority Chinese feel a certain duty and desire to maintain their HLs, insufficient attention has been paid to how it can be done successfully both inside and outside the home, and how home-language literacy can bootstrap subsequent language and literacy learning as well. Furthermore, in some minority homes (e.g. in our study), parents themselves have had relatively little formal education and are not literate in the home/HL or in Mandarin, which makes biliteracy all the more difficult and unlikely for their children. Bilingual programmes in schools involving HLs often appear to be transitional only. Once students shift to a Mandarin-dominant curriculum, their next opportunity to learn the HL may be universities offering courses in the larger minority languages (e.g. Tibetan).

In our interviews (in Chinese) with high-school students from non-Mandarin speaking cultural backgrounds within China who also produced narratives in English about their language histories, we observed some of the issues, dilemmas, opportunities and identities associated with multilingualism in Yunnan. Students described, often very poignantly, their experiences of learning and/or losing their HLs. Indeed, this shift is well underway in some small villages and counties. For many students, as in British Columbia, it begins when they enter public schools where Mandarin (and later, English) is taught. Although according to their language education policy their exposure to Putonghua (and English) should begin in primary school, in rural areas it is often later, in late primary or secondary school, based on the availability of local teachers who are proficient in Putonghua.

One student captured his sense of regret, sadness and frustration at not knowing the ancestral language of his village, Yi, which is still spoken elsewhere in Yunnan, and his desire to learn it. In his still-developing English (edited lightly below for spelling and mechanics, but not grammar), he wrote:

> [It] is a special language. Long long ago it was invented by our ancestors. But now, even my grandfather can't speak it. So does all my relatives and I! It's too bad, isn't it? I have ever looked for someone who can teach the language in my hometown. But no one can do it. I feel so sad about the facts. It's our cultural relics, also human race's, all the world's! We should protect it as to protect ourselves.

Another student, from a Hui (Muslim) background, remarked that everyone in her Hui village spoke Chinese, but that her mother, a farmer, had started to teach her English – not Arabic – when she was very young (age 3) so she would not be 'forgotten by the world'.

The region where we carried out our research has a large population of Bai minority students. One wrote about her distress at not being able to speak Bai: 'I am Bai Chinese. So are my family's members. But I cannot speak Bai language very well, that is very terrible for me.'

Another Bai student wrote about her inability to speak Bai because her parents refused to teach it to her, using Mandarin instead. She conveyed a sense of being disadvantaged by this home language policy particularly because she could not communicate well with Bai speakers, and perhaps feels regret or shame as a result:

> My parents and I speak Mandarin Chinese, my father also can speak Bai native language, but my father doesn't teach me. So I can't speak and understand Bai native language. When a Bai speak with me they use Bai native language, I will be nervous, and don't know how to tell he or she that I can't understand what he or she is saying . . .

One girl came from a Yi village and had Yi-speaking grandparents. Given the choice between learning Yi and learning English, she wrote that she would choose Yi because 'Yi dialect is a heritage language in China. We should promote it. [But] I wouldn't necessarily give up English.' Another Yi person wrote that he could not speak his language either, but noted its similarity to classical or literary Chinese and the richness of the culture and 'ancient stories and particular styles':

> My hometown is in mountains, I am Yi, but most of people in my village are Han. So I can't speak or write Yi language. But I know a lot about its culture, which is full of colourful histories, ancient stories and particular styles. I love it. Our languages are similar to formal Chinese.

A student from the Shangri-La (Diqing) region in northwest Yunnan, next to Tibet, disclosed that although her parents spoke some Lisu (which she apparently did not, speaking several dialects of Chinese instead), only some 'old people' in her community could still write the language, but 'probably not' her own grandparents. She observed that researchers were now in the region to 'study', and perhaps document, the written language.

As another Lisu student explains below, his community was Christian and their language has (or had) a special Romanised script but that the language was 'lost', at least to his own community, in his father's generation:

> My hometown has his own culture. We are Lisu people. It has own language. And Lisu language it has written form. But I can't speak this language. Because the language gets lost in my father's time. Lisu language is a special language in Nujiang Prefecture. The written form is very interesting, like the English writing [Roman alphabet].

In one interview, the participant was asked why, if he was Bai, he and his family spoke Chinese (Binchuan dialect) at home and in his village instead of Bai as he had mentioned. He replied (in Chinese, translated into English below):

> Because my parents were concerned about my studies in the future. If I spoke Bai language, I would develop an accent. If I spoke for a long time, it could affect

my Mandarin. My Mandarin would have an accent. My English would have an accent too. When I was playing with my childhood friends, they spoke Bai language but I only spoke Mandarin. So they could understand what I was saying, but I was unable to understand what they were saying. So I learnt Bai language. I learnt from them.

This case illustrates that parents' language ideologies and choices – dismissing home languages and local dialects of Chinese in favour of a more standard variety – despite their good intentions, have the potential to hasten linguistic and cultural obsolescence, unless students are as resourceful as this one and both choose and have the opportunity to learn the local languages on their own from their peers. The students may also become ostracised from their village peer groups if they do not learn local vernaculars, and in that way become alienated from the older generations as well.

To summarise, a body of recent research describes issues with bilingual education in minority languages and Mandarin in China, in Yunnan and other provinces. As in other research, the Chinese minority students who participated in our research communicated their misgivings and concerns about their experiences with language shift and their apprehension about the future sustainability of their treasured cultural heritage.

Conclusion

Several implications for language policy and pedagogy emerge from this brief exposition of HL maintenance in Sinophone contexts in Canada and China. If parents, teachers and peers can foster pride and model multilingualism and multiliteracies in minority languages, literacies and cultures, as well as in the dominant languages, they can be more effective agents of additive versus subtractive or transitional bi/multilingualism. They can also demonstrate the pragmatic, emotional and intellectual value of multilingualism. Educational policies that reward and support people's multilingualism and multiliteracies at home, in communities and schools legitimise these 'knowledges' as well.

Indeed, a growing literature on bi-/multilingualism and HL retention confirms that for many people a knowledge of their HLs and other languages allows them an expanded, more nuanced sense of 'self,' of family, and of global citizenship. However, the dominance of English and official languages, such as Putonghua in China, can also foment resistance to, and resentment of, HL education because of its increasing influence and gatekeeping role of the other two more internationally powerful languages. Negative (or neutral) attitudes toward HL preservation also coincide with the belief that an on-going commitment to one's HL precludes efficient and expedited learning of official languages and thus potential upward mobility.

The integration of teachers' and students' multilingual knowledge and identities in the Chinese school curricula, and its valorisation within local communities for students' personal, social/cultural, cognitive and educational wellbeing, requires much more investigation, advocacy and intervention. In addition, the varied interests, profiles and histories of learners in the same classes need to be explored and accommodated. For some HLs, as in the Yunnanese context, millions of students from minority populations risk linguistic and cultural severance from their millennia-old roots, traditions and local languages/dialects – the kinds of multilingualism and syncretism that many in our studies in both Canada and China (in the larger studies) reported to be a source of happiness and deep fulfillment (despite also being an ongoing struggle). Furthermore, they lose the well-documented benefits of building upon their prior knowledge and various forms of symbolic, social and cultural capital when learning mandated additional languages such as Chinese or English (e.g. Bourdieu 1991; Cummins 1996; Gao 2009). Also lost, eventually, are connections with their heritage and extended families and over time the languages themselves – especially those that are 'small,' relatively isolated and unwritten – may die. Thus, despite the push-and-pull effects of modernisation and globalisation on the one hand, and local knowledge and rootedness on the other, commitments and mechanisms are needed to ensure that powerful standard (inter)national languages can co-exist productively with beloved local or ancestral ones.

We must also take into account more fully issues connected with desire, voice, identity, heteroglossia and agency in HL learning (Duff 2012). Agency, though socioculturally mediated, includes the ability to resist, to make choices, to be self-directed and not only other-directed in terms of one's linguistic, cultural and other goals. Unlike the learning of Mandarin by young children of Chinese descent in Canada or in minority homes in China whose parents usually make the 'choice' for them, adolescents and young adults typically have more agency and autonomy with respect to their language learning decisions, behaviours and identities. They are not always aware of the trade-offs or consequences of *not* embracing their HLs for them, their families, their worldview and opportunities, and their languages. Once HLs become obligatory and institutionalised – particularly if not taught in an engaging manner – students may feel alienated by the experience and much less invested in the HL. This is, unfortunately, one of the dilemmas of HL education in many contexts. In the Yunnan context, furthermore, with the passing of time, as in the case of all too many 'small' Canadian indigenous languages, undocumented or unlearned local knowledges and habitus (Gao 2009) may be lost completely – truly 'forgotten by the world' to use the expression the Hui student used earlier. These issues therefore deserve the same kind of urgency and attention that is now (too late) associated with indigenous languages in other regions, as societies and governments rethink HLs and their value to humanity.

REFERENCES

Anderson, B. (2006). *Imagined Communities* (second ed.). London: Verso.

Ang, I. (2001). *On Not Speaking Chinese: Living Between Asia and the West.* London: Routledge.

Ashworth, M. (1988). *Blessed with Bilingual Brains: Education of Immigrant Children with English as a Second Language.* Vancouver: Pacific Educational Press.

Beckett, G. and MacPherson, S. (2005). 'Researching the Impact of English on Minority and Indigenous Languages in Non-Western Contexts'. *TESOL Quarterly* 2, 299–307.

Beynon, J. and Toohey, K. (1991). 'Heritage Language Education in British Columbia: Policy and programmes'. *Canadian Modern Language Review,* 47, 606–16.

Blachford, D.R. (1990). 'Language Planning and Bilingual Education for Linguistic Minorities in China: A Case Study of the Policy Formulation and Implementation Process'. Unpublished PhD dissertation, Ontario Institute for Studies in Education/ University of Toronto.

Blackledge, A. and Creese, A. (2008). 'Contesting "Language" as "Heritage": Negotiation of Identities in Late Modernity'. *Applied Linguistics* 29 (4), 533–54.

Bourdieu, P. (1991). *Language and Symbolic Power.* (B. Thompson (ed.); G. Raymond and M. Adamson, trans.). Cambridge: Cambridge University Press.

Brinton, D., Kagan, O. and Bauckus, S. (eds). (2008). *Heritage Language Education: A New Field Emerging.* New York: Routledge/Taylor and Francis.

Chen, Y.J. (2006). 'Balancing Goals and Emotional Responses to Learning Chinese as a Heritage Language'. Unpublished PhD dissertation. University of Texas, Austin.

Chiu, L. (2011). 'The Construction of the "Ideal Chinese Child": A Critical Analysis of Textbooks for Chinese Heritage Language Learners'. Unpublished MA thesis, University of British Columbia, Canada.

Cobbey, H. (2007). 'Challenges and Prospects of Minority Bilingual Education in China— An Analysis of Four Projects'. In A. Feng, ed., *Bilingual education in China,* 182–99. Clevedon: Multilingual Matters.

Comanaru, R. and **Noels, K.** (2009). 'Self-Determination, Motivation, and the Learning of Chinese as a Heritage Language'. *The Canadian Modern Language Review* 66 (1), 131–58.

Cummins, J. (1992). 'Heritage Language Teaching in Canadian Schools'. *Journal of Curriculum Studies* 24, 287–96.

— (1993). 'The Research Basis for Heritage Language Promotion'. In M. Danesi, K. McLeod and S. Morris (eds), *Heritage Language and Education: The Canadian Experience*, 1–21. Ontario, Canada: Mosaic Press.

— (1996). *Negotiating Identities: Education for Empowerment in a Diverse Society*. Los Angeles: California Association for Bilingual Education.

— (ed.). (1983). *Heritage Language Education: Issues and Directions*. Ottawa: Minister of Supply and Services Canada.

— (ed.). (1991). 'Heritage languages' (special issue). *Canadian Modern Language Review*, 47 (4).

Cummins, J. and **Danesi, M.** (1990). *Heritage languages: The Development and Denial of Canada's Linguistic Resources*. Montreal: Our Schools/Our Selves Education Foundation.

Curdt-Christiansen, X.L. (2008) 'Reading the World Through Words: Cultural Themes in Heritage Chinese Language Textbooks'. *Language and Education* 22 (2), 95–113.

Danesi, M., McLeod, K. and **Morris, S.** (eds). (1993). *Heritage Languages and Education: The Canadian experience*. Oakville, ON: Mosaic Press.

Duff, P. (2007). 'Multilingualism in Canadian schools: Myths, Realities, and Possibilities'. *Canadian Journal for Applied Linguistics* 10 (2), 149–63.

— (2008). 'Heritage Language Education in Canada'. In D. Brinton, O. Kagan and S. Bauckus (eds), *Heritage Language Education: A New Field Emerging*, 71–90. New York: Routledge/ Taylor and Francis.

— (2012). 'Identity, Agency, and SLA'. In A. Mackey and S. Gass (eds), *Handbook of Second Language Acquisition*, 410–26. London: Routledge.

— (forthcoming). 'Language Socialization into Chinese Language and "Chineseness" in Diaspora Communities'. In X.L. Curdt-Christiansen and A. Hancock, eds, *Learning Chinese in Diasporic Communities: Many Pathways to Becoming Chinese*. Amsterdam: John Benjamins.

Duff, P. and **Lester, P.** (eds). (2008). *Issues in Chinese Language Education and Teacher Development*. University of British Columbia Centre for Research in Chinese Language and Literacy Education.

Duff, P. and **Li, D.** (2013). 'Learning Chinese as a Heritage Language'. In C. Mady and K. Arnett, eds, *Minority Populations in Second Language Education: Broadening the Lens from Canada*, 87–100. Bristol: Multilingual Matters.

Duff, P., Anderson, T., Ilnyckyj, R., Lester, P., Wang, R. and **Yates, E.** (2013). *Learning Chinese: Linguistic, Sociocultural and Narrative Perspectives*. Berlin/Boston: De Gruyter.

Feng, A.W. (ed.). (2007). *Bilingual education in China: Practices, Policies and Concepts*. Clevedon: Multilingual Matters.

Gao, Y. (2009). 'Sociocultural Contexts and English in China: Retaining and Reforming the Cultural Habitus. In J. Lo Bianco, J. Orton, and Y. Gao (eds), *China and English: Globalisation and the Dilemmas of Identity*, 56–78. Bristol: Multilingual Matters.

He, A.W. (2006). 'Toward an Identity Theory of the Development of Chinese as a Heritage Language'. *Heritage Language Journal* 4 (1), 1–28.

— (2008). 'An Identity-based Model for the Development of Chinese as a Heritage Language. In A. He and Y. Xiao, eds, *Chinese as a Heritage Language: Fostering Rooted World Citizenry*, 109–24. Honolulu: National Foreign Language Resource Center, University of Hawaii.

He, A.W. (2010). 'The Heart of Heritage: Sociocultural Dimensions of Heritage Language Acquisition'. *Annual Review of Applied Linguistics* 30, 66–82.

Hornberger, N.H. and **Wang, S.** (2008). 'Who are our Heritage Language Learners? Identity and Biliteracy in Heritage Language Education in the United States'. In D. Brinton, O. Kagan, and S. Bauckus, eds, *Heritage language education: A New Field Emerging*, 3–35. New York: Routledge.

Jiang, H. (2010). 'A Socio-Historical Analysis of Chinese Heritage Language Education in British Columbia'. Unpublished MA Thesis, University of British Columbia, Canada.

Kelleher, A. (2008). 'Placements and Re-Positionings: Tensions around CHL Learning in a University Mandarin Program'. In A.W. He and Y. Xiao, eds, *Chinese as a Heritage Language: Fostering Rooted World Citizenry*, 239–58. Honolulu: National Foreign Language Resource Center, University of Hawaii at Manoa.

Kelleher, A. (2010). 'Policies and Identities in Mandarin Education: The Situated Multilingualism of University-Level "Heritage" Language Learners'. Unpublished PhD dissertation. University of California, Davis.

Kouritzen, S.G. (1999). *Face[t]s of First Language Loss*. Mahwah, NJ: Lawrence Erlbaum.

Lei, J. (2007). 'A Language Socialization Approach to the Interplay of Ethnic Revitalization and Heritage Language Learning – Case Studies of Chinese American Adolescents'. Unpublished PhD dissertation. State University of New York (SUNY), Albany.

Leung, C., Harris, R. and **Rampton, B.** (1997). 'The Idealised Native Speaker, Reified Ethnicities, and Classroom Realities'. *TESOL Quarterly* 31 (3), 543–60.

Li, D. (2008). Issues in Chinese language curriculum and materials development. In P. Duff and P. Lester, eds, *Issues in Chinese Language Education and Teacher Development*, 49–69. University of British Columbia Centre for Research in Chinese Language and Literacy Education.

Li, D. and **Duff, P.** (2008). 'Issues in Chinese Heritage Language Education and Research at the Postsecondary Level'. In A.W. He and Y. Xiao, eds, *Chinese as a Heritage Language: Fostering Rooted World Citizenry*, 13–33. Honolulu: National Foreign Language Resource Center, University of Hawaii at Manoa.

— (forthcoming). 'Chinese Language Learning by Adolescents and Young Adults in the Chinese Diaspora: Motivation, Ethnicity, and Identity'. In X. L. Curdt-Christiansen and A. Hancock, eds, *Learning Chinese in Diasporic Communities: Many Pathways to Becoming Chinese*. Amsterdam: John Benjamins.

Li, G. (2006). 'Biliteracy and Trilingual Practices in the Home Context: Case Studies of Chinese Canadian Children'. *Journal of Early Childhood Literacy* 6 (3), 359–85.

— (2007). 'Second Language and Literacy Learning in School and at Home: An Ethnographic Study of Chinese-Canadian First Graders' Experiences'. *Journal of Language Teaching and Learning* 11 (1), 1–40.

Li, L. (2011). 'Decentralizing Unitary Foreign Language Education Policy, Localizing Foreign Language Education and Practices: A Case Study in Southwest China,Yunnan Province'. Paper presented at the World Congress of Applied Linguistics, Beijing, August, 2011.

Li, P.S. (1998) *The Chinese in Canada*. Toronto: Oxford University Press.

Liu, G-Q. and Lo Bianco, J. (2007). 'Teaching Chinese, Teaching in Chinese, and Teaching the Chinese'. *Language Policy* 6, 95–17.

Lo Bianco, J., ed. (2007). 'The Emergence of Chinese' (special issue). *Language Policy* 6 (1).

Lo Bianco, J., Orton, J. and Gao, Y., eds (2009). *China and English: Globalization and the Dilemmas of Identity*. Clevedon: Multilingual Matters.

Louie, A. (2004). *Chineseness Across Borders: Renegotiating Chinese Identities in China and the United States*. Durham, NC: Duke University Press.

— (2009). Pandas, Lions, and Dragons, Oh My! How White Adoptive Parents Construct Chineseness'. *Journal of Asian American Studies* 12 (3), 285–320.

Lu, X. and Li, G. (2008). 'Motivation and Achievement in Chinese Language Learning: A Comparative Analysis. In A.W. He and Y. Xiao, eds, *Chinese as a Heritage Language: Fostering Rooted World Citizenry*, 89–108. Honolulu: University of Hawai'i Press.

Ma, J. (2011). Press release on major figures of the 2010 national population census. http://www.stats.gov.cn/english/newsandcomingevents/t20110428_402722237.htm (retrieved October 23, 2012).

McCarty, T. (2003). 'Revitalising Indigenous Languages in Homogenising Times. *Comparative Education* 39 (2), 147–63.

McDonald, E. (2011). *Learning Chinese, turning Chinese: Challenges to Becoming Sinophone in a Globalised World*. New York: Routledge.

Mizuta, A. (forthcoming). 'Bilingualism for All? Chinese Language Education in Metro Vancouver'. PhD dissertation, University of British Columbia.

Norton, B. and Toohey, K. (2011). 'Identity, Language Learning, and Social Change'. *Language Teaching* 44 (4), 412–46.

Pavlenko, A. and Lantolf, J.P. (2000). 'Second Language Learning as Participation and the (Re)Construction of Selves'. In J.P. Lantolf, ed., *Sociocultural Theory and Second Language Learning*, 155–77. New York: Oxford University Press.

Ross, H. (2005). 'China Country Report: Literacy for Life'. (Paper commissioned for the *EFA Global Monitoring Report 2006, Literacy for Life*). http://unesdoc.unesco.org/images/0014/001461/146108e.pdf (retrieved December 2012).

Statistics Canada (2011). 'Census in Brief: Immigrant Languages in Canada. Language, Census of Population, 2011. http://www12.statcan.gc.ca/census-recensement/2011/as-sa/98-314-x/98-314-x2011003_2-eng.pdf (retrieved January 2013).

Tao, H., ed. (2006). Chinese as a Heritage Language' (special issue). *Heritage Language Journal* 4 (1).

Taylor, C. (1994). 'The Politics of Recognition'. In A. Gutmann, ed., *Multiculturalism: Examining the Politics of Recognition*, 25–73. Princeton: Princeton University Press.

Tsung, L. and Cruickshank, K., eds (2011). *Learning and Teaching Chinese in Global Contexts: Multimodality and Literacy in the New Media Age*. London: Continuum.

Wiley, T. (2008). 'Chinese "Dialect" Speakers as Heritage Language Learners: A Case Study. In D. Brinton, O. Kagan, and S. Bauckus, eds, *Heritage Language Education: A New Field Emerging*, 91–105. New York: Routledge.

Xu, H. (2009). 'Ethnic Minorities, Bilingual Education and Globalization'. In J. Lo Bianco, J. Orton, and Y. Gao, eds, *China and English: Globalisation and the Dilemmas of Identity,* 181–91. Bristol: Multilingual Matters.

Zhou, M. (2000). 'Language Policy and Illiteracy in Ethnic Minority Communities in China'. *Journal of Multilingual and Multicultural Development* 21 (2), 129–48.

NOTES

1   We acknowledge, with gratitude, funding received from SSHRC in the form of two Standard Research Grants that supported this research and the writing of this chapter.

2   www.stats.gov.cn/english/newsandcomingevents/t20110429_402722516.htm.

3   According to Ross (2005), 'Ninety percent of China's minority population speaks 15 languages – Zhuang, Uigher, Miao, Tibetan, Mongol, Buyei, Korean, Dong, Hani, Bai, Kazak, Dai, Li, and Yao. Of China's 120 languages only 35 have more than 50000 speakers. Twenty-two of these languages have less than 10000 speakers and are expected to become extinct' (p. 23).

4   THE PLACE OF HERITAGE LANGUAGES in Languages Education in Australia: A Conceptual Challenge

Angela Scarino (University of South Australia)

Introduction: heritage language learning in the Australian context

As an integral part of languages education in Australia, heritage languages (HLs)[1] need to be viewed in both the global and the distinctively local contexts. The local context is shaped by the history of migration to this country and the language policies developed to address the distinctive ecology of languages within it. The global context is shaped by the processes of globalisation. I examine aspects of the global and local contexts to set the scene for understanding the nature of HL learning in Australia. These contexts have implications for the very nature of language learning in general and HL learning in particular in Australian education.

The context of globalisation

The unprecedented scale and speed of movement of people and their ideas, languages and cultures across the globe has altered the face of social, cultural and linguistic diversity in societies and in education. The term 'super-diversity', coined by Vertovec (2010), is intended to capture a level of complexity surpassing anything that many migrant-receiving communities have previously experienced. This context has implications for our understanding not only of the very nature of language, language use and multiculturalism (Blommaert and Rampton 2012), but also of the nature of language learning (Stroud and Heugh 2011). Languages are no longer assumed to be in a one-to-one relationship with ethnic or cultural groups or nations, but are viewed more expansively as expressive and personal resources for exchanging meaning (Shohamy 2007). In multilingual and multicultural contexts, language use is no longer 'pure', but hybrid, multiple, with a mixing of languages across the repertoire. Language learning needs to build on the diversity of languages and semiotic modes that learners as individuals bring to the classroom, and it needs to draw upon the collective diversity and its resources in the classroom. The global context provides a frame of reference for considering HL learning in Australia, recognising at the same time that each context of multilingualism and multiculturalism has its own distinctive nature and history. The consequences of global mobility are that in each local setting there is generally a larger number of languages in society and in education, a different distribution of languages, diverse personal affiliations with particular languages, and multiple motivations for and expectations about language use and language learning. This means that there is a need to provide one set of learning pathways and experiences for students who are HL learners and another for those who are not.

Responses to the context of globalisation and its impact on linguistic and cultural diversity can be polarised. On the one hand there is, in recent times, an increasing xenophobia, with concerns about security and religious fundamentalism; on the other hand, there is an increased awareness of the benefits of multilingualism and multiculturalism for the individual in terms of cross-generational communication, increased linguistic and cultural capital, and intellectual benefits. At the same time there are benefits for society in terms of international trade, diplomacy and defence, marketing of goods, and cultural experiences.

The context of language policy in Australia

HL learning in Australia resides in a context of continuously changing ideologies, motivations and language policy goals. Since the high point in Australia's language policy-making with the release of the *National Policy on Languages* (NPL) (Lo Bianco 1987) as an explicit, pluralistic, national policy, there has been a constant move towards seeking to reduce the diversity and complexity of languages provision (Liddicoat, Scarino, Curnow, Kohler, Scrimgeour and Morgan 2007; Lo Bianco with Slaughter 2009; Liddicoat 2013). There is a double irony in that, firstly, this reduction is part of an effort on the part of the field of languages education to ensure that language learning is a part of mainstream education and, secondly, it is taking place at the very time of increasing linguistic and cultural diversity. There has been no lack of policy activity in the period since the NPL; in fact, Lo Bianco and Gvozdenko (2006) identify 67 policy statements or plans on languages articulated at a national level. There has also been a continuous struggle for the inclusion and legitimacy of languages in educational goals and structures, and to sustain the diversity of languages offered (Scarino 2008). This struggle has necessitated a willingness to conform to general educational goals, policies, constructs and values that do not necessarily articulate well with linguistic and cultural diversity — and HLs are an integral part of the diversity of languages offered in Australian education. At the present time, despite immense activity on the part of all those involved and interested in languages education, there is a pervasive fragility in policy, participation and provision. The ambivalence that Scarino and Papademetre (2001) identified over a decade ago remains (See Colic-Peisker and Farquharson 2011 for a discussion of multilicultural policy in Australia).

Thus HLs in Australia are situated in a context of globalisation that is increasing the multilingualism and multiculturalism of localities, including Australia, while at the same time the policy settings and provision for languages learning and participation are fragile. This fragility means that HL communities and teachers, as advocates for their particular languages, face a continuous struggle for legitimacy. This struggle, however, should not take energy away from a focus on student learning.

The place of heritage languages in Australian educational provision

The history of HLs in Australia is directly linked to the history of migration and its linguistic and cultural consequences. The term 'community languages' has been in use since about 1975 to denote languages other than English and other than Aboriginal languages that are employed within the Australian community (Clyne 1991; see also Clyne 2005 for a more recent account). It was intended to capture the fact that these languages were actively used in the community. Like all such terms (including the term 'heritage language' in the US), it becomes problematic in relation to what is included and what is excluded. The term was intended to capture the languages of the immigrant communities, whose languages, up to the 1970s, were underrepresented in Australian education; and yet for all languages there is a community of users. Taking Italian, the most widely-taught language in Australia, as an example, its place in education is a result of its presence and active use in the community — it is a language of the community, with its own newspaper, radio and television programmes. It is a community language that is learnt both by those who have a family heritage in the language and by those who are interested in learning the language because it is widespread in the Australian community and is a language of 'cultural prestige' (see Lo Bianco and Aliani 2013). Given the migration vintage of the Italian community in Australia (generally post-World War II migrants), does 'community' refer to the countries where the language is used? Or to the community of Australian-born children of immigrant parents? Or is it the community of recent arrivals?

One of the important achievements in languages education in Australia is the provision in the school education system for a range of languages. Although not all are necessarily available in mainstream education, HLs are available through so-called 'complementary' providers, of which there are two major forms: government 'schools of language' and 'ethnic schools'. The government schools of language are Ministry of Education schools that focus on offering heritage languages, world languages such as French and, more recently and increasingly, Aboriginal languages. These language programmes are provided in mainstream school sites and are governed by the same regulations, requirements and accountabilities as mainstream schools, but they are offered out of regular school hours. The ethnic schools are supported through government funding and run by community groups, but are not governed by the education ministry. These complementary providers are well networked locally and nationally and provide a full range of languages, but are not subject to mainstream school governance.

A snapshot of participation in languages education in Australian schools in 2005 is provided in Liddicoat et al. (2007, 30–1). Of the 133 languages taught, 45 were indigenous Australian languages and 88 were non-indigenous languages, taught either as foreign languages or as community languages. The ethnic schools sector taught 77 languages, 22 of which were available only in ethnic schools (see Table 1). In all the schools sectors (government, non-government and ethnic schools), 47 languages were taught.

Table 1: Languages taught only in ethnic schools in Australia, 2005

Amharic	Fijian	Nepalese	Tatar
Assyrian	Finnish	Nuer	Telugu
Bari	Gujerati/Gujarati	Oromo	Tok Pisin
Bulgarian	Harari	Romanian	Uighur
Danish	Mandaean	Slovak	
Dinka/Madi	Mon	Swedish	

Source: Liddicoat et al. 2007, 30

Although a wide range of languages are taught in Australia, a much smaller number is taught widely. The 20 most widely studied languages taught around the country in 2005 (see Table 2) are a mixture of world languages, community languages, a classical language and an Aboriginal language.

Table 2: Languages taught in all school sectors

1.	Japanese	11. Auslan
2.	Italian	12. Hebrew
3.	Indonesian	13. Korean
4.	French	14. Turkish
5.	German	15. Latin
6.	Chinese*	16. Macedonian
7.	Modern Greek	17. Serbian
8.	Vietnamese	18. Khmer**
9.	Arabic	19. Pitjantjatjara
10.	Spanish	20. Tamil

* Chinese includes reports of Mandarin or unspecified Chinese.

** Khmer includes Cambodian.

Source: Liddicoat et al. 2007, 31

Perhaps the most robust achievement for HL learning in Australia is the availability of a wide range of these languages for formal examination at Year 12 level (the final year of the secondary cycle) and that students' results can be used in the calculation of the Australian Tertiary Admission Rank that determines students' access to university education. This means that the results of HL learning can contribute to a high-stakes process in the students' futures. This is achieved through a national collaborative scheme called the Collaborative Curriculum and Assessment Framework for Languages (CCAFL), which has been in place for more than two decades. It has involved the development of a shared framework for languages and a system for sharing syllabus development and examination.

Under the current CCAFL scheme, syllabuses are developed at three levels: beginners, continuers (second language) and background/first language speakers (for languages with significant 'background'-speaker cohorts). These levels are defined as:

- Beginners: for students who have little or no previous knowledge of the target language.
- Continuers: for students who have studied the language for 400–500 hours by the time they have completed Year 12, or who have an 'equivalent' level of knowledge.
- Background speakers: for students who have a background in the language and more than one year's education in a country where the language is spoken.

The table below illustrates the range of languages that were available for examination in 2012 through the SACE Board of South Australia, which administers the South Australian Certificate of Education (SACE). Overall, 40 languages were available in 2012, provided through 52 different courses.

Table 3: Languages offered by the SACE Board 2012

Locally Assessed Languages	Nationally Assessed Languages	Interstate-Assessed Languages
Australian Languages	Albanian (continuers)	Arabic (beginners) from BOS NSW
Chinese (background speakers)	Armenian (continuers)	Arabic (continuers) from BOS NSW
Chinese (continuers)	Auslan (continuers)	Chinese (beginners) from BOS NSW
French (continuers)	Bosnian (continuers)	French (beginners) from BOS NSW
German (continuers)	Croatian (continuers)	German (beginners) from BOS NSW
Indonesian (continuers)	Dutch (continuers)	Indonesian (beginners) from BOS NSW
Italian (continuers)	Filipino (continuers)	Italian (beginners) from BOS NSW
Japanese (continuers)	Hebrew (continuers)	Japanese (background speakers) from
Language and Culture	Hindi (continuers)	BOS NSW
Modern Greek (continuers)	Hungarian (continuers)	Japanese (beginners) from BOS NSW
Spanish (continuers)	Khmer (continuers)	Korean (first language) from VCAA
Vietnamese (background speakers)	Macedonian (continuers)	Modern Greek (beginners) from
Vietnamese (continuers)	Malay (background speakers)	BOS NSW
	Maltese (continuers)	Spanish (beginners) from BOS NSW
	Persian (background speakers)	
	Polish (continuers)	
	Portuguese (continuers)	
	Punjabi (continuers)	
	Romanian (continuers)	
	Russian (background speakers)	
	Russian (continuers)	
	Serbian (continuers)	
	Sinhala (continuers)	
	Swedish (continuers)	
	Tamil (continuers)	
	Ukrainian (continuers)	
	Yiddish (continuers)	

Source: SACE Board of South Australia

In the table, the locally assessed languages are those offered and examined locally by the SACE Board. The nationally assessed languages are those languages for which the syllabus and examinations are developed collaboratively, based on the CCAFL framework. The interstate-assessed languages are those syllabuses and examinations that the SACE Board borrows from other states. 'BOS' stands for Board of Studies of New South Wales; 'VCAA' stands for Victorian Curriculum and Assessment Authority.

The wide diversity of HLs and HL courses made available to Australians has been possible only because of national collaboration. It is likely that the languages of more recently arrived migrant groups will gradually be added to the collaborative scheme. Such a request has been made recently by the Dinka-speaking community. Achieving this status as a Year 12 subject confers legitimacy to the HL and symbolic value in the eyes of the community. There is a point of complexity, however, that warrants explanation.

Because some languages, such as Italian, are learnt both as HLs and as second or foreign languages, assessment authorities in the different states of Australia have found it necessary to differentiate courses by learner background. There are courses for beginners at senior secondary level; courses for continuers, second language learners who have studied the language at least since Year 7/8, throughout the secondary cycle; and courses for background speakers (who learnt it as their first language and are HL learners, also called 'first language speakers' in different states). In addition, more recently, in the state of New South Wales, a course has been developed specifically for HL learners for the four Asian languages (Chinese, Indonesian, Japanese and Korean) that have been prioritised in Australian language policy.

The diversity of learner background is particularly salient in Asian languages education just now because of: 1) current patterns of migration; 2) their use in the wider community; 3) opportunities for community schooling, and 4) the participation of an increasing number of international students from the Asian region in primary and secondary school education in Australia.

In a typical secondary school classroom for Chinese language learning in Australia, for example, there are students learning Chinese as second language beginners, alongside learners with prior experience of learning Chinese in their primary years, students learning Chinese as additional language learners (e.g. Vietnamese home users learning Chinese), and Chinese HL learners. Given this context and the high-stakes nature of assessment at Year 12, students need to be placed in the course that is most appropriate to their background. There is concern, for example, that HL learners have an advantage.

Eligibility criteria have been developed for participation in courses at both continuers and background speaker levels. These criteria were designed to exclude students with knowledge or experience beyond that anticipated from the target group. In general, students deemed ineligible for continuers level (that is, those with prior language learning knowledge) are permitted to enrol at background speakers level. These eligibility criteria have been established and are implemented in different ways in each of the states (for a detailed discussion see Scarino, Elder, Iwashita, Kim, Kohler and Scrimgeour 2011), which renders the implementation of this system even more complex.

Although eligibility criteria screen students into separate groupings for assessment purposes, they are frequently taught in the same classroom.

In recent times, the increasing diversity has placed pressure on these eligibility criteria. Issues have been raised about definitional criteria and perceptions of particular students as 'advantaged' or 'disadvantaged'. These issues arise because the achievements of learners of different backgrounds do, in fact, differ and in Australia these students study side-by-side and sit a high-stakes examination where the difference in achievements is relevant. This complex issue has been studied extensively by Elder (1996, 2000a, 2000b), and most recently in the Student Achievement in Asian Languages Education (SAALE) study undertaken by Scarino, Elder, Iwashita, Kim, Kohler and Scrimgeour (2011). This empirical study examined the impact of learner background and time-on-task on student achievements in Asian languages (Chinese, Japanese, Indonesian and Japanese). In a context where, for more than three decades, learner achievements in language learning have been described generically (that is, using one description for all languages), this study was the first in the history of languages education in Australia that specifically examined the influence of learner background and the related variable of time-on-task on learner achievements in K-12 in four specific languages. It targeted the end of Years 6/7 (the end of the primary cycle), Year 10 and Year 12 (the end of the secondary cycle; see Scarino et al. 2011, for a detailed discussion). Three key findings from the study related to language background of the students:

- The quantitative analyses support language groupings used to generate descriptions of learner achievement that are sensitive to learner backgrounds.
- First language learners consistently achieve at higher levels than second language learners.

- The achievements of background language learners are highly variable; they are not always distinct from first and second language learner groups.

Further investigation of the achievements of HL learners in a range of languages is warranted. The generic descriptions do not do justice to the variation across languages and learner groups, both of which need to be better understood. It is worth highlighting that for HL learners, being able to study the language of their home and to count this learning both in the formal certification that marks the completion of secondary schooling and for tertiary entrance, adds legitimacy and value. At the same time, they are also caught in the assumption of 'advantage', which does not always hold.

Federal policy over the past three decades has included languages in general, as well as HLs, in the statements of the national goals of Australian schooling (see Scarino 2010). The most recent statement of goals includes the note 'especially Asian languages' (see Ministerial Council for Education, Early Childhood Development and Youth Affairs 2008). This prioritisation of a particular group of languages, all of which are both second languages and HLs, has the potential to create limits to diversity, especially in a context where policies for multilingualism and multiculturalism have lost ground. I discuss this issue further below.

Thus, there is provision for HLs in the Australian education system, but there is also a price to be paid for sustaining this diversity. HLs are included with all other languages, including world languages and Aboriginal languages. There are pressure points for eligibility criteria and differentiation of courses to provide for fairness.

Having described the context of globalisation, some aspects of the context of language policy in Australia, and the place of HLs in Australian educational provision, I now turn to a discussion of the implications of the increasing linguistic and cultural diversity for learning HLs and, specifically, the need to reconceptualise the nature of HL learning to do justice to students' language use and language learning practices. I then discuss HL learning in the context of the current development of the Australian (national) curriculum.

Much of the discussion that follows is broadly applicable to language learning in general, but applies all the more intensely to HLs because of the lived reality of the community of users of HLs. Arguably, more than all other language learners, HL learners, are in an 'in-between' space. Their family background in the HL and culture creates a different affiliation with the language than that of second language learners; and yet, because of the reduced exposure to their language and culture, they cannot be considered to be first language learners. This phenomenon needs to be better understood and captured in the languages education for these learners.

Implications of the increasing linguistic and cultural diversity for learning heritage languages

The global reality of increasing linguistic and cultural diversity puts a premium on communicating and learning to communicate multilingually across languages and cultures. As a consequence of globalisation, there is an increasing diversity of learners and an increasing diversity of languages in the communities of schools.

Given the diversity of students in Australian education, it is important to recognise that a range of HLs are brought to and used as part of learning in the formal curriculum and/or in the students' primary socialisation in families and the local target language-speaking community in Australia. Most recently, a number of the languages of Africa are beginning to be introduced as HLs in response to changing patterns of migration. All learners also encounter English as the language of instruction at school. In contemporary understandings of language learning and development, *all* the languages that learners experience in their socialisation and education form part of the learners' distinctive linguistic and cultural repertoires. These repertoires are an integral part of their identities. The languages are no longer conceptualised as being held separately in students' minds. Rather, they are understood as being interrelated and developed through what Cenoz and Gorter (2011) call a 'holistic' approach. As such, for students with a home background in the language being learned, HLs play an important role in students' overall language learning and development, and in their learning in general. Traditionally, HLs have been seen as part of a learners' home or community backgrounds, but this notion of background diminishes their role. These languages are not simply 'in the background'; they are part of the learners' life-worlds, integral to the framework of interpretive resources that they bring to learning. It is through their frameworks of knowledge, mediated through language in the context of culture, that new learning takes place (see Halliday 1993). In this way, the HL can be understood as constitutive of learners' learning and, through this learning, it is also constitutive of their identity. Whether they are learning and using their language in classrooms, at home or in their communities, HL learners navigate social relations through the use of their language and it is from these social interactions that their hybrid and emergent identities are formed (Rampton 1995). The researcher He (2006, 7) highlights the problems with the notion of background and the central role of identity for heritage learners as follows:

> . . . learner identity [is] the centerpiece rather than the background of Heritage Language development. In other words, identity is understood not as a collection of static attributes or as some mental construct existing prior to and independent of human actions, but rather as a process of continual emerging and becoming, a process that identifies what a person becomes and achieves through ongoing interactions with other persons.

HL learners have a distinctive social, cultural and emotional affiliation with their language. This affiliation is often a complex one of perception and positioning between their home language and the mainstream language. For each of these unique social and cultural beings, with his or her own distinctive trajectory of life and learning experiences, language learning involves developing sophisticated communication and literacy capabilities and working towards 'high functional multilingualism in diverse hybrid spaces' (Byrnes 2006, 244). It is through holistic approaches connected to the social, cultural and historical context that learners develop their multilinguality and extend their overall learning and identify formation.

Reconceptualising the nature of language learning

In the context of heightened linguistic and cultural diversity there is a need to conceptualise language learning beyond communicative language teaching and learning. This is true for all language learning, but it is true in a distinctive way for HL learners. Language use and language learning need to be conceived not as learning a separate language, but as bilingual or multilingual acts, because for all learners there are always at least two languages at play. For second language learners in Australia, this is English and the language being learnt. For HL learners, it is the home/community language (or languages and dialects) that is learnt in relation to English, the mainstream language. Communication involves more than just an exchange of words; it involves the mutual or reciprocal exchange of meanings – personal meanings, experiences, memories and resonances that are linguistically and culturally constructed. This (at least) dual-language orientation means that communication in multilingual contexts will always involve comparison. In communication, HL learners become linguistic and cultural mediators, moving between two or more linguistic and cultural systems, developing understanding and explaining different perspectives, reactions and responses to themselves and others. Furthermore, in communicating, HL learners consider who they are and who they can be when they use diverse languages, as well as how they are perceived by others (He 2010). This process leads to reflection about their own identity, languages and cultures in the context of their own multilinguality. Thus, communicating successfully also entails reflecting on communication, comparing one's own interpretations, perspectives and reactions with others', respecting the different linguistic and cultural worlds that exist in the classroom and in the community, and gradually coming to understand why their interlocutors see things as they do. This is how people make and exchange meaning. In an interconnected and reciprocal way, each individual reflects on, interprets, judges, compares and interconnects ideas and experiences in the exchange. In this way, language learning for HL learners needs to be conceptualised as inter-linguistic and inter-cultural.

The reconceptualisation of language learning is signalled in a range of terms from sociolinguistic theories of globalisation and language contact. These include 'plurilingualism' (Council of Europe 2001), 'multicompetence' (Cook 2008), 'languaging' (Swain 2006), 'translanguaging' (Garcia 2009), 'multilinguality', 'multimodality' and 'code-and mode-switching' (Li 2011a; 2001b), 'code-meshing' (Canagarajah 2011), 'metrolingualism' (Pennycook 2010) and 'considerations of identity theory' (Norton 2000). All of these terms seek to capture the nature of language use inside and beyond the classroom when people are embedded in a multilingual environment.

These terms describe the reality of the language use of HL learners. Li (2011a, 1223) summarises the practice of translanguaging for HL learners as:

> ... both going between different linguistic structures and systems ... and going beyond them. It includes the full range of linguistic performances of multilingual language users for purposes that transcend the combination of structures, the alternation between systems, the transmission of information and the representation of values, identities and relationships. The act of translanguaging then is transformative in nature; it creates a social space for the multilingual language user by bringing together different dimensions of their personal history, experience and environment, their attitude, belief and ideology, their cognitive and physical capacity into one coordinated and meaningful performance, and making it into lived experience. (Li 2011a, 1223)

It is this conceptualisation of language learning that begins to do justice to the diverse goals, experiences, expectations and desired learnings that come from HL learning. To Li's conceptualisation of language use and language learning I would add a conception of language learning as interpretive, respecting the notion that meaning-making is central to both language use and language learning and that meaning-making through language is inherently interpretive. Furthermore, language use and language learning, especially when understood as inter-linguistic and inter-cultural, involve reflection on the process of reciprocal meaning-making: ideas, perspectives, responses, persons, roles, positions, and how and why they are as they are (see Scarino, forthcoming, and Liddicoat and Scarino 2013, for a more detailed discussion).

The section that follows looks at the complexity of ensuring an adequate place for HLs in the Australian Curriculum, which is currently in development. This is based on my experience of contributing to the shaping of languages in the Australian Curriculum. My role was specifically as an academic invited to write the *Shape Paper for Languages* (ACARA 2011), a paper which was intended to provide the conceptual base for the development of the national curriculum for languages.

Heritage language learning in the Australian Curriculum

The Australian Curriculum is being developed as a national endeavour in a context where legislative responsibility for school education resides with six states and two territories in a complex relationship with the Federal Government, and all previous attempts have met with limited success. It is a curriculum that specifies, at a national level, content and achievement standards, leaving to the states and territories and their teachers the responsibility for pedagogy and implementation. Its development includes three dimensions: learning areas (The Arts, English, Health and Physical Education, Languages, Mathematicss, Science, Technologies, Humanities and Social Sciences, Economics and Business, Civics and Citizenship, Geography, History); a set of capabilities intended as cross-curricular learning (literacy, numeracy, information and communication technological competence, critical and creative thinking, ethical behaviour, personal and social competence and inter-cultural understanding); and three cross-curricular priorities (Aboriginal and Torres Strait Islander histories and cultures, Asia, and Australia's engagement with Asia and sustainability).

A range of policies govern the development of the Australian Curriculum. The one which might be expected to be most relevant to HL learning is the Student Diversity Policy (ACARA 2013). This policy identifies three categories of diversity: students with disability, gifted and talented students and students with English as an additional language or dialect. The absence of any specific recognition of linguistic and cultural diversity is noteworthy. It signals the monolingual conception of the curriculum as a whole, a conception that renders an argument for HL learning within and across the curriculum particularly difficult to make.

Specific languages in the Australian Curriculum

In the languages learning area, all languages are included in the Australian Curriculum: world languages (European and Asian), Australian languages, classical languages and Auslan. In the past two decades in Australia, as in other parts of the world where frameworks of standards for curriculum and assessment have been developed, these have been generic (see the *Common European Framework of Reference*, Council of Europe 2001, and the framework of the American Council for the Teaching of Foreign Languages; ACTFL). In education this has been justified as a way of encompassing *all* languages and ensuring a certain commonality of conception and design, but it has also had the effect of minimising the inherently diverse nature of languages and their histories of development in education. This generic approach has also minimised the clear differences in learning achievements that pertain in learning different languages in the educational context of Australia. In terms of curriculum content and achievement standards, there has been an assumption that these are common to all languages, when clearly they cannot be. The consequence has been a generalisation and standardisation of language learning towards a foreign language norm that does not do justice to the distinctive inter-linguistic and inter-cultural language practices of HL learners.

Contrary to curriculum and assessment framework developments to date, the *Shape Paper for Languages* specifies that the curriculum will be language-specific, though this was a major point of contestation. As the curriculum development proceeds, this remains a contested matter. Although it represents a major step forward for curriculum development in the field, it has meant that ACARA has had to determine which specific languages would be developed. The languages curricula being developed in the first instance are Arabic, Chinese, French, German, Italian, Indonesian, Japanese, Korean, Modern

Greek, Spanish, Vietnamese and a framework for Australian languages (that is Aboriginal languages and Torres Strait Islander languages). Language-specific development means that it is possible to take into account, at least in a general way, the specificity of each language and its learners as well as the distinctive history of that language in the Australian educational context. Many of the HLs (e.g. Khmer, Polish, Tamil, Turkish and Hindi) have not been included in the plans for development at this time. The communities of speakers of these languages are rightly signalling the need for their languages also to be developed and in that way included in the Australian Curriculum.

Multiple pathways in language learning in the Australian Curriculum

In developing languages in the Australian Curriculum, a further decision was made to provide for two major variables in language learning: learner background and time-on-task. In language learning in Australia it cannot be assumed that all learners will have a regular K-12 sequence of language learning as is the case for other learning areas. This means that, at the very least, there needs to be an entry point (or more than one) at primary level and another at secondary level, providing for variations of time-on-task. In addition, in deciding the architecture for languages in the Australian Curriculum, it was recognised that differences in learner backgrounds needed to be captured. Provision has been made in the *Shape Paper* for different pathways for second language learners, background or Heritage learners and first language learners. In Chinese, therefore, curricula are being developed for three distinct pathways to cater for the immense diversity of learners learning Chinese in Australia: a second language pathway, a background or HL learner pathway and a first language learner pathway. Chinese is the language where, at present, there is the greatest degree of difference in learner backgrounds (see Orton 2008). Although the overall architecture allows for three different pathways, at the present time all three pathways are being developed only for Chinese. In all other languages only the pathway that is most prevalent is being developed, and this decision is also contested. Thus, at this stage, second language pathways are being developed for all languages except for Arabic and Vietnamese, where pathways are being developed for background or HL learners. The distinctiveness of languages and learners requires differences to be taken into account if provision is to be made for different languages and pathways. Overriding these differences reduces the complexity in a way that makes it manageable for education systems, but forces a generalisation and standardisation that is unhelpful to learning. This remains a tension.

Conceptualisation of language learning in the Australian Curriculum: Languages

Given the expanded conception of language learning for contemporary times as inter-linguistic and inter-cultural, discussed earlier, the *Shape Paper* begins with a conceptualisation of the three fundamental concepts in language learning: language, culture and learning. In this way, it seeks to capture the relationships between language and culture; language, culture and learning; language and learning; language and content; and language and literacy, as a way of depicting a relational and holistic conception of language learning (see Cenoz and Gorter 2011). This conception was considered to be too complex for practical implementation and was simplified in the development process. These relationships are particularly important for pathways for background or HL learners, who differ significantly in the extent to which they are active users of the language.

In line with curriculum and assessment framework development of this kind internationally, the curriculum is defined through a set of organisers called 'strands'. The development of strands is a complex, conceptual task that involves translating important ideas of the field into curriculum constructs that are sufficiently generative to carry the specification of content and achievement standards. Traditionally in languages education these have been: listening, speaking, reading and writing. This traditional formulation, however, depicts no more than the surface skills of communication, without capturing the richness of the experiences of language use and language learning that background or HL learners need to accomplish. The strands proposed originally in the *Shape Paper* were as follows:

- **Communicating:** using language for communicative purposes in interpreting, creating and exchanging meaning

- **Understanding:** analysing language and culture as a resource for interpreting and creating meaning

- **Reciprocating:** reflecting upon and interpreting self in relation to others in communication as language users and language learners (self-awareness as user and learner). (ACARA 2011, 23–4)

The reciprocating strand was proposed as a way of pushing the boundaries, especially for background or HL learners, to highlight the nature of communication as described by Kramsch (2006, 245) when she notes that: 'Today it is not sufficient for learners to know how to communicate meanings; they have to understand the practice of meaning-making itself.'

The emphasis on reflection and reflexivity through the 'reciprocating' strand was intended to ensure that students would develop meta-cognitive and meta-linguistic awareness, not only of the way the linguistic system works but also of the ways in which language and culture shape meanings, the significance of particular linguistic choices and the reality of alternative interpretations. Refection and reflexivity help students to understand themselves and others as inter-linguistic and inter-cultural communicators, operating with the dual role of performers and analysers of language. The reciprocating strand was intended to introduce processes such as decentering, positioning, comparing, questioning assumptions, reinterpreting and referencing all the languages in students' repertoires simultaneously, as background or HL learners do, and re-examining the self in relation to others, and others in relation to self, intra-culturally and inter-culturally. This re-examination is a process that recognises the linguistic and cultural construction of meaning and of self in relation to others in the act of communicating.

In the extensive consultation process with teachers and, importantly, the states and territories, without whose endorsement the national curriculum would cease to be national, the reciprocating strand was removed from the design. Though not a linguistic category *per se*, the paper deliberately sought to include a lever that would invite curriculum developers and teachers to acknowledge that communication is not a superficial and trivial process (as it becomes in some realisations of communicative language teaching). As a compromise, it was agreed that the reciprocating strand would be integrated in the communicating and understanding strands. The process of translating important concepts of the field into curriculum constructs that need to carry the descriptions of content and achievement standards is complex. Inevitably, education systems seek to reduce the complexity in order to render a new curriculum acceptable to teachers and, in the present instance, to the states and territories. Such reduction, however, does not do justice to the language learning of background or to HL learners as mediators of language and culture.

The curriculum design sets out intentions and constructs, but of course these need to be interpreted in the first instance by curriculum writers and subsequently by teachers. The process involves the movement from intention to interpretation to enactment. This too is a highly complex process. In order to clarify intended meanings, the paper provided an elaboration of the two strands that would be used to define the content of the curriculum by identifying a set of sub-strands (see Appendix 1). Then, for each sub-strand, it provided a further elaboration of the sub-strand itself and related concepts, processes and text-types. Naturally, these have been interpreted differently by the writing teams established to develop curricula for specific languages.

Although the language-specific curriculum writers are all working with the design, its acceptance remains to be negotiated. Initial feedback suggests that it is seen as too complex. There has been some resistance to sub-strand 1.4: 'translating'. This is because participants in the consultation process feared the return of traditional translation exercises in the curriculum rather than the understanding of translation as an act of linguistic and cultural mediation – a role that is frequently performed by background or HL learners. As a result of the consultation process, a sub-strand focused on 'expressing and performing identity' has been subsumed under a sub-strand 'reflecting on intercultural language use'. Again, this gives less prominence to discussions of identity formation as an important dimension of learning for background or HL learners. These strands represent the very dimensions of language learning that I consider to be of particular value to background or HL learners. Their retention, albeit in a reduced form, has required complex negotiation.

I have indicated two layers of interpretation in the current curriculum development process: 1) the interpretation of the design by curriculum writers, and 2) the interpretation of the design and the specific language curriculum by teachers. The curriculum cannot simply be 'given' in advance. Rather, it has to be worked with and interpreted by teachers, and subsequently enacted interactively with students. The strands that are being resisted may well be those that currently are least developed in teacher practice. Nevertheless, not to engage with the ideas that they are intended to capture reduces the span of experiences and learning through which all learners, and especially background or HL learners, would extend their linguistic repertoires.

The value of such frameworks of curriculum and assessment standards resides first and foremost in their conceptualisation of the constructs and, secondly, in the desire to provide a sense of the scope and sequence of learning across the K-12 continuum. The conceptualisation needs to encompass the learning requirements of diverse students – those who are learning the particular language as an additional language and those who are learning the particular language as background or HL learners. Such scoping is useful in providing an overview of possible trajectories of development. Both of these processes are intricate and, at the moment, the research base to inform such scoping remains insufficient. And yet all frameworks hypothesise such trajectories. There is an important tension here in that these frameworks inevitably reduce and generalise when, for the purposes of teaching and learning HLs, it is the distinctiveness of these trajectories that needs to be captured.

In the design of the Australian Curriculum there is an acknowledgement of the diversity of languages, indicating that they are not the same and that indeed each has its own learner groups and distinctive history in Australian education. Not all languages are currently in development as part of the Australian Curriculum and how many more will be developed remains to be seen. There is provision in the design for a designated pathway for HLs, although this has not been fully utilised at the current stage of development of language-specific curricula. The design of strands and sub-strands signals an expansive set of learning that incorporates interpretive, reflective and reflexive dimensions, but substantial work is needed in translating these ideas into enactments as language-specific curricula and classroom programmes for teaching, learning and assessment. There are implications for teacher development that remain to be considered.

Conclusion

There are many political challenges in the fragility around policy and in the provision for languages in a way that sustains the diversity that makes up the linguistic and cultural landscape of Australia. The current diversity in languages education is not a random accumulation of programmes, but rather an ever-evolving response to diverse needs for language learning and use within the Australian population. The fragility is also linked to debates about inclusion and exclusion of minorities, settlement of refugees and the place of their home languages in society and in education. Nevertheless, in the process of developing the Australian Curriculum, I have come to see the real challenge as a conceptual one of imagining, scoping and enacting the learning of HLs through to advanced levels. This necessitates working against the tendency of frameworks towards generalisation and standardisation, which fails to do justice to the diversity of background or HL students and their language learning in the context of diversity. It means conceptualising the teaching and learning of languages within a multilingual perspective that reflects and builds upon the learners' language practices as they live in diversity. Value and linguistic justice for background or HL learners resides in developing in them the sophisticated capability of interpreting meaning that occurs through their learning of the language of their primary socialisation, and reflecting on their resulting sense of identity and well-being.

Appendix: Strands and sub-strands for languages in the Australian Curriculum

Strand	Sub-strand	Description
Communicating: Using language for communicative purposes in interpreting, creating and exchanging meaning.	1.1 Socialising and taking action	Interacting orally and in writing to exchange ideas, opinions, experiences, thoughts and feelings; and participating in planning, negotiating, deciding and taking action.
	1.2 Obtaining and using information	Obtaining, processing, interpreting and conveying information through a range of oral, written and multimodal texts; developing and applying knowledge.
	1.3 Responding to and expressing imaginative experience	Engaging with imaginative experience by participating in, responding to and creating a range of texts, such as stories, songs, drama and music.
	1.4 Translating	Moving between languages and cultures orally and in writing, recognising different interpretations and explaining these to others.
	1.5 Reflecting on intercultural language use	Participating in intercultural exchange, questioning reactions and assumptions; and considering how interaction shapes communication and identity.
Understanding: Analysing and understanding language and culture as resources for interpreting and shaping meaning in intercultural exchange.	2.1 Systems of language	Understanding language as a system, including sound, writing, grammatical and textual conventions.
	2.2 Language variation and change	Understanding how languages vary in use (register, style, standard and non-standard varieties) and change over time and place.
	2.3 The role of language and culture	Analysing and understanding the role of language and culture in the exchange of meaning.

REFERENCES

ACARA (Australian Curriculum, Assessment and Reporting Authority) (2011). *Shape of the Australian Curriculum: Languages*. Sydney: ACARA. www.acara.edu.au/verve/_resources/Languages_-_Shape_of_the_Australian_Curriculum.pdf (retrieved 24 September 2013).

— (2013). *Student Diversity*. www.acara.edu.au/curriculum/student_diversity/student_diversity.html (retrieved 24 September 2013).

Blommaert, J. and **Rampton, B.** (2012). 'Language and Superdiversity: A Position Paper'. *Working Papers in Urban Language and Literacies*. Göttingen: Max Planck Institute for the Study of Religious and Ethnic Diversity.

Byrnes, H. (2006). 'Perspectives: Interrogating Communicative Competence as a Framework for Collegiate Foreign Language Study'. *Modern Language Journal* 90 (2), 244–6.

Canagarajah, A.S. (2011). 'Code-Meshing in Academic Writing. Identifying Teachable Strategies of Translanguaging'. *Modern Language Journal* 95 (3), 401–17.

Cenoz, J. and **Gorter, D.** (2011). 'A Holistic Approach to Multilingual Education: Introduction'. *Modern Language Journal* 95 (3), 339–43.

Clyne, M. (1991). *Community Languages: The Australian Experience*. Cambridge: Cambridge University Press.

Clyne, M. (2005). *Australia's Language Potential*. Sydney: University of New South Wales Press.

Colic-Peisker, V. and **Farquharson** (2011). 'Introduction: A New Era in Australian Multiculturalism? The Need for Critical Interrogation'. *Journal of Intercultural Studies* 32 (6), 579–86.

Cook, G. (2008). 'Multi-Competence: Black Hole or Wormhole for Second Language Acquisition Research?' In Z. Han (ed.), *Understanding Second Language Process*. Clevedon: Multilingual Matters.

Council of Europe (2001). *Common European Framework of Reference for Languages: Learning, Teaching, Assessment*. Cambridge: Cambridge University Press.

Elder, C. (1996). 'The Effect of Language Background on 'Foreign' Language Test Performance: The Case of Chinese, Italian and Modern Greek'. *Language Learning* 46 (2), 233–82.

— (2000a). 'Learner Diversity and its Implications for Outcomes-based Assessment'. In C. Elder (ed.), *Defining Standards and Monitoring Progress in Languages Other Than English*. Guest-edited issue of the *Australian Review of Applied Linguistics* 23 (2), 36–61.

— (2000b). 'Outing the "Native Speaker": The Problem of Diverse Learner Backgrounds in Foreign Language Classrooms'. *Language Curriculum and Culture* 13 (1), 86–108.

Garcia, O. (2009). *Bilingual Education in the 21st Century: Global Perspectives*. Malden, MA: Blackwell.

Halliday, M.A.K. (1993). 'Towards a Language-based Theory of Learning'. *Linguistics and Education* 5 (2), 93–116.

He, A.W. (2006). 'Toward an Identity Theory of the Development of Chinese as a Heritage Language'. *Heritage Language Journal* 4 (1), 1–28.

— (2010). 'The Heart of Heritage: Sociocultural Dimensions of Heritage Language Learning'. *Annual Review of Applied Linguistics*, 30, 66–82.

Kramsch, C. (2006). 'From Communicative Competence to Symbolic Competence'. *Modern Language Journal* 90 (2), 249–52.

Li, W. (2011a). 'Moment Analysis and Translanguaging Space: Discursive Construction of Identities by Multilingual Chinese Youth in Britain'. *Journal of Pragmatics*, 43:5, 1222–35.

— (2011b). 'Multilinguality, Multimodality, and Multicompetence: Code- and Modeswitching by Minority Ethnic Children in Complementary Schools'. *Modern Language Journal* 95 (3), 370–84.

Liddicoat, A.J. (2013). *Language-in-education Policies: The Discursive Construction of Intercultural Relations*. Bristol, UK: Multilingual Matters.

Liddicoat, A.J. and Scarino, A. (2013). *Intercultural Language Teaching and Learning*. Malden, MA: Wiley-Blackwell.

Liddicoat, A.J., Scarino, A., Curnow, T.J., Kohler, M., Scrimgeour, A. and Morgan, A.-M. (2007). *An Investigation of the State and Nature of Languages in Australian Schools*. Canberra: Report to Department of Education, Science and Training.

Lo Bianco, J. (1987). *National Policy on Languages*. Canberra: Australian Government Publishing Service.

Lo Bianco, J. and Aliani, R. (2013). *Student Voices, Policy Ambitions: Language Planning Interactions*. Bristol: Multilingual Matters.

Lo Bianco, J. and Gvozdenko, I. (2006). *Collaboration and Innovation in the Provision of Languages Other Than ENGLISH in Australian Universities*. www.lcnau.org/pdfs/LO%20BIANCO%20GVOZDENKO%20LOTES%20in%20Australian%20Universities.pdf (retrieved 24 September 2013).

Lo Bianco, J. with Slaughter, Y. (2009). 'Second Languages and Australian Schooling'. *Australian Education Review* 54. Melbourne. Australian Council for Educational Research.

MCEECDYA (Ministerial Council for Education, Early Childhood Development and Youth Affairs) (2008). 'The Melbourne Declaration on Educational Goals for Young Australians'. http://www.mceecdya.edu.au/verve/_resources/national_declaration_on_the_educational_goals_for_young_australians.pdf.

Norton, B. (2000). *Identity and Language Learning: Gender, Ethnicity and Educational Change*. London: Longman.

Orton, J. (2008). *Chinese Language Education in Australian Schools*. Melbourne: The University of Melbourne.

Pennycook, A. (2010). *Language as a Local Practice*. London: Routledge.

Rampton, B. (1995). *Crossing Language and Ethnicity Amongst Adolescents*. New York: Longman.

Scarino, A. (2008). 'Community and Culture in Intercultural Language Learning'. *Australian Review of Applied Linguistics* 31 (1), 5.1–5.15.

— (2010). 'Language and Languages and the Curriculum'. In A. Liddicoat and A. Scarino (eds), *Languages in Australian Education: Problems, Prospects and Future Directions*. Newcastle-Upon-Tyne: Cambridge Scholars.

— (2013). *The Australian Curriculum Languages Design*. ACARA.

— (forthcoming). 'Learning as Reciprocal, Interpretive Meaning-Making'. To appear in the *Modern Language Journal*.

Scarino, A., Elder, C., Iwashita, N., Kim, H., Kohler, M. and **Scrimgeour, A.** (2011). *Student Achievement in Asian Languages Education. Report to Department of Education, Employment and Workplace Relations (DEEWR)*. Adelaide: Research Centre for Languages and Cultures. www.saale.unisa.edu.au/ (retrieved 24 September 2013).

Scarino, A. and **Papademetre, L.** (2001). 'Ideologies, Languages, Policies: Australia's Ambivalent Relationship with Learning to Communicate in "Other" Languages'. In J. Lo Bianco and R. Wickert (eds) *Australian Policy Activism in Language and Literacy*. Canberra: Language Australia.

Shohamy, E. (2007). *Language Policy: Hidden Agendas and New Approaches*. London: Routledge.

Stroud, C. and **Heugh, K.** (2011). 'Languages in Education'. In R. Mesthrie (ed.), *Cambridge Handbook of Sociolinguistics*. Cambridge: Cambridge University Press.

Swain, M. (2006). 'Languaging, Agency and Collaboration in Advanced Second Language Proficiency'. In H. Byrnes (ed.), *Advanced Language Learning: The Contribution of Halliday and Vygotsky*. London: Continuum.

Vertovec, S. (2010). 'Towards Post-multiculturalism: Changing Communities, Conditions and Contexts of Diversity'. *International Social Science Journal* 61 (199), 83–95. doi: 10.1111/j.1468-2451.2010.01749.x.

NOTES

1   The term used in Australia that is closest to the term 'heritage languages' used in the US is the term 'community languages'. Although I discuss the Australian situation, I use the term 'heritage language' as it is likely to be more readily understood. Alternative terms used in this chapter, derived from Australian studies, are 'background language learners' and 'first language learners'. Subjects in Australia that are designed for heritage or community language users are designated 'background speakers level'. In the development of languages in the Australian Curriculum the term 'background language learners' is used to designate 'heritage language learners'.

COURSES IN THE LANGUAGE AND CULTURE OF ORIGIN AND THEIR IMPACT ON YOUTH DEVELOPMENT IN CULTURAL TRANSITION: A Study Amongst Immigrant and Dual-Heritage Youth in Switzerland

Elena Makarova (University of Bern, Switzerland)

Immigrants in Switzerland

Switzerland is amongst those European countries that have a high proportion of immigrants in relation to native population. Today more than one third (34.7%) of the Swiss population have an immigrant background, 12.7% of those have Swiss citizenship and 22% are persons with foreign citizenship of the first or second immigrant generation. Most immigrants living in Switzerland (86.3%) are of European origin. However, since 1980 an increasing number of foreigners have been coming from more distant countries, leading in turn to an increase in the proportion of non-European nationals to 13.7% (Swiss Federal Statistical Office 2013a). Moreover, according to the census (2000), the highest proportion of foreigners was amongst children. Amongst children under the age of six, 25.8% were foreigners, and in the five largest Swiss cities, the percentage of foreign children has even reached 45% (Swiss Federal Department of Foreign Affairs 2013). The large proportion of foreign children in the Swiss resident population is due to the low number of naturalisations in Switzerland compared to other European countries (Swiss Federal Statistical Office 2013b).

There are two main reasons for the low naturalisation rate in Switzerland. Firstly, the naturalisation law of Switzerland is based on *jus sanguinis* (right of blood), and not on *jus soli* (right of the soil). Thus, Swiss naturalisation law is very strict: before applying for naturalisation in Switzerland one needs to have been a resident in the country for at least 12 years.[1] In case of marriage to a Swiss citizen, one needs five years of residency in Switzerland and three years of marriage before applying for citizenship (Swiss Federal Office for Migration 2013). Secondly, under Swiss federalism, three levels of authorities are responsible for naturalisation matters: federal, cantonal and local community level (Bianchi 2003; Hofhansel 2008). Moreover, differences in the procedural costs at the cantonal and communal levels make naturalisation in some cases a privilege of wealthy foreigners (Bianchi 2003, 185). Finally, in Switzerland every applicant for citizenship has to prove that they are 'socially and culturally integrated in Switzerland' (Swiss Federal Office for Migration 2013). The integration of applicants is usually measured by language proficiency in one of the state languages, and by knowledge about Swiss customs, political order and civil rules (Bianchi 2003, 179).

The high proportion of foreigners in the resident population of Switzerland has the effect of increasing the number of intercultural marriages. Thus, 37.5% of marriages are currently bi-national marriages between a Swiss citizen and a foreign citizen. Accordingly, the proportion of bi-national children rose to nearly half (47.5%) of all births by married women in 2007 (Swiss Federal Statistical Office 2008, 8).

To summarise, Switzerland has a large proportion of immigrants in its resident population. The constantly growing number of immigrants as well as individuals of bi-national origin leads to high cultural diversity in Swiss society. However, Swiss policy with respect to the naturalisation of immigrants is exclusive and the governmental strategy of immigrant integration is based on the cultural assimilation of immigrants.

The establishment of LCO courses in public schools in Switzerland

The high cultural heterogeneity of the Swiss population is reflected in the proportion of highly culturally heterogeneous school classes in Swiss compulsory schools,[2] currently 41.8% on average, of which the vast majority of such classes are in schools in urban cantons (Swiss Federal Statistical Office 2013c).

Since 1991 the Swiss Conference of Cantonal Ministers of Education (EDK) has provided a principled recommendation for the education of foreign students. This affirms the integration of all foreign children and youth living and attending public schools in Switzerland, and the avoidance of any discrimination. It furthermore stresses that integration should respect the rights of children to maintain the language and culture of their country of origin (EDK 1991). The latest inter-cantonal agreement on the harmonisation of compulsory education (HarmoS-Concordat) supports the previous recommendation for the education of foreign students and states that cantons should provide organisational support for the implementation of Language and Culture of Origin courses (LCO) for students with an immigrant background (EDK 2013a).

The first impetus for the establishment of LCO courses came from Italian immigrant parents in 1930 (Serra 1991; Caprez-Krompàk 2010). In 1970 this motion was supported by the EDK, recommending that the school authorities of the cantons should implement the LCO courses into the regular school timetable (EDK 1995, 11 and 43). At that time immigrant students were regarded as being temporarily in the schools of the host society. Only in 1990, when temporary labour migration turned into permanent migration, were the foreign children in Swiss schools interpreted as a 'permanent component' in the student population (Allemann-Ghionda 1993). Accordingly, during that period the objectives of the LCO courses also changed. Whereas in the 1970s and 1980s the objectives of the LCO courses were aimed at preparing immigrant youth for a possible return migration, since the 1990s bilingual development and the integration of immigrant youth into the host society have become leading objectives (Serra 1991). The EDK responded to this development with recommendations to integrate the LCO courses into the school curriculum for at least two hours a week and to investigate the possibility of considering achievement in LCO courses for academic selection (EDK 1995, 161).

Currently, each of the 26 cantons in Switzerland has its own guidelines for the integration of LCO courses in public schools. More than two thirds of the cantons regulate the LCO courses by law or executive directives, although with substantial differences in the cantonal legal framework. However, only three cantons regulate LCO course organisation by cantonal law, while most of the cantons provide executive directives for this purpose. Some cantons formulate, additionally or solely, recommendations with respect to LCO course organisation for communities, schools and teachers (EDK 2013b).

The LCO courses in all cantons are organised and sponsored by non-governmental organisations or embassies of foreign countries in Switzerland. Nearly a third of the cantons apply an authorised procedure for the recognition of LCO course organisers. However, the employment of teachers and the supervision of the teaching is usually the responsibility of the LCO course organisers, with a few cantons participating in this process. Only two cantons provide mandatory courses for LCO course teachers (ibid.).

Current practice in LCO course implementation varies greatly amongst the cantons. Generally speaking, LCO courses are provided for immigrant students from Grades 1 to 9. They typically consist of two to four lessons per week. LCO courses are seldom conducted during regular school hours, but often after school or on Saturdays. In almost all cantons, classrooms and school infrastructure are generally provided for LCO classes free of charge, although this often falls within the competence of the municipalities or schools (ibid.). LCO course attendance and/or achievement in the first language are recorded on the school certificate in most cantons. However, achievement in the first language is not relevant for selection processes during the school career of immigrant youth (ibid.), and thus remains unvalued in the selection processes of compulsory education in Switzerland.

In conclusion, it would appear that up to the present, the contribution of LCO courses in the development of immigrant children and youth is not valued in the Swiss educational system, and therefore that the cultural heritage of children and youth with an immigrant background is rejected in Swiss compulsory education.

The effects of multilingual education on the development of immigrant youth

The inclusion of LCO courses for immigrant youth in the school curriculum of host countries is encouraged through the concept of intercultural education in German-speaking European countries (Herzog and Makarova 2007, 262–3). The argument for the implementation of LCO courses in the national education curriculum is widely supported through empirical evidence from studies on the various positive effects of ethnic language maintenance for immigrant youth development (e.g. Allemann-Ghionda 1999; Caprez-Krompàk 2010; Dollmann and Kristen 2010; Gogolin 2009; Hesse, Göbel and Hartig 2008; Oksaar 2003; Reich and Roth 2002; Siebert-Ott 2003). First, the formal maintenance of the mother tongue improves academic achievement, especially with respect to performance in the instructional language. Second, a multilingual education contributes to the recognition and appreciation of languages and cultures of ethnic minorities. Third, the inclusion of LCO courses in the public schools of host countries increases language awareness not only amongst immigrant youth but also amongst native youth. These effects positively influence the intercultural competencies of young people, including their willingness to establish and maintain contact with individuals of other cultural backgrounds, their knowledge about specific and general aspects of culture and communication, and their mastery of interaction-based strategies in multilingual environments. As a result, the overall quality of intercultural communication between immigrant and native youth can be improved.

Furthermore, it is assumed that the maintenance of traditional languages and cultures has positive effects on the development of immigrant youth in the new society of settlement. In particular, it has been suggested that participation in LCO courses increases the self-esteem of immigrant youth, facilitates the development of their bicultural identity and improves their integration in the host society (Salm 2000; Salm and Künzli 2001). However, there is a lack of empirical evidence on the precise effect of LCO course attendance on immigrant youth's acculturation and on their cultural identity. Likewise, even less is known about the impact of LCO courses on the cultural identity of dual-heritage youth.

Acculturation and cultural identity of youth in cultural transition

Acculturation was originally conceptualised and defined by anthropologists Redfield, Linton and Herskovits (1936, 149). Following their definition, 'acculturation' refers to:

> . . . those phenomena which result when groups of individuals having different cultures come into continuous first-hand contact, with subsequent changes in the original culture patterns of either or both groups. (Redfield, Linton and Herskovits 1936, 149)

Today the issue of acculturation and its effects on group relations and individual development has gained a prominent place in the social sciences in general (Sam and Berry 2006; Trimble 2003), and especially in 'cross-cultural psychology' (e.g. Berry 2003, 2005; Ward 2001).

In cross-cultural research, the widely established conceptualisation of acculturation consists of two main dimensions that are independent of each other: 1) maintenance of heritage culture and identity, and 2) relationships sought amongst groups (Berry 2005, 705; Berry 2006, 35). Alternatively, Bourhis, Moise, Perreault and Sénécal (1997) proposed an interactive acculturation model in which the second dimension of contact and participation is replaced by issues of culture adoption. At the same time Bourhis and his colleagues accept that acculturation takes place in both groups – the immigrant group and the majority group of the receiving society – and has reciprocal effects on each other's preferences (Bourhis 1997, 94). The acculturation attitudes of immigrants are commonly clustered into four acculturation strategies:

- An integration strategy aimed at the maintenance of the ethnic origin culture as well as at the adoption of the host culture.
- An assimilation strategy aimed at the adoption of the host culture and rejection of the ethnic origin culture.
- A separation strategy aimed at the maintenance of the ethnic origin culture and rejection of the host culture.
- A marginalisation strategy aimed at the rejection of the ethnic origin culture as well as the host culture.

Proficiency in ethnic and national languages as well as language use 'are generally regarded as key indicators of acculturation' (Phinney, Berry, Vedder and Liebkind 2006, 78). However, short-term acculturation outcomes should be distinguished from 'adaptation' as a long-term outcome (Sam 2006, 16). The latter is a 'highly variable process' that includes more than one aspect (Berry 2006, 40). Moreover, a distinction is warranted between psychological adaptation, which involves individual psychological and physical well-being, and sociocultural adaptation, which refers to immigrants' success in dealing with daily life in the new cultural environment of their receiving country. In contemporary approaches, sociocultural adaptation is divided into competence in the ethnic culture (i.e. interaction with co-nationals, maintenance of ethnic language and traditions), and competence in the mainstream culture (i.e. interactions with hosts, acquisition of skills and behaviours of the majority culture, academic and job performance; Arends-Tóth and Vijver 2006, 143).

The acculturative process is, furthermore, fundamental for 'cultural identity development' (Phinney 1990, 2003). According to the social identification approach, the choice of an ethnic group label which derives from group membership is 'the most obvious and straightforward aspect' of ethnic identity (Phinney 2003, 66). Moreover, ethnic identity

> . . . is not only a psychological phenomenon, but also a social phenomenon in the sense that the internal psychological states express themselves objectively in external behavior patterns that come to be shared by others'. (Isajiw 1990, 35)

Thus, the external components of ethnic identity refer to aspects that are obvious to everyone, such as the maintenance of ethnic traditions or acquisition of ethnic language, while the internal components refer to individuals' thinking, feeling and attitudes about their cultural heritage and belonging (ibid., 36–7). However, there is inconsistent research evidence with respect to the role of ethnic language maintenance for ethnic identity. Some studies report that ethnic group membership and a sense of belonging do not depend on ethnic language maintenance, while others show that ethnic language maintenance is crucial for ethnic identity (Phinney et al. 2006).

Contemporary research on cultural identity distinguishes between 'objective' (i.e. alter-ascribed) and 'subjective' (i.e. self-recognised) social or cultural identity. Thus, ethnic self-identification should not be conceptually confused with the objective ethnicity of a person, which is related to the individual cultural heritage given by birth. Therefore, individual ethnic self-identification can differ from one's objective ethnicity and can even combine self-identification with more than one ethnic group (Liebkind 2001). Consequently, national identity involves 'feelings of belonging to, and attitudes toward, the larger society' (Phinney, Horenczyk, Liebkind and Vedder 2001, 497), and ethnic identity refers to 'strength, valence, or understanding of one's ethnicity' (Phinney 2003, 66). Self-identification with both ethnic and national identity refers to a bicultural identity which is 'not simply a midpoint' between an ethnic and national identity but 'rather the result of identification with two cultures' (ibid., 64). Thus, the identification with two cultural origins corresponds to the bi-dimensional models of acculturation, with one dimension of culture maintenance and the other dimension of adoption of the mainstream culture (Bourhis et al. 1997). Cultural identity can consequently be described as one of the cognitive outcomes of the acculturation process (Ward 2001).

With respect to the cultural identity development of dual-heritage youth, Stephan and Stephan (1989) demonstrate that dual-heritage youth of two mixed-heritage groups (part-Japanese and part-Hispanic) living in the US commonly developed multiple identities. However, the results also indicate that no respondents consistently used a single mixed-heritage identity. The authors suggest that 'the mixed-heritage identities are less stable or more sensitive to situational variation than is single heritage identity' (ibid., 515).

Another European study investigated the link between acculturation and cultural identity amongst native, immigrant and dual-heritage youth in multicultural schools in Switzerland (Makarova 2008). With respect to the cultural identity of youth with an immigrant background, the results show that most dual-heritage youth reported a monocultural identity using either an ethnic or national label. At the same time, most of the immigrant youth identified a monocultural ethnic identity by choosing an ethnic label. Moreover, immigrant youth reported multicultural self-identification with more than one ethnic group more often than dual-heritage youth (ibid., 134). Based on the overall results, this study argues that a dual-heritage origin does not necessarily lead to bicultural identity and suggests that the common conceptualisation of acculturation as a process initiated through first-hand contact between individuals with different cultural backgrounds is not in fact sufficient to describe the acculturation and cultural identity development of dual-heritage youth.

In summary, positive attitudes towards the maintenance of ethnic language and traditions are fundamental for acculturation and cultural identity development. Since research on bicultural development has predominantly focused on ethnic minorities by comparing them with the majority of the host country, little is known about the acculturation and identity development of dual-heritage youth. However, the results of the studies referred to concur that the patterns of cultural identity amongst dual-heritage youth differ from those of immigrant youth. Moreover, the acculturation of dual-heritage youth is a highly complex process that cannot be adequately captured by the bi-dimensional acculturation model.

Aims of the study

In light of this, the aim of this study is to examine the meaning of LCO courses for youth development in the cultural transition process. In particular, the current study has the following aims:

- To examine the attendance of LCO courses and attitudes towards such courses amongst immigrant youth and dual-heritage youth.
- To explore the link between LCO courses and acculturation attitudes amongst immigrant youth.
- To analyse the impact of LCO course attendance and attitudes towards such courses on the cultural self-identification, intensity and evaluation of self-identification amongst immigrant and dual-heritage youth.

Method

Sample

The study had a cross-sectional design and was conducted in the German-speaking part of Switzerland. Students in Grades 7, 8 and 9 were surveyed during regular classes. The participants completed a pen-and-paper questionnaire during class time.

For the purposes of this study, a survey of 682 students (female 50.7% and male 49.3%) with an immigrant background was employed. The youths' age ranged between 12.62 and 17.92 years ($M = 14.79$, $SD = 1.11$).

The students were clustered into two groups according to their origin: 1) students for whom both parents were born abroad were denoted as 'immigrant youth' ($N = 488$, 71.6%), and 2) students for whom one parent was born in Switzerland and the other abroad were considered 'bi-national youth' ($N = 194$, 28.4%).

The immigrant student sample consisted of the following ethnic origins: Albanians ($N = 87$, 17.8%), Bosnians ($N = 46$, 9.4%), Italians ($N = 39$, 8%), Macedonians ($N = 41$, 8.4%), Serbians ($N = 34$, 7%), Tamils ($N = 42$, 8.6%), Turks ($N = 98$, 20.1%), and youth of other origins combined in the group 'other origins' ($N = 101$, 20.7%).

The vast majority of bi-national youth ($N = 156$, 81.7%), as well as the majority of the immigrant students ($N = 304$, 62.6%), were born in Switzerland. The length of residence in Switzerland amongst those immigrant and bi-national youth who were born abroad ranged from 1 to 15 years (immigrant youth: $M = 5.24$, $SD = 3.89$ and bi-national youth: $M = 6$, $SD = 4.20$). However, only 26.8% ($N = 129$) of immigrant youth were naturalised in Switzerland, whereas 74.0% ($N = 142$) of bi-national youth had Swiss citizenship.

Measures

Attendance of LCO courses amongst immigrant youth was measured with the question: 'In addition to school classes do you attend a course in which you learn the language and culture of your ethnic group?' This question was slightly reformulated for bi-national youth: 'In addition to school classes do you attend a course in which you learn the language and culture of an ethnic group other than Swiss?' The answer options were 'Yes' / 'No' / 'Not any more'. For further analyses the students who attended the courses at the time of the survey or had attended such courses previously were arranged into one group.

The importance of LCO course attendance amongst immigrant youth was measured with the question: 'Do you consider it important that youth of your ethnic origin attend those courses?' The answer utilised a five-point scale (ranging from 1 = 'not at all', to 5 = 'very important'). Amongst bi-national youth this question was reformulated as follows: 'Do you consider it important that youth of an ethnic origin other than Swiss attend those courses?'

'Cultural identity' was measured with questions about individuals' self-identification with the ethnic group of origin and/or with the ethnic group of the ethnic majority, as well as about the intensity and evaluation of ethnic self-identification.

'Subjective' (self-recognised) cultural identity was measured as proposed by Phinney (1992) with an open question: 'With respect to your ethnicity to which ethnic group or groups do you belong?' According to their responses, immigrant and bi-national youth were than clustered into three groups: 1) youth who identified themselves only with an ethnic group of origin were referred to as youth with 'monocultural ethnic identity'; 2) youth who identify themselves only with the Swiss were referred to as youth with 'monocultural national identity', and 3) youth who identify themselves with an ethnic group of origin as well as with the Swiss were denoted as youth with 'bicultural identity'.

Following Piontkowski, Florack, Hoelker and Obdrzálek (2000), the 'intensity of ethnic self-identification' was measured with the question: 'How much do you feel like a member of your ethnic group?'; the response was rated on a five-point scale (ranging from 1 = 'not at all', to 5 = 'very').

Following the suggestion of Kinket and Verkuyten (2003), the 'evaluation of ethnic self-identification' was measured with three items on a five-point scale (ranging from 1 = 'strongly disagree', to 5 = 'strongly agree'): 'It is something special to be a member of my ethnic group'; 'I am glad to be a member of my ethnic group', and 'I am proud to be a member of my ethnic group'. After a principal component analysis one factor was used for further analysis (Cronbach's alpha = .82, R^2 = 75%).

According to the Interactive Acculturation Model (Bourhis et al. 1997), 'students' attitudes towards acculturation' were measured along two dimensions: 1) students' attitudes towards the maintenance of the culture of ethnic origin, and 2) students' attitudes towards the adoption of the culture of the host society. Each dimension of acculturation was measured by five items on a five-point scale (ranging from 1 = 'strongly disagree', to 5 = 'strongly agree').

Immigrant students' acculturation attitudes towards culture maintenance were assessed by the following statements: 'It is important that youth from my ethnic group living in Switzerland preserve their own language/ religion/ clothing style/lifestyle/cultural traditions.' The immigrant students' attitudes towards adoption of the Swiss culture were assessed with statements such as 'It is important that youth from my ethnic group living in Switzerland adopt Swiss German language/religion/clothing style/lifestyle/cultural traditions.'

After a principal component analysis two factors were extracted for further analysis: 1) youth acculturation orientations towards the maintenance of the ethnic culture (Cronbach's alpha = .84, R^2 = 61%); 2) youth acculturation orientations towards the adoption of the Swiss culture (Cronbach's alpha = .80, R^2 = 56%). In order to indicate 'students' acculturation strategies', the factor values of both dimensions of acculturation were split at the scale midpoint. Afterwards, the dichotomous values of both factors were combined to form the four acculturation strategies, namely: 'integration' (i.e. high value in maintenance of the culture of ethnic origin as well as high value in adoption of the culture of the host society); 'assimilation' (i.e. low value in maintenance of the culture of ethnic origin and high value in adoption of the culture of the host society); 'separation' (i.e. high value in maintenance of the culture of ethnic origin and low value in adoption of the culture of the host society), and 'marginalisation' (i.e. low value in maintenance of the culture of ethnic origin and low value in adoption of the culture of the host society).

Results

LCO course importance and attendance amongst immigrant and bi-national youth

The analysis of variance illustrates that immigrant students rated the 'importance of LCO courses' significantly higher than bi-national youth (F (1, 667) = 6.50, $p < .05$, η^2 = .01; immigrant students: N = 479, M = 3.35, SD = 1.14 and bi-national students: N =192, M = 3.11, SD = 1.02; Cohen's d = .22). However, there were no significant differences with respect to students' gender (F (1, 667) = .02, p = .90).

However, immigrant students' attitudes towards the importance of LCO courses differ significantly between ethnic groups (F (6, 379) = 5.48, $p < .001$, η^2 = .08) (see Graph 1). The post-hoc Bonferroni tests indicate that Albanian ($p < .05$), Tamil ($p < .001$), and Turkish ($p < .001$) students rated the importance of LCO courses significantly higher than Bosnian students. In addition,

Tamil students ($p < .001$) rated the importance of LCO courses significantly higher than Serbian students.

Graph 1: Rating of LCO course importance amongst immigrant youth

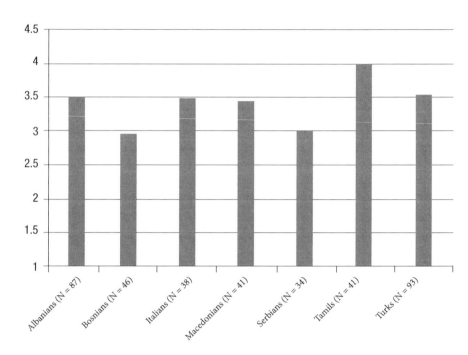

With respect to 'LCO course attendance', significantly more immigrant youth attended such courses than did bi-national youth (X^2 (1, 575) = 9.29, $p < .01$; immigrant youth: $N = 167$, 43.7%; bi-national youth: $N = 59$, 30.6%). Amongst both immigrant youth and bi-national youth, slightly more female students attended LCO courses than did male students. More specifically, amongst immigrant youth 49.5% ($N = 91$) of female and 38.1% ($N = 75$) of male students attended an LCO course, while amongst bi-national youth 33.7% ($N = 35$) of female and 27.3% ($N = 24$) of male students attended an LCO course. However, the gender difference turned out to be significant only amongst immigrant youth (X^2 (1, 381) = 5.02, $p < .05$), but not amongst bi-national youth (X^2 (1, 192) = .91, $p = .35$).

Moreover, amongst immigrant youth, attendance at such courses differed significantly according to ethnic origin (X^2 (6, 382) = 56.88, $p < .001$).

Table 1: LCO course attendance amongst immigrant students

		LCO course attendance		
		Yes	No	Total
Albanians	N	27	60	87
	%	31.0	69.0	100.0
	R_{adj}	-2.7**	2.7**	
Bosnians	N	14	32	46
	%	30.4	69.6	100.0
	R_{adj}	-1.9	1.9	
Italians	N	26	12	38
	%	68.4	31.6	100.0
	R_{adj}	3.2***	-3.2***	
Macedonians	N	10	31	41
	%	24.4	75.6	100.0
	R_{adj}	-2.6**	2.6**	
Serbians	N	10	24	34
	%	29.4	70.6	100.0
	R_{adj}	-1.8	1.8	
Tamils	N	35	6	41
	%	85.4	14.6	100.0
	R_{adj}	5.7***	-5.7***	
Turks	N	45	50	95
	%	47.4	52.6	100.0
	R_{adj}	0.8	-0.8	
Total	N	167	215	382
	%	43.7	56.3	100.0

Note: R_{adj} = Adjusted Residual; $R_{adj} \geq \pm 2.6 = p < .01$**; $R_{adj} \geq \pm 3.3 = p < .001$***.

Thus, Italian and Tamil youth were significantly over-represented amongst immigrant youth attending such courses. In contrast, Albanian and Macedonian students were under-represented amongst immigrant students who attended LCO courses (see Table 1).

LCO courses, acculturation and cultural identity of immigrant youth

With respect to the effect of the LCO courses on the 'acculturation of immigrant youth', an analysis of variance illustrates (F (3, 359) = 5.57, p < .01, η^2 =

.04) that immigrant youth who favoured an 'integration strategy' (N = 102, M = 3.52, SD = 1.01) or a 'separation strategy' (N = 188, M = 3.55, SD = 1.20) in their acculturation rated the importance of LCO courses significantly higher than those favouring an 'assimilation strategy' (N = 39, M = 2.85, SD = 1.07). The tests of effect size indicated moderate effects of mean differences for an integration strategy and an assimilation strategy (Cohen's d = .66) as well as for a separation strategy and an assimilation strategy (Cohen's d = .60). Moreover, those students who preferred a separation strategy attended LCO courses more often than youth preferring other acculturation strategies, but this was only significant for immigrant youth of Italian origin (X^2 (3, 34) = 10.38, p < .05).

Regarding the meaning of LCO course attendance for the 'cultural identity of immigrant youth',[3] our findings show that immigrant youth with a monocultural ethnic self-identification were significantly over-represented amongst those who attended LCO courses, while youth with a bicultural identity were significantly under-represented amongst LCO courses attendants (X^2 (1, 366) = 5.01, p < .05) (see Table 2).

Table 2: LCO course attendance and cultural identity of immigrant youth

		LCO course attendance		
		Yes	No	Total
Bicultural identity	N	40	74	114
	%	35.1	64.9	100.0
	R_{adj}	-2.2*	2.2*	
Monocultural ethnic identity	N	120	132	252
	%	47.6	52.4	100.0
	R_{adj}	2.2*	-2.2*	
Total	N	160	206	366
	%	43.7	56.3	100.0

Note: R_{adj} = Adjusted Residual; $R_{adj} \geq \pm 2.0 = p < .05$*.

Furthermore, a multivariate analysis of variance shows that the intensity and evaluation of self-identification with an ethnic group of origin vary significantly according to LCO course attendance (MANOVA Pillai-Spur-Test: F (2, 371) = 3.06, p < .05, η^2 = .02). Thus, the intensity and the evaluation of self-identification with an ethnic group of origin are significantly higher amongst youth who attended LCO courses (intensity of self-identification: F (2, 373) = 4.60, p < .05; evaluation of self-identification: F (2, 373) = 4.34, p < .05) (see Graph 2).

Graph 2: Evaluation and intensity of ethnic identity amongst LCO course attendance and non-attendance: immigrant youth

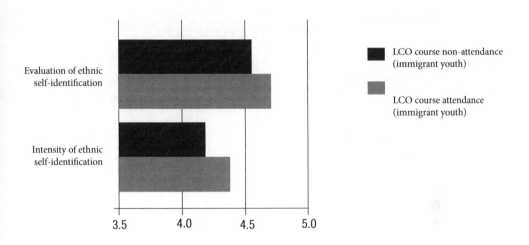

However, amongst immigrant youth the effect sizes of mean differences turned out to be rather small for the intensity of ethnic self-identification (LCO course attendants: $N = 162$, $M = 4.36$, $SD = .75$, and LCO course non-attendants: $N = 212$, $M = 4.18$, $SD = .85$; Cohen's $d = .22$), and for evaluation of ethnic self-identification (LCO course attendants: $N = 162$, $M = 4.70$, $SD = .52$ and LCO course non-attendants: $N = 212$, $M = 4.56$, $SD = .73$; Cohen's $d = .22$).

Finally, amongst immigrant youth, the rating of the importance of LCO courses correlates significantly positively with the intensity of ethnic self-identification ($r = .22$, $p < .01$), and with the evaluation of ethnic self-identification ($r = .13$, $p < .05$).

LCO courses and cultural identity of bi-national youth

With respect to the meaning of LCO courses for the 'cultural identity of bi-national youth', our results show that bi-national youth with a monocultural ethnic self-identification were significantly over-represented amongst those who attended LCO courses, while youth with a monocultural national self-identification were significantly under-represented amongst LCO course attendants (X^2 (2, 184) = 22.29, $p < .001$) (see Table 3).

Table 3: LCO course attendance and cultural identity of bi-national youth

		LCO course attendance		
		Yes	No	Total
Bicultural identity	N	13	22	35
	%	37.1	62.9	100.0
	R_{adj}	.8	-.8	
Monocultural ethnic identity	N	34	35	69
	%	49.3	50.7	100.0
	R_{adj}	4.0***	-4.0***	
Monocultural national identity	N	11	69	80
	%	13.8	86.2	100.0
	R_{adj}	-4.6***	4.6***	
Total	N	58	126	184
	%	31.5	68.5	100.0

Note: R_{adj} = Adjusted Residual; $R_{adj} \geq \pm 3.3 = p < .001$***.

Moreover, a multivariate analysis of variance shows that intensity and evaluation of self-identification with an ethnic group of origin vary significantly according to LCO course attendance (MANOVA Pillai-Spur-Test: F (2, 127) = 6.15, $p < .01$ $\eta^2 = .09$). Thus, the intensity and the evaluation of self-identification with an ethnic group of origin are significantly higher amongst youth who attended LCO courses (intensity of self-identification: F (2, 129) = 6.94, $p < .01$; evaluation of self-identification; F (2, 129) = 10.57, $p < .01$) (see Graph 3). Amongst bi-national youth the effect sizes of mean differences turned out to be moderate for the intensity of ethnic self-identification (LCO course attendants: N = 53, M = 4.30, SD = .70 and LCO course non-attendants: N = 77, M = 3.94, SD = .83; Cohen's d = .50), as well as for evaluation of ethnic self-identification (LCO course attendants: N = 53, M = 4.72, SD = .44 and LCO course non-attendants: N = 77, M = 4.29, SD = .90; Cohen's d = .62).

Graph 3: Evaluation and intensity of ethnic identity amongst LCO course attendants and non-attendants: bi-national youth

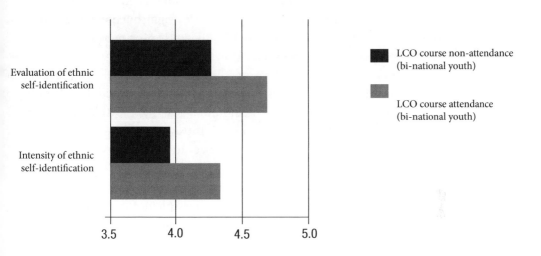

Finally, our results indicate that amongst bi-national youth the rating of LCO course importance correlates positively with the evaluation of ethnic self-identification ($r = .20$, $p < .05$). However, there were no significant correlations of LCO course importance with the intensity of ethnic self-identification ($r = .17$, n.s.).

Discussion

LCO courses and their impact on the development of immigrant youth

Overall, 43.7% of immigrant youth and 30.6% of dual-heritage youth in our survey attended LCO courses during their compulsory schooling in addition to the regular school curriculum. Amongst immigrant youth, LCO course attendance was significantly higher amongst female youth than amongst male youth, whereas, amongst the youth of dual heritage, LCO course attendance did not differ between female and male youth. At the same time, youth of dual heritage rated the importance of the LCO courses less highly than did immigrant youth.

Amongst immigrant youth there were considerable differences in LCO course attendance depending on both gender and origin. Thus, while the vast majority of the Tamil (85.4%) or Italian youth (68.4%) attended such courses, only 24.4% of Macedonians attended them. Opinion about the importance of LCO courses also differed according to ethnic origin, but not in the same way. While Italian and Tamil youth were significantly over-represented amongst immigrant youth attending such courses, their opinion concerning the importance of the LCO courses varied: Tamil youth rated the importance of LCO course attendance highest, whereas Italian youth rated the importance of such courses as average. We, therefore, suggest that the differences in LCO course attendance and attitudes towards those courses amongst immigrant youth can be explained by analysing the contextual factors in the society of settlement.

In the context of Swiss society the high attendance of LCO courses amongst immigrant youth from Italy can be explained by the following contextual factors. First, the Italian language is one of the national languages in Switzerland, which can also be chosen as a school subject and therefore has its relevance for the academic career of immigrant youth. Second, the Italian immigrants belong to one of the oldest and largest immigrant groups in Switzerland. Immigration from Italy has its roots in the second half of the 19th century and reached its peak during labour immigration in 1975. Finally, the courses in Italian language and customs were the first LCO courses in Switzerland (Serra 1991).

Compared to Italian immigrants, Tamils belong to the group of recent immigrants to Switzerland. Since 1980 immigrants from Sri Lanka have been arriving in Switzerland as refugees, but currently most of them have a long-term residence permit. Tamil immigrants are part of a well-organised diaspora which supports a wide range of ethnic-based activities, highlighting the maintenance of language and culture of origin. This maintenance of culture amongst Tamil youth is reinforced by their parents, who try to prevent their Swiss-resident children from forgetting traditional values and their native language (Moret, Efionayi and Stants 2007).

With respect to the immigrant youth from Albania and Macedonia, who were under-represented amongst LCO course attendants, our results are consonant with those reported by Reich and Roth (2002): as in Germany, the immigrant youth from former Yugoslavia were under-represented in LCO courses compared to immigrant youth of other origins. In analysing the reasons for this weak interest in LCO courses of youth from former Yugoslavia, the authors suggested that the experience of war might have influenced their language loyalty. We cannot support or reject this suggestion based on our data. However, the indication of loyalty towards ethnic language amongst Albanian youth in our sample is their relatively high rating of the importance of the LCO courses. According to another Swiss study amongst Albanian students of Grades 5 to 9, the low attendance of LCO courses was predominantly motivated by lack of interest and by the distant location of the courses from the place of residence (Schader 2006, 117). The inconvenient organization of the LCO courses was also the reason for negative judgments about such courses amongst immigrant students who attended them (Binder, Tuggener, Trachsler and Schaller 2002). Thus, immigrant youth reported being limited in their contacts with peers because the courses were conducted during a time that was free of schooling for their classmates. Also, in the schools that participated in our survey, the courses were not integrated into the regular school template but were conducted outside regular school hours. Moreover, the Macedonian LCO courses were not even explicitly listed amongst other LCO courses announced on the education department homepages of the cantons surveyed. We therefore suppose that the inopportune implementation of the LCO courses is the main reason for the low attendance of LCO courses amongst Albanian and Macedonian youth in our survey.

In conclusion, our findings indicate that LCO course attendance amongst immigrants greatly depends on the conditions of their implementation in the educational system of the host society or on the status and establishment of the immigrant group in question in the society of settlement. Our findings also confirm the great influence of the host society on the effectiveness of ethnic language learning amongst immigrants (Phinney et al. 2006, 79). Moreover, we suggest that for youth of dual heritage these effects could be even greater because their attitudes towards the ethnic culture of their parents are influenced by the status of their heritage groups in society (Stephan and Stephan 1989).

LCO courses and their impact on youth development

With respect to the link between LCO courses and the acculturation of immigrant youth, our findings indicate that youth who favoured the maintenance of the heritage culture – either as part of an integration strategy or solely as a separation strategy – rated the importance of LCO courses significantly higher than did youth who aimed at adoption of the host society culture. There are a large number of studies examining the impact of acculturation preferences of immigrants on their adaptation into new societies of settlement (review in Berry and Sam 1997). The results of European studies show that integration is usually the most successful acculturation strategy of immigrant youth, while a separation strategy has an intermediate impact on immigrants' adaptation in the society of settlement (Berry and Sabatier 2010; Pfafferott and Brown 2006). At the same time the strong pressure to assimilate is associated with a developmental risk for immigrant youth in the new society of settlement (Coll and Marks 2012). Thus, the attendance of LCO courses is important for the sociocultural adaptation of immigrants because it allows the acquisition of competencies in the ethnic culture (Arends-Tóth and Vijver 2006). However, it is important to note that the preference for culture maintenance as part of acculturation attitudes does not necessarily lead to a corresponding acculturative behaviour. As shown in our study, amongst all immigrant youth who preferred a separation strategy, only Italian students attended LCO courses more often than youth preferring other strategies. As discussed above, the establishment of Italian immigrants in Swiss society and the solid implementation of courses promoting Italian language and culture in Switzerland facilitate the accessibility of LCO courses for those Italian youth who favour maintenance of the heritage culture. Thus, LCO courses can facilitate the acquisition of ethnic language and traditions, but only if the immigrants' culture is accepted and appreciated in the new society of settlement.

With respect to youth cultural identity, our results show that immigrant and dual-heritage youth who attend LCO courses are more likely to identify themselves with an ethnic group of origin from the cultural background of their parents. Moreover, the strength and valence of the ethnic identity were significantly greater amongst immigrant and dual-heritage youth who attended the LCO courses. Thus, LCO course attendants felt a stronger sense of belonging to the ethnic group with which they identified themselves and were prouder to belong to the chosen ethnic group than youth who did not attend the courses. These effects were even stronger for the ethnic identity of dual-heritage youth than for immigrant youth. Based on these findings we assume that LCO courses contribute greatly to ethnic identity development, but are limited to facilitating bicultural identity development amongst immigrant and dual-heritage youth. However, bicultural identification is not *per se* advantageous for adaptation amongst youth. When the integration of different cultural origins in one's cultural identity fails, one can experience the feeling of being 'torn between one's two cultural identities' (Benet-Martínez and Haritatos 2005, 1026). At the same time the overall results of a cross-cultural study conducted in 13 countries[4] show that ethnic identity correlates significantly positively with the psychological adaptation (i.e. life-satisfaction and self-esteem) of immigrant youth as well as with their sociocultural adaptation (i.e. school adjustment) in the society of settlement (Sam, Vedder, Ward and Horenczyk 2006, 134).

We conclude that the LCO courses play a crucial role in the development of youth with an immigrant background in the process of cultural transition by facilitating their successful psychological and sociocultural adaptation in the society of settlement. However, our results illustrate that LCO course attendance amongst immigrants is influenced by contextual factors such as the conditions of LCO course implementation in the educational system of the host society or the status and establishment of certain immigrant groups in the society of settlement.

Conclusion and limitations

Overall, our study provides empirical evidence for the impact of courses in the language and culture of origin on the cultural identity development of immigrant and dual-heritage youth. Our findings provide strong support for Jim Cummins' statement: 'To reject a child's language in the school is to reject the child' (ibid. 2001, 19). They highlight the need for schools in receiving societies to recognise the potential for cultural heterogeneity afforded by students with an immigrant background in creating a multilingual learning and teaching environment for students of all origins.

However, our study also has some limitations. First, it employed a cross-sectional design and therefore cannot ascertain the causality of the suggested relations between LCO course attendance and the development of immigrant youth in the host society. A longitudinal study would be needed to confirm the causality of the reported findings. Secondly, the generalisability of the present results is limited to the context of one European country; more research on the meaning of LCO courses for youth development in cultural transition is needed in other countries.

REFERENCES

Allemann-Ghionda, C. (1993). 'Die Schweiz und ihr Bildungswesen: von Babylonia zu MultiKulti'. *Zeitschrift für Pädagogik* 3, 127–45.

Allemann-Ghionda, C. (1999). 'Die kulturelle und sprachliche Vielfalt – eine für den Schulerfolg notwendige Dimension der Lehrerbildung' ('Cultural and Language Diversity – An Essential Dimension of School Success and Teacher Training'). *Beiträge zur Lehrerbildung* 17 (3), 297–306.

Arends-Tóth, J. and Vijver, F.J.R. van de (2006). 'Assessment of Psychological Acculturation'. In D.L. Sam and J.W. Berry, eds, *Cambridge handbook of acculturation psychology*, 142–62. Cambridge: Cambridge University Press.

Benet-Martínez, V. and Haritatos, J. (2005). 'Bicultural Identity Integration (BII): Components and Psychosocial Antecedents'. *Journal of Personality* 73, 1015–49.

Berry, J.W. (2003). 'Conceptual Approaches to Acculturation'. In K.M. Chun, P. Balls Organista and G. Marin, eds, *Acculturation: Advances in Theory, Measurement, and Applied Research*, 17–38. Washington: American Psychological Association.

Berry, J.W. (2005). 'Acculturation: Living Successfully in Two Cultures'. *International Journal of Intercultural Relations* 29, 697–712.

— (2006). 'Contexts of Acculturation'. In D.L. Sam and J.W. Berry, eds, *Cambridge Handbook of Acculturation Psychology*, 27–42. Cambridge: Cambridge University Press.

Berry, J.W., Phinney, J.S., Sam, D.L. and Vedder, P., eds (2006). *Immigrant Youth in Cultural Transition. Acculturation, Identity, and Adaptation Across National Contexts*. Mahwah, NJ: Lawrence Erlbaum.

Berry, J.W. and Sabatier, C. (2010). 'Acculturation, Discrimination, and Adaptation Amongst Second Generation Immigrant Youth in Montreal and Paris'. *International Journal of Intercultural Relations* 34, 191–207.

Berry, J.W. and Sam, D.L. (1997). 'Acculturation and Adaptation'. In J.W. Berry, M.H. Segall and C. Kagitcibasi, eds, *Handbook of cross-cultural psychology*, 291–326. Boston, MA: Allyn and Bacon.

Bianchi, D. (2003). *Die Integration der ausländischen Bevölkerung: der Integrationsprozess im Lichte des schweizerischen Verfassungsrechts (The Integration of Foreigners: The Integration Process in the Light of Swiss Constitutional Law)*. Zürich: Schulthess.

Binder, H., Tuggener, D., Trachsler, E. and Schaller, R. (2002). *Qualität in multikulturellen Schulen (QUIMS) (Quality in Multicultural Schools)*. Zürich: Bildungsdirektion des Kantons Zürich.

Bourhis, R.Y., Moise, L.C., Perreault, S. and Senécal, S. (1997). 'Towards an Interactive Acculturation Model: A Social Psychological Approach'. *International Journal of Psychology* 32, 369–86.

Caprez-Krompàk, E. (2010). *Entwicklung der Erst- und Zweitsprache im interkulturellen Kontext. Eine empirische Untersuchung über den Einfluss des Unterrichts in heimatlicher Sprache und Kultur (HSK) auf die Sprachentwicklung (Development of the first and second languages in an intercultural context. An empirical study of the impact of education in the native language and culture on language development)*. Münster: Waxmann.

Coll, C.G. and Marks, A.K., eds (2012). *The Immigrant Paradox in Children and Adolescents: Is Becoming American a Developmental Risk?* Washington: American Psychological Association.

Cummins, J. (2001). 'Bilingual Children's Mother Tongue'. *Sprogforum* 19, 15–20.

Dollmann, J. and Kristen, C. (2010). 'Herkunftssprache als Ressource für den Schulerfolg? Das Beispiel türkischer Grundschulkinder' ('Native Language as a Resource for School Success? An Example of the Turkish Primary School Children'). *Zeitschrift für Pädagogik*, 55, 123–46.

Herzog, W. and Makarova, E. (2007). *Interkulturelle Pädagogik* (*Intercultural Education*). In J. Straub, A. Weidemann and D. Weidemann, eds, *Handbuch Interkulturelle Kommunikation und Kompetenz*, 261–72. Stuttgart: Metzler.

Hesse, H.-G., Göbel, K. and Hartig, J. (2008). 'Sprachliche Kompetenzen von mehrsprachigen Jugendlichen und Jugendlichen nicht-deutscher Erstsprache ('Language Skills of Multilingual Youth and Youth of non-German Mother Tongue). In E. Klieme, ed., *Unterricht und Kompetenzerwerb in Deutsch und Englisch. Ergebnisse der DESI-Studie*, 208–30. Weinheim: Beltz.

Hofhansel, C. (2008). *Citizenship in Austria, Germany, and Switzerland: Courts, Legislatures, and Administrators.* Faculty Publications: Paper 103. digitalcommons.ric.edu/faculty-publications/103 (retrieved March 2013).

Gogolin, I. (2009). 'Bilinguale Schulen ('Bilingual schools). In S. Blömeke u.a., eds, *Handbuch Schule*, 414–17. Bad Heilbrunn: Klinkhardt (UTB).

Isajiw, W.W. (1990). 'Ethnic-Identity Retention'. In R. Breton, W.W. Isajiw, W.E. Kalbach and J.G. Reitz, eds, *Ethnic Identity and Equality*, 34–91. Toronto: University of Toronto Press.

Kinket, B. and Verkuyten, M. (2003). 'Levels of Ethnic Self-Identification and Social Context'. *Social Psychology Quarterly* 60 (4), 338–54.

Liebkind, K. (2001). 'Acculturation'. In R. Brown and S. Gaertner, eds, *Blackwell Handbook of Social Psychology: Intergroup Processes* (386–406). Oxford: Blackwell.

Makarova, E. (2008). *Akkulturation und kulturelle Identität. Eine empirische Studie bei Jugendlichen mit und ohne Migrationshintergrund in der Schweiz* (*Acculturation and Cultural Identity. An Empirical Study Amongst Native Youth and Youth with an Immigrant Background in Switzerland*). Bern: Haupt.

Moret, J., Efionayi, D. and Stants, F. (2007). *Die srilankische Diaspora in der Schweiz* (*The Sri Lankan Diaspora in Switzerland*). Bern: Bundesamt für Migration (BFM).

Oksaar, E. (2003). *Zweitspracherwerb. Wege zur Mehrsprachigkeit und zur interkulturellen Verständigung* (*Second Language Acquisition. Ways to Multilingualism and Intercultural Understanding*). Stuttgart: Kohlhammer.

Pfafferott, I. and Brown, R. (2006). 'Acculturation Preferences of Majority and Minority Adolescents in Germany in the Context of Society and Family'. *International Journal of Intercultural Relations* 30, 703–17.

Phinney, J.S. (1990). 'Ethnic Identity in Adolescents and Adults'. *Review of Research, Psychological Bulletin* 108 (3), 499–514.

— (1992). 'The Multigroup Ethnic Identity Measure: A New Scale for Use with Diverse Groups. *Journal of Adolescence Research* 7 (2), 156–76.

— (2003). 'Ethnic Identity and Acculturation'. In K.M. Chun, P. Balls Organista and G. Marin, eds, *Acculturation: Advances in Theory, Measurement, and Applied Research*, 63–82. Washington: American Psychological Association.

Phinney, J.S., Horenczyk, G., Liebkind, K. and Vedder, P. (2001). 'Ethnic Identity, Immigration, and Well-Being: An Interactional Perspective'. *Journal of Social Issues*, 57 (3), 493–510.

Phinney J.S., Berry, J.W., Vedder, P. and Liebkind, K., eds (2006). 'The Acculturation Experience: Attitudes, Identities and Behaviors of Immigrant Youth'. In J.W. Berry, J.S. Phinney, D.L. Sam and P. Vedder, eds, *Immigrant Youth in Cultural Transition: Acculturation, Identity, and Adaptation across National Contexts*, 71–116. Boston, NJ: Lawrence Erlbaum.

Piontkowski, U., Florack, A., Hoelker, P. and Obdrzálek, P. (2000). 'Predicting Acculturation Attitudes of Dominant and Non-Dominant Groups'. *International Journal of Intercultural Relations* 24, 1–26.

Redfield, R., Linton, R. and Herskovits, M.J. (1936). 'Memorandum of the Study of Acculturation'. *American Anthropologist* 38, 149–52.

Reich, H.H. and Roth, H.-J. (2002). *Spracherwerb zweisprachig aufwachsender Kinder und Jugendlicher. Ein Überblick über den Stand der nationalen und internationalen Forschung (Language Acquisition Amongst Bilingual Children and Youth. An Overview of the State of National and International Research)*. Hamburg: Behörde für Bildung und Sport.

Salm, E. (2000). *Schulerfolg der Migrantinnen und Migranten (School Success of Immigrants)*. Bern: Amt für Bildungsforschung der Erziehungsdirektion des Kantons Bern.

Salm, E. and Künzi, A.M. (2001). *Der HSK-Unterricht im Kanton Bern: Rechtliche Grundlagen, Bestandesaufnahme und Konzeptvorschläge für die Integration des Unterrichts in heimatlicher Sprache und Kultur (HSK) (LCO Courses in the Canton of Bern: Legal Framework, Inventory and Concept Proposals for the Integration of Courses in the Language and Culture of Origin (LCO))*. Bern: Amt für Bildungsforschung der Erziehungsdirektion des Kantons Bern.

Sam, D.L. (2006). 'Acculturation: Conceptual Background and Core Components'. In D.L. Sam and J.W. Berry, eds, *Cambridge Handbook of Acculturation Psychology*, 11–26. Cambridge: Cambridge University Press.

Sam, D.L. and Berry, J.W. (2006). *Cambridge Handbook of Acculturation Psychology*. Cambridge: Cambridge University Press.

Sam, D.L., Vedder, P., Ward, C. and Horenczyk, G. (2006). 'Psychological and Sociocultural Adaptation of Immigrant Youth'. In J.W. Berry, J.S. Phinney, D.L. Sam and P. Vedder, eds, *Immigrant Youth in Cultural Transition*, 117–42. Mahwah, MA: Lawrence Erlbaum.

Schader, B. (2006). *Albanischsprachige Kinder und Jugendliche in der Schweiz. Hintergründe, schul- und sprachbezogene Untersuchungen (Albanian-speaking Children and Youth in Switzerland. Background-, School- and Language-related Research)*. Zürich: Pestalozzianum.

Siebert-Ott, G. (2003). 'Mehrsprachigkeit und Bildungserfolg' ('Multilingualism and Educational Success'). In G. Auernheimer, ed., *Schieflagen im Bildungssystem: Die Benachteiligung der Migrantenkinder*, 161–76. Opladen: Leske und Budrich.

Serra, A. (1991). *Kurse in heimatlicher Sprache und Kultur (HSK) (Courses in the Language and Culture of Origin (LCO))*. Schlussbericht über die Versuchsphase gemäss

Erziehungsratsbeschluss vom 8. November 1983. Zürich: Erziehungsdirektion des Kantons Zürich.

Stephan, C.W. and **Stephan, W.G.** (1989). 'After Intermarriage: Ethnic Identity Amongst Mixed-Heritage Japanese-Americans and Hispanics'. *Journal of Marriage and Family* 51 (2), 507–19.

Swiss Conference of Cantonal Ministers of Education (EDK) (1991). *Empfehlungen zur Schulung der fremdsprachigen Kinder vom 24. Oktober 1991 (Recommendations and Resolutions: Recommendations for the Education of Foreign Children from 24 October 1991).* www.edk.ch/dyn/11984.php (retrieved March 2013).

— (1995). *Empfehlungen und Beschlüsse. Erklärung zur Förderung des zweisprachigen Unterrichts in der Schweiz vom 2. März 1995 (Recommendations and Resolutions. Declaration on the Encouragement of Bilingual Education in Switzerland from 2 March 1995).* www.edk.ch/dyn/11984.php (retrieved March 2013).

— (2013a). *Interkantonale Vereinbarung über die Harmonisierung der obligatorischen Schule (HarmoS-Konkordat) (Intercantonal Agreement on the Harmonisation of Compulsory Education (HarmoS-Concordat)).* www.edk.ch/dyn/11659.php (retrieved March 2013).

— (2013b). *Unterricht in Migrationssprache (Classes in the Language of Origin).* www.edk.ch/dyn/19191.php (retrieved March 2013).

Swiss Federal Department of Foreign Affairs (2013). *Foreigners.* www.swissworld.org/en/people/the_swiss_population/foreigners/ (retrieved March 2013).

Swiss Federal Office for Migration (2013). *Swiss Citizenship/Naturalization.* www.bfm.admin.ch/content/bfm/de/home/themen/buergerrecht.html (retrieved March 2013).

Swiss Federal Statistical Office (2008). *Ausländerinnen und Ausländer in der Schweiz, Bericht 2008. (Foreigners in Switzerland, Rapport 2008).* Neuchâtel: BFS.

— (2013a). *Population with an Immigration Background.* www.bfs.admin.ch/bfs/portal/de/index/themen/01/07/blank/key/04.html (retrieved March 2013).

— (2013b). *Acquisition of Swiss Citizenship.* www.bfs.admin.ch/bfs/portal/en/index/themen/01/07/blank/key/03.html (retrieved March 2013).

— (2013c). *Unterrichts- und Lernbedingungen – Kulturelle Heterogenität der Schulabteilungen (Teaching and Learning Conditions – The Cultural Heterogeneity of School Departments).* www.bfs.admin.ch/bfs/portal/en/index/themen/01/07/blank/key/03.html (retrieved March 2013).

Trimble, J.E. (2003). 'Introduction: Social Change and Acculturation'. In K.M. Chun, P. Balls Organista and G. Marin, eds, *Acculturation: Advances in Theory, Measurement, and Applied Research*, 3–14. Washington, DC: American Psychological Association.

Ward, C. (2001). 'The ABCs of Acculturation'. In D. Matsumoto, ed., *The Handbook of Culture and Psychology*, 411–45. Oxford: Oxford University Press.

NOTES

1 Years spent in Switzerland between the ages of ten and twenty count double (Art. 15, Federal Law on Acquisition and Loss of Swiss Citizenship; Bürgerrechtsgesetz).

2 According to the Swiss Federal Statistical Office (2013), classes with more than 30% of students with foreign nationality or foreign mother tongue are referred to as 'culturally highly heterogeneous' classes.

3 Because few immigrants identified themselves solely with Swiss natives, the group monocultural national identity was excluded from further analyses of immigrant youth.

4 The International Comparative Study of Ethnocultural Youth (ICSEY) was carried out in Australia, Canada, Finland, France, Germany, Israel, the Netherlands, New Zealand, Norway, Portugal, Sweden, the UK and the US (Berry, Phinney, Sam and Vedder 2006).

6 LANGUAGE POLICIES IN THE CONTEXT OF AUSTRALIAN CIVIC PLURALISM

Eugenia Arvanitis (University of Patras)
Mary Kalantzis (University of Illinois)
Bill Cope (University of Illinois)

Introduction

As a result of its extensive migration programme since World War II, Australia is one of the most multicultural and multilingual countries in the world. Currently more than 350 languages (including 150–55 indigenous languages) are in use to cover a wide spectrum of social needs. About 20.4% of Australians (2011 Census) have a dominant language other than English in their homes, an indication that second language use is present in a much higher proportion in Australians' everyday professional, personal and social life (Lo Bianco 2009).[1]

The strong multilingual profile of Australian society (with more than 300 ancestries) has at times been contrasted to a 'monolingual mindset' (Clyne 2005) as policy-making in Australian society has been characterised as persistently Anglocentric. The Australian narrative on language policies, however, has been closely related to the country's nation-building process and thus has taken on different ideological orientations over time. This can be interpreted as a general movement from *nationalism*, to *neoliberalism* and to *social pluralism* (Kalantzis and Cope 2012). More specifically, in the 19th century, the prevailing public attitudes towards languages was tolerance and openness (a *laissez faire* approach in Clyne's (1991) terms) followed by hostility periods of 'closure and opposition' due to world events (e.g. the closure of German bilingual programmes in World War II). Exclusion and assimilation served a nationalist ideology of the newly established Commonwealth in 1901. The *White Australia Policy* (social and cultural sameness), adopted as the official policy in dealing with difference for a vast period of time, coincided with Australian nationalism and the formation of 'a consoling narrative of kinship and national belonging' (Kalantzis and Cope 2012, 115).

In more recent times, during the 1970s and 1980s, neoliberalism emerged as a new ideology which dictated a smaller role for the state (privatisation), greater regulation by markets and an ethics of self-reliance (or 'survival of the fittest') as opposed to a welfare state (Kalantzis and Cope 2012, 118). Social inequality became an individual issue in a globalised world, which paradoxically fuelled both uniformity and diversification trends. Thus, the narrative of belonging transformed to allow multiple identifications, disconnected from the idea of 'one people, one land and one nation'. In addition, exclusion and discrimination were not acceptable in a multicultural context of recognition and acceptance.

The 21st century has created a new impetus in national building, with the important impact of learning technologies, global media, transnational networks and the emergence of the so-called 'knowledge society'. 'Civic Pluralism', according to Kalantzis and Cope (2012, 128), better represents the new narrative of 'the changing shape of the state and its relationship to civil society'. As the authors state, it is a narrative of 'diversity, inclusion, collaboration and cosmopolitanism' (p. 129), where citizens acquire agency, new social competences and forms of ethics, multiple roles of civic participation, multiple citizenships and self-governing roles in many divergent communities.

As far as education is concerned in multicultural societies such as Australia, this process of national building was centred on the dynamics of citizenship/belonging and the character building of its citizens ('learning civility'). Participating as a member of two or more states, as well as connecting with two or more cultures, brought a monumental change in the way people perceived their status as local/global citizens. Education in a globalising world could ensure comparable learning outcomes, negotiate differences (material conditions, corporeal attributes and symbolic differences), and enhance autonomy and responsibility (Kalantzis and Cope 2012). Further, ethnic and diasporic community networks in the frame of 'triangular relationships' (Arvanitis 2000) are significant paradigms of local/global interconnection where a new multicultural citizenship can be forged based on a new basics such as multicultural awareness, cultural openness, civic and ethical commitment, communication and intercultural competences (Arvanitis 2004, 2006).

Symbolic differences such as culture or ethnicity and language were seen as the most prominent components of cultural diversity in Australia as policies regarding diversity evolved (Ozolins 1993). The position and survival of languages within a multicultural society are closely associated with power relations, self-determination and access (Kalantzis Cope and Slade 1989). Languages and their respective communities potentially formulate a totally new social space of interaction, transformation and multicultural national building. However, they can be either ignored/killed/abandoned, or recognised but not funded or partially supported, or promoted as a national priority.

This chapter discusses the narrative of Australian language policy based on official attempts to accommodate various aspirations as set out in selected aims and objectives regarding language teaching and programme development that seek consensus in ensuring national unity within the context of the recognition of the legitimacy of ethnic interests ('consociational' theories – Lijphart 1977a and 1977b, 1984). It also describes the inconsistency between theory (language policy rhetoric) and practice (language planning) as it emerges from the language policy tensions at federal and state levels. In Australia, efforts were primarily made to increase the numbers of language speakers ('acquisition planning' in Djite's terms; 1994) and expand the provision of 'Languages Other Than English' (LOTES) due to the *de facto* declaration of English as the national language of the country and the assumption that it is the only fundamental requirement for professional and social mobility (Djite 2011). In addition, language planning revolved around priority decisions over which languages were to be taught and/or funded, together with other associated language issues.

Finally, this chapter discusses a new context of language teaching and learning for global purposes that serves a new multicultural citizenship. This in fact re-interprets the traditional nexus between ethnicity and language,[2] and rethinks the ethno-specific perception of language teaching as well as the great emphasis put on English as the exclusive marker of Australian identity which has deprived language policy of its educational and global dimensions.

The narrative of Australian language policy

Language policy rhetoric in Australia represents the dominant ideology for managing diversity. A generic scheme (Kalantzis and Cope 2012) to highlight this evolution refers to three phases, namely: 1) exclusion/assimilation/integration (up to the mid-1970s); 2) recognition (last quarter of the 20th century); and, finally, 3) inclusion (1990s and early 21st century).[3] However these phases overlap, and certain characteristics re-emerge or are submerged due to the dynamism of significant 'actors' (language professionals, policy makers, indigenous and ethnic communities, diplomatic, commercial/trade and security representatives). Overall, language policy and planning in Australia became a messy and quite 'unplannable' process due to competing ethnic interests and their access to resources for their diverse culture and linguistic needs. This aspect was present during all stages of the planning process (the 'mixing of interests' in Ozolins' (1993) terms).

The following sections discuss major characteristics of language policy in each phase based on federal documents and initiatives. The term 'policy' is used as a general notion to accommodate 'textual' statute positions (policy documents), 'discourse' or debates around decision making, and practical/ performance applications. In other words, the discussion is centred on dimensions of 'intended, enacted and experienced' policy elements and especially the influence of inside (stakeholders) and outside ('those who are on the receiving end') actors in policy development who serve as *change agents,* able to transform or subvert it (Lo Bianco 2009, 17).

Australian nationalism: exclusion, passive tolerance, assimilation and integration

Australia's colonial past was characterised by Anglo-conformity and a tendency to replicate British society. Australia was the 'British outpost' in the South Pacific and the national character was built on the consensus that Australia should be white, British, monolingual and naturally affiliated with the United Kingdom (Ozolins 1993, 14), restricting the richness and multilingual character of the continent. Although more than 250 indigenous languages were spoken before colonisation, they were subsequently repressed and forced into extinction. However, colonies did not remain monolingual as the first English settlers and convicts were supplemented by Chinese, German, Irish, French, Scottish Gaelic, Italian and Welsh settlers, alongside free arrivals of adventurers and workers headed for the gold fields, ports and rural industries.[4]

In the 19th century, 'foreign language teaching reflected essential British prestige choices' (Lo Bianco 2009, 15). A 'comfortably British' society allowed instances of language promotion (e.g. 100 French, German, Hebrew and Gaelic bilingual schools), yet, during these early years, repression alternated with periods of toleration or neglect. Indigenous and immigrant languages, even though present in various domains (e.g. ethnic media, community language and bilingual schools), were neglected or repressed in a context of a *laissez-faire* approach.

In 1901 the federated Commonwealth introduced a 'textual' policy model, starting with the adoption of the Immigration Restriction Act, the first legislative action of the Federal State. The so-called *White Australia Policy* (until its dismantling in 1969) ensured that languages where tolerated but restricted within their ethnic limits. An aggressive English monolingualism, based on the Western cannon of strict literacy use and accuracy, enforced uniformity.[5] At the same time, hostility and rejection emerged towards certain languages (e.g. the German language) due to political tensions in Europe and the role of Germany in World War I, while in 1918 several states banned instruction in any language other than English.

The post-World War II mass migration programme changed Australia's ethnic composition (which up to 1947 was overwhelmingly British) with northern Europeans, displaced persons, Mediterranean and, finally, Asian migrants. This explosion coincided with English second language provision (for adults starting from classes in the ocean liners and migrant reception centres, and later on for children; Vogiazopoulos 2006).[6]

The period up to 1970 has been characterised as one of separatism, rejection or 'aggressive assimilationism' (Cahill 1996, 8) that encouraged the total sociocultural and linguistic absorption of migrants in the interest of securing the national identity, unity and homogeneity of the Australian nation. Assimilation operated as both an ideological mechanism facilitating the acceptance of the large immigration programme by a largely xenophobic population as well as a sociocultural and political construct that implicitly asserted the superiority of the Anglophone population and culture (Castles, Kalantzis, Cope and Morrisey 1988, 45). A softer form of assimilation (Ozolins 1993) assured Australians that 'cultural differences were not immutable, while paving the way for the softening of a racist popular culture and for a quietly successful mass migration programme' (Kalantzis, Cope, Noble and Poynting 1990, 17).

The mass migration programme and the policy of assimilation after World War II had an immense impact on schooling because of the enormous expansion of students in Australian schools (57% increase in 1961). Ethnic children (Non-English Speaking Background students; NESB) were asked to become entirely Australianised 'new Australians', forgetting their past cultural backgrounds in doing so – in other words, they had to 'sink or swim'. The Federal focus in the early 1960s (the 'rejecting' phase in Australian language politics) was on migration expansion rather than on the educational predicament of migrant children, who were expected to assimilate quietly and easily (Ozolins 1993, 82).

However, the *White Australia Policy* became 'an embarrassment' during the 1960s and early 1970s due to the gradual halt of European migration to Australia, the fact that migration was a source of skilled manpower and due to Australia's trading activities with Asia region. Overt assimilation was replaced (not easily though) by integration (according to the declaration of the Liberal Immigration Minister, Snedden). Integration, however, also served the basic assimilationist ideology as it was aimed at the sociocultural homogeneity of the nation. The educational system became the prime mechanism for imposing sameness and the English language was regarded, especially by conservative policies in the 1950s and 1960s, as the only means for migrants to assimilate. The non-existence of mother tongue provision and the poor funding to the various programmes did little to facilitate integration, and it became obvious that migrant children had poor educational retention rates and were disadvantaged. An explosion of detailed knowledge about the immigration-schooling nexus characterised the move away from assimilation by revealing that neither assimilation nor integration was occurring within the Australian classes and that migrant education required something broader than English as a Second Language (ESL) education (Cahill 1996).

However, the policy of integration took a significant new direction in the political sphere after 1972 with the election of the Whitlam Labor government (1972–1975), the first radical social democratic government since 1949. The Whitlam government made a considerable effort to endorse social participation[7] and equity as well as general reformist welfare policies. Issues such as equal economic opportunity for migrants, migrant participation in Australian cultural and social life, migrant disadvantage and socioeconomic division and discrimination were key policy areas. The Labor government moved beyond the denial of migrant problems and saw migrants (whose massive urban concentrations were obvious) as a 'social problem' and 'disadvantaged', accepting at the same time that they were an integral part of Australian society. A new self-understanding of Australian society began with Al Grassby (Minister for Immigration 1973–74), and his notion of the 'Family of the Nation', which implied that the different elements of Australian society should be seen in relationship to one another as if members of a family. Al Grassby laid the groundwork for the emergence of multiculturalism, as he frequently used this concept in the public domain as 'an over-idealistic but certainly an attention-taking metaphor' (Foster and Stockley 1988, 29).

In education, federal funding increased and new reform initiatives were taken up under the Commonwealth Schools Commission with, for example, the establishment of the Child Migrant Education Program (CMEP) in 1970, which secured extended funding for education from $1.8 million in 1970 to $26.4 million by 1977. These actions were aimed at further developing the concept of multicultural education and overcoming the educational disadvantage in schools with high migrant density. In this period there was some movement towards curricula innovation and the establishment, for example, of the Victorian Curriculum Advisory Board in 1966. Ethnic languages took a more permanently structured place in the education system in the Higher School Certificate (HSC) and tertiary education (Modern Greek was introduced in 1973). However, the CMEP was entirely English language-orientated and was initially conceived as an 'equality of opportunity through the teaching of English' (Kalantzis et al. 1990, 19).

Language education in schools still remained at the periphery, although the Task Forces[8] raised issues of language maintenance and learning, and Al Grassby recognised languages as a valuable part of Australian life. During this period, controversy arose over the importance of bilingualism (Clyne 1983, 1986b; Rado 1978), and the value of language exposure in pre-school education (early start) as compared to the position of establishing English first and the broadening of language provision into tertiary level (not only for prestige languages).

During the integration period, migrant activism (late 1960s to mid-1970s rights-equality movement, and the active involvement of second generation new Australians in policy making) provoked a number of federal initiatives, although the nature of ethnic relations was characterised by differentiation. Ethnic communities and language professionals were discussing broader social and educational issues, such as bilingual/multicultural education, community languages, the curriculum implications of Australia's increasingly heterogeneous population, and ethnic schools, and were raising those issues before the broader Australian community (Martin 1978, 125). Djite (2011, 56) noted that these professionals were one important key driver of multiculturalism by producing 'an intellectual rationalisation of the intrinsic value of languages'.

Thus, great emphasis was given by professionals and communities to language and cultural maintenance (especially, after the mid-1970s) as a right, and as a national resource with broader relevance to Australian society. Migrant activism promoted the idea that cultural diversity allowed migrant children both to integrate and to retain their language and culture.

Language maintenance (inter-generational multilingualism) was discussed on the basis of rights, social justice and equal opportunity (Djite 2011; Lo Bianco 1990, 55–7; Lo Bianco 2003). Thus, a new 'ambitiously multicultural' phase (in Lo Bianco's terms; 2009, 16) commenced in the early 1970s which placed emphasis on 'the assertion of rights' rather than 'the eradication of problems'. Community languages, therefore, attracted a more positive and direct attention.

Overall, the integration doctrine accepted ethnicity as a marker of social classification, legitimised the entry of ethnic groups and their ethnic representatives into the political arena and, finally, triggered ethno-specific services to counter structural disadvantage. Migrants became a viable constituency and policies were orientated towards attracting the 'ethnic vote'. Ethnicity was recruited for purposes of control, mobilisation and political expediency, even though this became evident to voters in the later culturalist phase from the mid-1970s to the early 1980s. However, ethnic activism failed to force Australian institutions to translate language rights into practical programmes, as language programmes were entirely orientated towards ethnic interests and obtained a marginal status without broader relevance to the wider population.

Australian neoliberalism: cultural recognition

The phase of cultural recognition coincides with the culturalist or multicultural phase (mid-1970s – early 1980s) and the polarisation phase (early 1980s – early 1990s) where the notion of multilingualism was promoted, legitimising language teaching in the frame of 'egalitarianism, inclusiveness and cultural open-mindedness' (Djite 2011, 56). From the 1980s and throughout the 1990s, new economic conditions (e.g. detachment from British economy), aligned Australia more to its neighbouring region, enabling more 'energetically Asian' approaches to the teaching of Asian languages, which in fact reversed the traditional preference for European and community languages (Lo Bianco 2009).

This period brought cultural maintenance issues and culturalist explanations of the position of migrants in a multicultural society into the public agenda. Cultural diversity, multilingualism and multiculturalism were strengthened by the forces of globalisation, whereas neoliberal ideology allowed for multiple forms of self-reliance. Ethnic groups were encouraged to develop their own structures and self-managed organisations in Australia. The ethnic school sector and its interconnected diasporic networks were significant actors in this movement and in the process of affirming and constructing social knowledge around language teaching (Arvanitis 2000; 2006). Authentic and progressive approaches in education dictated the affirmation of differences and their placement into the curriculum (e.g. country/cultural studies), although this took on a 'tokenistic', stereotyping and 'even patronising' character that obscured the issues of access to social power or resources (Kalantzis and Cope 2012, 163).

After the mid-1970s, multiculturalism became the dominant ideology of managing cultural pluralism in Australia. Australia's linguistic and cultural diversity attracted full federal recognition, combined with large-scale immigration from Asia. However, the concept itself was not clear and even today it is used either as a description or a prescription of Australian society. The uneven evolution of multiculturalism indicated the persistence of Anglo-conformity in Australian national building.

The following sections discuss the development of multiculturalism characterised by ideological and political shifts, contradictions and reversals. This evolution started with the Whitlam government and were continued by the Fraser and Hawke governments based on significant bipartisanship.

1. Culturalism

Fraser's government (1975–83) established 'conservative multiculturalism', which saw the issue of migrants as unproblematic (Castles et al. 1988) and ethnic groups as homogeneous, rather than class-divided. Fraser's neo-conservative philosophy, characterised by small state, individual self-reliance and economic recovery, indicated that ethnicity was a critical marker for social categorisation (Kalantzis et al. 1989, 59). The emergence of conservative multiculturalism signalled a clear shift from Grassby's 'family of the nation' and the concept of the welfare state to self-reliance and ethno-specific services. Multiculturalism was seen to be more an attitude to be encouraged. The policies on multiculturalism operated within 'a narrow systems-management framework', which implied that immigrants should integrate, be actively involved in policy implementation processes (but not in the actual construction of knowledge) and be self-reliant (Foster and Stockley 1988, 31).

Conservative multiculturalism therefore came with two main elements: The first was the growing social and political voice of the migrant communities. Federal funding was channelled through self-managed ethnic organisations, creating a powerful lobby of ethnic representatives (official government partners for consultation) that reinforced a 'patron-client' relationship. Potential social pressures could be eliminated at the State level[9] and become the responsibility of the community itself (Arvanitis 2000). Within this framework, ethnic communities were becoming self-help welfare agencies (Kalantzis et al. 1990), providing service delivery on the cheap.[10] This meant that these services would be characterised by a degree of voluntarism, but also that individual groups could be played off against each other in competition for extremely limited resource allocations. Ethnic politics became entwined with the politics of liberal social reform due to the numerical strength of migrants and the need to regulate the migrant vote, and address their social disadvantage. The contradiction in this was that up to a certain point, ethnic politics were *de facto* accepting their structural assimilation by desiring their entry to the same cultural act as the dominant group, but conversely were focused on ethnic disadvantage and the need for new skills to be acquired for upward social mobility (Kalantzis et al. 1989, 1990; Castles et al. 1988, 121).

The second element was the development of a 'cultural pluralist' model, focused on a descriptive approach to existent diversity, as something to be celebrated and maintained in an inexpensive way, obscuring any critical structural analysis or the fact that assimilation might be an ongoing process. At the same time, the criticism of simplistic pluralism emphasised the fact that community languages should be viewed as a tool of social access and not as means of cultural maintenance. From that point of view, the discussion over the benefits of transitional bilingualism and the teaching of community languages similar to foreign ones was triggered (Kalantzis et al. 1989, 60).

In education after the mid-1970s, major federal initiatives gave a degree of legitimacy to language teaching and maintenance issues as well as to ethnic schools with per capita funding (e.g. the *Report of the Committee on the Teaching of Migrant Languages in Schools* in 1976). However, a consecutive document, the *Report of the Review of Post-Arrival Programs and Services for Migrants* in 1978 (also known as the Galbally report), was a conservative proposition. The core features of multiculturalism were based on a past-orientated notion of culture and a general 'ethnic pacification' and social coherence function, as part of Fraser's systems-management approach. The report clearly promoted an ethnic model of disadvantage; it provided a framework of patronage through a community-based welfare system and, finally, provided a research mechanism to reinforce this ideology by establishing Australian Institution of Multicultural Affairs (AIMA) (Castles et al. 1988, 70). Nevertheless, this report made a significant contribution to language policy and practice as it signaled the acceptance of multiculturalism by the Australian conservative wing (who were still ignoring indigenous languages), directed public funding to multilingual services, and introduced the institutional recognition of ethnic schools as complementary language providers (Lo Bianco 2009, 22).

After the Galbally report, 'multicultural education' was the centre of national focus and action. Cultural diversity and linguistic maintenance became a recognised object of policy development, supplementing the teaching of English as a second language (ESL). Funding allocation led to an expansion of the so-called 'self-esteem programmes' 'in which one would end up feeling good about one's difference' (Kalantzis et al. 1990, 20-1). However, the quality of community language instruction was degraded due to low-level funding and short-term planning (Foster and Stockley 1988).

Language provision at that time was based on the concept that language teaching was that of 'cultural and linguistic maintenance as virtues and social or educational ends in themselves' (Kalantzis et al. 1989, 8) and it was characterised by rigorous debates involving political, community and academic circles (Kringas and Lewins 1981; Norst 1982). The main issue was about which system could efficiently accommodate language learning in a multicultural society (mainstream or the specialised ethnic schools system). Could accredited, largely voluntary and community funded ethnic schools[11] be an 'official' alternative or not, and what sort of multicultural education could be provided within a monocultural (non-Anglo) ethos?

The *Evaluation of Post-Arrival Programs and Services* (AIMA 1982) reviewed the first two years of the CMEP and found inconsistencies in funding allocation on behalf of the State Multicultural Education Co-ordination Committees. This report generated the terminology of mainstreaming and the idea that multicultural education should become part of the normal responsibilities of the school system rather than a specific, identifiable or marginal federal programme. The evaluation saw the government's role as one of setting guidelines and frameworks, while proposing the establishment of a National Advisory and Coordinating Committee on Multicultural Education (NACCME). The report had less provision for English as a second language (ESL) and signaled that states should take more responsibility in this area (Ozolins 1993, 177).

In this context, the regular school system was viewed to be the most appropriate place for language teaching, although it was impossible for all languages to be included. Ethnic schools were relegated to the periphery of federal concern and were regarded as a somewhat marginal phenomenon. The Ethnic Schools Program (ESP), even though it succeeded in expanding community languages and cultural maintenance provision, was replaced by the Community Language Teaching Program. This programme consisted of two elements: 1) the ethnic schools and classes (the previous per capita payments) and 2) a joint allocation element with direct funding to the schools in order to further integrate insertion classes (Arvanitis 2000). However, 'the exponential growth' of insertion classes (mainly Italian) within mainstream (usually Catholic) schools, and the allocation of most of the funding ($7.23 million in total) to language sensitisation programmes of low quality rather than authentic language learning programmes was 'an unintended outcome' during the early 1980s (Cahill 1996, 94; Harris 1984; Norst, 1982).

2. Mainstreaming ideology

Economic constraints and the deregulation of the Australian economy during the Hawke Labor government (1983–91) made impossible the return to Whitlam's welfare state system. Multiculturalism was now based on the notion of 'community sacrifice with equity'[12] (Foster and Stockley 1988, 22) and the concept of mainstreaming. An economic crisis and major budget cuts in 1986 brought the construction of mainstream rhetoric around 'access and equity'. The official policy after the mid-1980s created a notion of multiculturalism for all Australians, a mainstreaming notion contrary to multicultural practices in the transitional period which viewed 'ethnic groups as a focal point of social cohesion and mobilization in Australia' (Castles et at. 1988, 71). The 'mainstream' notion, in addition, ensured that the concern for ethnic populations became the concern of all other relevant federal agencies and services. Multiculturalism was accordingly linked to mainstream social justice and economic strategies and as such remained 'an ambiguous and ephemeral phenomenon in Australian politics', as social equity replaced cultural pluralism in the public rhetoric (Castles et al. 1988, 78).[13] However, it became an ideology with its own consistency and institutional basis.

This new policy direction emanated, as Castles et al. (1988) have outlined, from the new social democratic approach to multiculturalism[14] with no ethno-specific services that might stigmatise migrants as disadvantaged. Research directed public opinion away from ethnic disadvantage (e.g. the myth of second generation mobility), while the emergence of new market forces, able to take up the cost of post-arrival services, and the feeling that the migrant vote no longer counted, were other factors. According to Kalantzis, Cope and Slade, 'the general mainstreaming argument reasoned that relegating crucial social issues to specialist funding can, in effect, marginalise those issues and make them institutionally very vulnerable' (Kalantzis et al. 1990, 24).

At the same time, a consensus style was applied, stressing social cohesiveness (Castles et. al., 1988, 74–75), not least because ethnic communities' representatives were still able to act as consultants to the government in decision-making processes between 1983 and early 1986. The so-called 'corporatism' permitted government to handle the economic crisis by promoting 'simulation decisions'. According to Foster and Stockley (1988, 35), this practice meant that the real decisions were hidden. Ethnic and multicultural policy in this period became a low-profile matter.

3. A national policy on languages

In education, after a long political evolution, a significant development occurred with the bipartisan adoption of the first comprehensive *Australian National Policy on Languages* in 1987 (NPL; also known as the Lo Bianco Report). This document legitimised language policy as an issue in its own right, placing it outside ethnic origins. It represented a model of treating languages in a relatively discrete way, addressing a whole range of other issues such as indigenous languages, community and Asian languages, cross-cultural and intercultural training, adult literacy, and ESL and multilingual resources/services (e.g. interpreting and translating services, multilingual media, resources in libraries). It also required government bureaucracy to push language policy as an issue and ensured the participation of different stakeholders, language professionals and (ethnic) organisations into a workable coalition of interests in policy formulation, promoting multilingualism as a value in itself (Ozolins 1993, 260).

The threefold classification of needs/rights/resources, as crystallised within the NPL, provided an important 'organizing principle' for a previously amorphous set of language issues. Coordination, facilitation of effort and the setting of priorities rather than advocacy of additional programmes was the rationale behind this (Ozolins 1993, 213). The NPL was reported to be a unique model in English speaking countries (Clyne 2005; Romaine 1991), whereas its social goals of enrichment, economic opportunities, external relations and equality were envied by overseas commentators (Cummins and Danesi 1990).

The NPL built positively on the Fraser–Galbally concept of multiculturalism and consolidated the move towards the social equity principle of the 1980s (Kalantzis et al. 1989, 25). The NPL's principles of 'English for all', the support for Aboriginal and Torres Strait Islanders languages, 'languages for all', and equitable and widespread language services reflected a broader and comprehensive approach towards language policy. Nine languages of wider teaching (Arabic, Chinese, French, German, Modern Greek, Indonesian, Italian, Japanese and Spanish) were nominated, together with a complementary network of first language/heritage language provision.

However, the NPL also stressed the external and economic factors and geographical considerations. There is a predominant economic rationalism, which affected languages in this period; even the term 'community languages' was replaced by the acronym Languages Other Than English (LOTE), indicating a 'mainstreaming' ideology. It also pointed out that language policy should become broader and not exclude other language groups that wanted a place in education. This in fact reflected an emphasis on the efficient teaching of languages of trade and economic significance. In 1989 the National Languages Institute of Australia was established (together with its 32 constituent centres) in order to give greater institutional and research scope to the NPL. However, the shortcomings of this policy were related to insufficient funding and the assumption that the states should take responsibility for funding in language education. This allowed for cuts, for example, to federal programmes relevant to racism in schools.

Finally, from the mid-1980s, there was considerable development in state language education policies.[15] The decentralisation of the curriculum and decision-making processes that many states applied made it difficult to ensure that the aims of the language policy documents were implemented. Thus, although the official rhetoric for languages was increasingly pointing to their worth for all Australians and for the educational system as a whole, the mechanisms for infusing this perspective throughout the education system become looser and less easy to identify. The contradiction between rhetoric and practice was obvious (Arvanitis 2000).

Overall, during the cultural recognition period, representing the Whitlam, Fraser and Hawke era, many policies on multiculturalism were introduced which are still present today. This phase also saw the initiation of important national curriculum developments and language planning declarations such as the Galbally Report and the NPL, which were intended to be broadened and evolved in the years that followed. 'Practically', as Lo Bianco (2009, 20) asserts, 'the entire apparatus of Australia's response to linguistic pluralism was fashioned by these Prime Ministers.' Australia's response was unique due to the involvement of the ethnic groups in policy development and the considerable bipartisan consensus, which prevailed despite ideological differences: the Australian left connected cultural diversity with class and power relations, whereas the Australian right promoted a more celebratory aspect of diversity (Lo Bianco 2009, 20). Cultural diversity underpinned policy development until the early 1990s, when Asian languages with trade importance became an exclusive priority and attracted considerable funding. According to Lo Bianco (2009), domestic interests such as multiculturalism, and Asian engagement, shifted policy determinations away from traditional British attachments.

Civic pluralism and inclusion

The 1990s signalled an ongoing shift from language policy characterised as 'Asianist', or 'economic rationalism' (Keating Labor government), to an 'English as literacy' phase or 'economic assimilationism' (Howard, Liberal-National government). This focus has been embraced and retained during the years of Labor government (2008–13), with a strong commitment towards formulating a nationally coordinated curriculum (ACARA) with detailed 'Key Learning Areas' profiles, including languages and competencies essential for employment mobility.

More specifically, global economic imperatives in the 1990s, brought about by globalisation and economic and political crises following global terrorist attacks such as those in New York in 2001, Bali in 2002/2005 and London in 2005, gave a new perspective to language policy in Australia. This in turn brought new inequalities and in some instances a revamped assimilationist ideology. Multicultural affairs were depoliticised as multiculturalism had proven a dynamic ongoing process with inconsistencies and tensions. The notion of systems-management became more apparent as the government's role was to overcome inequalities arising from economic and social differences. Multicultural policy development was reinterpreted in terms of an economic rationale and a renewed social justice rhetoric (Castles et al. 1988), and away from its cultural emphasis in the 1980s. This caused the revamp of a 'hard-nosed' multiculturalism (Lo Bianco 1990), which defined the relationship of culture and economy under new conditions. Multiculturalism was seen both as a social theory for interpreting society (its descriptive sense of ethnic and cultural diversity), as well as a public policy of social equity and access and participation with three main dimensions: 'cultural identity', 'social justice' and 'economic efficiency'. This is evident in the *National Agenda for a Multicultural Australia* (1989), which supported language maintenance on an economic driven base noting that language education is a 'capital investment' (National Agenda 1989, 40). In the last part of the 1990s, multiculturalism was closely associated with Australian citizenship and inclusiveness. *Australian Multiculturalism for a New Century: Towards Inclusiveness* was published by the National Multicultural Advisory Council (NMAC) in 1999. This document included principles such as civic duty, cultural respect, social equity and productive diversity (Cope and Kalantzis 1997), highlighting a new understanding of multiculturalism. The vision of Australian multiculturalism for the new millennium is 'of a united and harmonious Australia, built on the foundations of our democracy, and developing its continually evolving nationhood by recognising, embracing, valuing and investing in this heritage and cultural diversity' (NMAC 1999, iii).

However, from the 1980s onwards, multiculturalism has been the target of concerted attacks revolving around the influx of Asian migrants, national security issues and border protection, and xenophobic rhetoric. Examples include the 1984 Blainey debate, during which controversial historian Geoffrey Blainey criticised what he saw as the high levels of Asian immigrants allowed by the government; the short-lived 1988 Liberal opposition to the Asian intake; the new dogma of 'one Australia'; the establishment of the 'One Nation' party, and the rise of so-called Hansonism in 1996–7, and finally, the Howard government's conservative and xenophobic reaction to multiculturalism. The denial of multiculturalism in such a way dictates the revival of an assimilationist ideology that is implicitly racist, while it denounces social equality and participation by maintaining the current structural and cultural relations with the various communities (Arvanitis 2000).

In the educational field, attacks were made against the specialist multicultural educational programmes and on the 'mythical' issue of the educational disadvantage of NESB students in a renewed rhetoric of budget constraints. However, this criticism tends to create another myth since, as Kalantzis et al. (1989, 67) have argued, there is a constant need for services and accommodation of cultural and linguistic diversity as the immigration programme is ongoing. This is more obviously due to the importance of education in the socialisation process as well as its impact on social participation and cohesion.

In the 1990s three major language policy documents had a tremendous impact on language policy and planning, namely: 1) the *Australian Language and Literacy Policy* (ALLP) in 1991; 2) the *National Asian Languages and Studies in Australian Schools* in 1994 (NALSAS); and 3) the *Commonwealth Literacy Policy* (CLP) in 1997.

More specifically, ALLP restrained the NLP in its scope, illustrating once again the change over language matters placing great emphasis both on Asian languages as languages in education and English literacy. The major policy position of the document was that Australians should become 'literate' and 'articulate' in the national language (Australian English). The importance of

LOTE was also recognised, although cultural maintenance was considered as being outside the province of education. Emphasis was shifted away from Australian cultural pluralism to 'a foreigner understanding of languages', initiating a financial incentive to promote language learning (Ozolins 1993, 253). The goals of ALLP were narrow in scope, while a major pillar of NLP, the multilingual services, were excluded from its planning, indicating the desire to decentralise the language issues to the states (Ozolins 1993).

Along with the internal language needs, ALLP paid attention to successful international contact via quality language services. Second language learning thus became a component of national policy, although it highlighted the introduction of development projects in languages relevant to economic development and the multicultural community. In addition, it proposed that each state should identify eight priority languages in Year 12 and to aim for a 25% increase of Year 12 enrolments by 2000. This goal has never been reached (Cahill 2001). In general terms, ALLP made a significant contribution to the maintenance and development of Australia's language resources. Nevertheless, it was criticised by academics and language professionals for its emphasis on economically significant languages and the fact that it is focused more on a language-in-education policy, rather than a more comprehensive national language policy (Djite 1994).

Another major language policy document was the *National Asian Languages and Studies in Australian Schools* (1994–2002), which availed significant budget allocations for just four languages (Chinese, Indonesian, Japanese and Korean), signalling mainly pragmatic and economic arguments (not community) for their value in relation to national survival. Even though this policy resulted in the temporary increase of student enrolments to almost a quarter, quality became an issue and the fading numbers alerted stakeholders to the country's Asian language capability by the mid-2000s (Lo Bianco 2009). According to Djite, NALSAS 'overlooked other language groups and weakened the intellectual and cultural claims of language policy' (Djite 2011, 60). For example, by 2007 only 29 languages were offered at tertiary level, implying that European and major languages of the Australasian region were not taught as student enrolments declined (Djite 2011, 64).

Finally, the *Commonwealth Literacy Policy* was adopted in 1997 by the Howard government, signalling a clear shift towards English literacy. This document was centred on a 'national crisis' of literacy standards and the poor performance of young Australians, asserting that English is the 'fundamental skill', 'educational objective' and 'achievement' for securing employment. This diverted funding from Second Language learning and ESL to literacy (Lo Bianco 2009, 22), and also signaled a conservative shift towards a renewed assimilationist ideology by promoting both the notion of 'traditional Australian values' and that of 'Fortress Australia' (Djite 2011, 61).

Other developments included the *Melbourne Declaration of Educational Goals for Young Australians* (MCEETYA 2008), a state, territory and Commonwealth ministerial provision to set a future framework for national schooling for the next decade and to identify priority learning areas (including languages). In 2009, Federal policy also produced another Asian programme directing considerable funding (approximately $62 million over 2008–11) targeted to increase proficiency and cultural understanding of Chinese, Indonesian, Japanese and Korean language, as well as a 12% increase of Year 12 enrolments by 2020.

Finally, in 2011 after wide consultation, extensive debate and research about the provision for learning languages (MCEETYA 2005), and much community agitation for accessing mainstream recognition and resources, a national curriculum on languages was adopted (ACARA 2011). Languages were nominated as a key learning area and the document provided a guide to curriculum development across the country to enable all students to engage in language learning.

The rationale of learning languages was grounded on communication proficiency skills, intercultural capability and the understanding of and reflection on the linguistic and cultural diversity of human experience in a globalising and interconnected world. The learning of languages was linked to the broader educational scope of educating global learners for personal, social and employment opportunities as well as to identity issues recognising students' diversified lifeworlds (biographies) and cultural repertoires. Language learning (i.e. learning the linguistics, the culture itself and generic knowledge) was viewed as an intercultural transformative process (by interpreting self and others and understanding the relationship between language and culture). The main focus was on communicating, interpreting and creating meaning on a mental, social, interactive and collaborative basis. It was also linked to the notion that language learning develops overall literacy capabilities that are transferable across languages, social domains and learning areas, together with meta-awareness in scaffolded learning repertoires (ACARA 2011).

The national curriculum was based on three organising strands for learning languages, namely: 1) communicating (via listening, speaking, reading and writing skills to interpret, create and exchange meaning); 2) understanding (the variable use of languages); and 3) reciprocating (developing a metacognitive and metalinguistic awareness of self as intercultural communicator/user). The national curriculum suggested time allocations for language learning (350 hours per year from Foundation to Year 6, 160 hours across Years 7–8, 160 hours across Years 9–10 and 200–240 hours across Years 11–12). The development of the language curriculum is an ongoing process and will be specified by state and territory authorities. The selected languages will be in different tiers of importance and inclusion, and will include Arabic, Auslan, Chinese, Classical languages, French, German, Hindi, Indonesian, Italian, Japanese, Korean, Modern Greek, Spanish, Turkish and Vietnamese.

Overall, this phase (especially in recent years) can be characterised by a shift to 'economic assimilationism' (Djite 2011), but with more stable and confident government intervention on national language planning. Language policy has been transformed to accommodate international language efficiency issues as well as return on investment for community or regional languages provision. International economic competitiveness became an issue concerning the dominance of English instruction as an export industry and attention was paid to its literary standards and global commercial use. Outcomes-based education and language provision were viewed as a vehicle for upgrading national skills and their relevance into a global/regional market.

Conclusion

Language education in the 21st century is central to the assistance of students in their efforts to become successful learners, confident and creative individuals, as well as active and informed citizens' in a knowledge society (Kalantzis and Cope 2012). According to Lo Bianco (2009), a holistic and a more comprehensive approach to language learning demands a new strategy with new arguments that extend beyond elitist notions or the economic rationale of language study, to meet broader and realistic cultural, intellectual and humanistic aims. The major components of this approach are quality teaching and learning, which addresses the issues of diversity, differentiated instruction and digital technologies as well as the preparation of language teachers to design and offer enriched and scaffolded learning repertoires to students. An example of an inclusive epistemological framework for learning and teaching is the *Learning by Design* approach (www.newlearningonline.com) which utilises multilingual digital media technology (www.neamathisi.com) and tools for collaborative learning and school-based training (Kalantzis, Cope and Arvanitis 2010). It also uses a comprehensive pedagogical framework that engages students' lifeworlds as well as multimodal experiential, conceptual, analytical, applied and transformative forms of learning for diverse global audiences (Kalantzis and Cope 2012).

Furthermore, the formation of a comprehensive and more inclusive language policy remains an imperative. Lo Bianco (2009) asserts four main components of a broader strategy to capitalise on Australia's breadth and depth of language skills in a context of life-long and life-wide learning. This means productive linkages between the non-formal capacity of language speaking (in homes, workplaces and in communities) as well as formal and explicit instruction, aiming at accuracy and outcomes-based learning in educational institutions. The first component of such a strategy refers to the cultivation of and investment in existing language competencies in non-formal settings and authentic sociolinguistic spaces. In other words, recognising and investing in the *productive diversity* that exists in Australia (Cope and Kalantzis 1997), and forging links with the whole spectrum of non-formal and semi-formal language providers and networks (e.g. ethnic schools, state based specialist language providers, etc). Research findings in Greek ethnic schools in Australia (Arvanitis 2000, 2004, 2006) had previously called for more alignment between formal and non-formal institutions, based on a collaborative and effective framework of joint curriculum development and professional learning, as well as international peer learning to promote a broader scope for language teaching in diasporic and global settings.

A second component to a comprehensive approach would be a 'universal apprenticeship in learning how to learn languages' (Lo Bianco 2009, 60), starting from the very early years due to young children's openness and natural disposition to acquire new languages, sounds, skills and experiences. This apprenticeship would offer a basic understanding of how to learn languages and of the importance of language learning in an interconnected world. This would allow students to become more aware of languages, to master practical language skills, to learn how to learn languages, and to be able to transfer language skills to different languages. The inclusion of language learning in early childhood would boost bilingual skills and intercultural awareness and competencies.

The other two components of a broader strategy refer to articulated learning, the reduction of attrition in language learning in upper secondary and university levels, and the certification of language competence to secure academic and professional mobility. Surprisingly, Australian students and undergraduates have lower participation rates in second language learning than any other OECD country (Djite 2011), resting on the assurances of their English as a global commodity. Finally, language learning should be promoted in vocational and adult education to serve the purposes of external relations, trade, diplomacy and recreation.

Australian language education constituted a long journey of political and social transformation. Reasoning for language learning took on different connotations, ranging from its close linkage to ethnic identity formation and maintenance to a mainstream ideology with narrower linkages to economic and regional rationalisations. Aggressive globalisation over recent years broadened the significance and reasoning behind language learning to include educational, cultural and intellectual considerations. Language education has proven to be an amazing apparatus of professional and academic mobility in the knowledge society and an exciting effort of nation building despite its fragility, tensions, antagonism regarding resources and programme proliferation. Quality language teaching has the potential to deepen intercultural understanding and awareness, stimulate reflexivity and communicative skills, and 'foster more reflective, and imaginative dispositions in citizens, as well as the principles of democratic discourse, participation and opportunity' (Lo Bianco 2009, 64).

REFERENCES

Arvanitis, E. (2000). *Greek Ethnic Schools in Transition: Policy and Practice in Australia in the Late 1990s.* Faculty of Education, Languages and Community Services. Melbourne: RMIT University. (PhD thesis).

— (2004). 'Greek Ethnic Schools in a Globalising Context'. *Journal of Modern Greek Studies Australia and New Zealand,* 11–12, 241–57.

— (2006). 'Community Building Education and Greek Diasporic Networks'. *The International Journal of Interdisciplinary Social Sciences* 1 (3), 153–62.

Australian Bureau of Statistics (2013). *2011 Census Quick Stats.* Available at www.censusdata. abs.gov.au/census_services/getproduct/census/2011/quickstat/0 (retrieved May 2013).

Australian Curriculum, Assessment and Reporting Authority (2011). *The Shape of the Australian Curriculum: Languages.* Sydney: ACARA.

Australian Institute of Multicultural Affairs (1982). *Evaluation of Post-Arrival Programs and Services.* Melbourne: AIMA.

Cahill, D. (1984). *A Greek-English Bilingual Education Program: Its Implementation in Four Melbourne Schools.* Melbourne: Language and Literacy Centre, Phillip Institute of Technology.

— (1996). *Immigration and Schooling in the 1990s.* Canberra: AGPS.

— (2001). 'The Rise and Fall of Multicultural Education in Australian Schools'. In C. Grant and J. Lei, eds, *Multicultural Education across the World.* USA: Lawrence Erblaum.

Castles, S., Kalantzis, M., Cope, B. and Morrisey, M. (1988). *Mistaken Identity: Multiculturalism and the Demise of Nationalism in Australia* (2nd ed.). London: Pluto.

Clyne, M. (1983). 'Bilingual Education as a Model for Community Languages in Primary Schools'. *Journal of Intercultural Studies,* 4 (2), 23–36.

— (1986). *An Early Start.* Melbourne: River Seine.

— (1991). *Community Languages: The Australian Experience.* Cambridge: Cambridge University Press.

— (2005). *Australia's Language Potential.* Sydney: University of New South Wales Press.

Cope, B. and Kalantzis, M. (1997). *Productive Diversity: A New, Australian Model for Work and Management.* Sydney: Pluto Press.

Cummins, J. and Danesi, M. (1990). *Heritage Languages. The Development and Denial of Canada's Linguistic Resources, our schools/ourselves.* Aurora, Ontario: Garamond Press.

DEET (Department of Employment, Education and Training) (1990). *The Language of Australia: Discussion Paper on an Australian Literacy and Language Policy for the 1990s* ('Green Paper'). Canberra: AGPS.

— (1991). *Australia's Language: The Australian Language and Literacy Policy* ('White Paper'). Canberra: AGPS.

Department of the Prime Minister and Cabinet (1989). *National Agenda for a Multicultural Australia: Sharing Our Future.* Canberra: AGPS.

Djite, P. (1994). *From Language Policy to Language Planning: An Overview of Languages Other Than English in Australian Education.* Canberra: NLLIA.

— (2011). 'Language Policy in Australia: What goes Up Must Come Down'. In C. Norbby and J. Hajek, eds, *Uniformity and Diversity in Language Policy: Global Perspectives.* Clevedon: Multilingual Matters.

Foster, L. and **Stockley, D.** (1988). *Australian Multiculturalism: A Documentary History and Critique.* Clevedon: Multilingual Matters.

Gilchrist, H. (1992). *Australia and Greeks I: The Early Years.* Sydney: Halstead Press.

— (1997). *Australia and Greeks vol. II: The Middle Years.* Sydney: Halstead Press.

Harris, J. (1984). *Study of Insertion Classes Funded under the Commonwealth Ethnic Schools Program.* Canberra: AGPS.

Kalantzis, M., Cope, B. and **Slade, D.** (1989). *Minority Languages and Dominant Culture: Issues of Education, Assessment and Social Equity.* London: The Falmer Press.

Kalantzis, M., Cope, B., Noble, G. and **Poynting, S.** (1990). *Cultures of Schooling. Pedagogies for Cultural Difference and Social Access.* London: The Falmer Press.

Kalantzis, M., Cope, B. and **Arvanitis, E.** (2010). 'Towards a Teaching Ecology for Diversity, Belonging and Transformation'. In P. Mata, ed., *Intercultural Education as a Project for Social Transformation. Linking Theory and Practice. Towards Equity and Social Justice.* Malta: EU Interwork Programme-Commenius.

Kalantzis, M. and **Cope, B.** (2012). *New Learning: Elements of a Science of Education* (2nd ed.). New York: Cambridge University Press.

Kringas, P. and **Lewins, F.** (1981). *Why Ethnic Schools? Selected Case Studies.* Canberra: ANU Press.

Lijphart, A. (1977a). *Democracy in Plural Societies: A Comparative Exploration.* New Haven: Yale University Press.

— (1977b). *Political Theories and the Explanation of Ethnic Conflict in the Western World.* New Haven: Yale University Press.

Lijphart, A. (1984). 'Democracies: Patterns of Majoritarian and Consensus Government in Twenty-One Countries'. In M.J. Esman, ed., *Ethnic Conflict in the Western World Ithaca.* Ithaca, NY: Cornell University Press.

Lo Bianco, J. (1987). *National Policy on Languages.* Canberra: AGPS.

— (1989). *Victoria Language Action Plan.* Melbourne: Ministry of Education.

— (1990). 'Making Language Policy: Australia's Experience'. In Jr, R. Baldauf and A. Luke, eds, *Language Planning and Education in Australasia and the South Pacific.* Clevedon: Multilingual Matters.

Lo Bianco, J. (2003). *A Site for Debate, Negotiation and Contest of National Identity, Language Policy in Australia.* Strasbourg: Council of Europe.

— (2009). *Second Languages and Australian Schooling.* Melbourne: ACER.

Martin, J. (1978). *The Migrant Presence.* Sydney: Allen and Unwin.

MCEETYA (2005). *National Statement for Languages Education in Australian Schools: National Plan for Languages Education in Australian Schools 2005–2008.* Adelaide: The State of South Australia, Department of Education and Children's Services.

— (2008). *Melbourne Declaration on Educational Goals for Young Australians.* Available at www.mceecdya.edu.au/verve/_resources/national_declaration_on_the_educational_goals_for_young_australians.pdf (retrieved May 2013).

Mills, J. (1982). *Bilingual Education and Australian Schools.* Melbourne: ACER.

National Multicultural Advisory Council (1999). *Australian Multiculturalism for a New Century: Towards Inclusiveness.* Canberra: AGPS.

— (1999). *Australian Multiculturalism for a New Century: Towards Inclusiveness.* Canberra: AGPS.

Norst, M. (1982). *National Ethnic Schools Survey.* Canberra: Commonwealth Schools Commission.

Ozolins, U. (1993). *The Politics of Language in Australia.* Melbourne: Cambridge University Press.

Rado, M. (1978). 'Multilingualism in the Australian context'. *New Education* 1 (1), 47–62.

Review of Migrant and Multicultural Programs and Services (1986). *Don't Settle for Less! (Chair Jupp).* Canberra: AGPS.

Review of Post-Arrival Programs and Services to Migrants (1978). *Migrant Services and Programs* (Chair Galbally). Canberra: AGPS.

Romaine, S. (1991). 'Introduction'. In S. Romaine, ed., *Language in Australia.* Cambridge: Cambridge University Press.

Vogiazopoulos, Z. (2006). *Bonegilla: Memories and Recollections of an Insider.* E. Arvanitis, ed., Melbourne: Australian Greek Resource and Learning Centre, RMIT University.

NOTES

1   For example, in Sydney and Melbourne this rises to over 30% (ABS census 2011). In Sydney's Haymarket, around Chinatown, 85% of dwellings reported more than one language. The biggest language groups there were Mandarin (17%) and Thai (14.4%), followed by Indonesian, Korean and Cantonese (continuing the Australian shift away from Cantonese towards Mandarin in the Chinese community). Also in 2011, the Census revealed that over a quarter (27%) of Australia's population was born overseas and a further one fifth (20%) had at least one overseas-born parent. The most common languages spoken at home (other than English) were Mandarin (1.7%), Italian (1.5%), Arabic (1.4%), Cantonese (1.3%) and Greek (1.3%).

2   Namely, the one-to-one relation, without taking into account the variant language use at an ethnic group's development such as the language revival (Hebrew) or symbolic valuing of a language (Welsh) or language separatism (Belgium) or even global citizens multilingual identifications.

3   Other scholars have suggested a different categorization including five phases, namely, the 'laissez-faire approach', the 'tolerant but restrictive phase', the 'rejecting phase', the 'accepting even fostering' or 'multicultural phase' and finally the 'Asianist', 'economic rationalism' or 'English as literacy phase' (Clyne 1991). In addition, language ideologies refer to overlapping periods of *Britishism, Australianism, Multiculturalism, Asianism and Economism* (Lo Bianco 2009).

4   It has been recorded that the first Greek settlers were seven islanders from Hydra after the Greek revolution in 1921 (Gilchrist 1992 and 1997).

5   The dominance of British literacy was gradually replaced by local Australian literary and communication norms due to the influence of Irish and the new environment of the

20th century. As Lo Bianco (2009, 15) noted, 'Australianist approaches to understanding language and communication issues, and their link with national identity emerged in the documenting of local forms of expression and their literary forms, but they have also been used as a bolster of assimilation of immigrants and Aborigines'.

6   The adoption of the Child Migrant Education Act in 1969 signaled the first attempt to teach English in a systematic way to children.

7   Greeks and Italians were the most organised and large groups. The Italians mostly demanded for migrant language recognition and their introduction into the mainstream school system at the end of the 1960s. Also, in 1973 at the Greek Community of Melbourne was signed the Statement of Immigrant Education, Cultures and Languages, indicating that assimilationist English-only language policy no longer could be sustained (Ozolins 1993, 87).

8   The Task Forces were one of the most significant of Grassby's initiatives. Their principal function was to look at settlement problems and to produce recommendations that could be placed on departmental agendas (Ozolins 1993, 115).

9   The states accepted greater responsibility for ethnic affairs and education, alongside the Commonwealth Multicultural Educational Program (CMEP). Thus an Ethnic Affairs Commission (EAC) was established in NSW and Victoria to advise government on ethnic issues.

10   This trend could be interpreted in terms of middle-class western governments in a late-capitalist society which limit governmental intervention, and constantly look for self-help and community assistance as well as non-government agencies and to prescribe the spheres of governmental action (Foster and Stockle 1988, 33).

11   Norst provided an encouraging picture of ethnic schools and their role in language maintenance as a distinct fourth sector in language teaching operating in alignment with the full-time mainstream sector (Norst 1982). More recent findings regarding Greek ethnic schools indicate what constitutes an authentic milieu for language teaching and an important factor of cultural maintenance, namely identity formation and multicultural awareness. In the late 1990s, ethnic schools still operated as a mechanism in promoting education 'on the cheap', even though efforts were made to address quality. Closer articulation with the day school system was still equivocal (Arvanitis 2000).

12   For example, the 50% budget cuts in Teaching English as a Second Language programme were based on the hope that mainstream institutions would provide the necessary services without discrimination.

13   Labor policy of multiculturalism during the 1980s, although it merged multicultural programmes and services into general ones, retained the rhetoric of the word. The Liberals, on the other hand, abandoned the ideas of the 1970s and concentrated on the celebration of cultural diversity and encouragement of small ethnic businesses, lacking, however, a specific framework in implementing such policy.

14   A major policy document, which expressed the official understanding over multiculturalism, was the Jupp Report on Multicultural and Migrant Programs and Services (1986). The key notion of this report was 'equitable participation' as an ideal serving cultural diversity. Furthermore, the mainstream notion was triggered by the rhetoric of Federal policy to reinforce ethnic institutions to become part of the infrastructure and ongoing

recurrent commitment of State Education Departments and other State programmes (ROMAMPAS 1986, 286).

15   In Victoria the two main policy bodies (BOS and MACMME) produced an implementation paper in 1985 about '*The Place of Community Languages in Victorian Schools*'. According to Ozolins, this paper was 'probably the most thorough language education policy up to this time in Australia' (Ozolins 1993, 183). The paper gave a comprehensive rationale of the community language programmes for all children, while it continuously referred to community language maintenance, emphasizing the development of bilingual language skills of NESB students through the school programme). However the progress over bilingual education despite the research in this area (Cahill 1984; Clyne 1983; Mills 1982; Rado 1978) was very slow. Victoria was the state which in 1989 demonstrated a wide provision in services in education such as ESL teachers and teacher-aides on the basis of the mainstreaming notion. Multiculturalism was also supported by two main guiding documents: the 1986 *Education in and for a Multicultural Society: Policy Guidelines for School Communities* and the 1989 *Languages Action Plan* by Lo Bianco.

COMMUNITIES TAKING THE LEAD: Mapping Heritage Language Education Assets

Themistoklis Aravossitas (University of Toronto)

Introduction

Canada is a multicultural state that acknowledges and celebrates the contribution of its vibrant ethnic communities and the importance of their cultural and linguistic resources (Cummins and Danesi 1990; Duff 2008). Even in such a fertile sociopolitical environment, intergenerational transmission of immigrant languages, also known as heritage languages (HLs), remains an extremely complex task that entails various challenges of a sociolinguistic, educational and organisational nature (Campbell and Christian 2003; Peyton et al. 2001). This chapter presents aspects of a collaborative investigation that explores the state of Greek HL programmes and attempts to illustrate the strengths and weaknesses of a polymorphous educational system mainly run by community organisations that are poorly documented and supported (Fishman 1979; 1985a; 1985b; 2001). The discussion begins with navigation in the field of heritage language education (HLE) with a particular focus on Greek language in Canada and the challenges that HL programme organisers and participants face. Then, frameworks of ethnolinguistic vitality and language maintenance are examined (Giles, Bourhis and Taylor 1977; Conklin and Lourie1983; Fishman 1985b; Grin 1990; Lo Bianco 2008a; 2008b), along with Community-Based Research (CBR) principles (Israel, Schulz, Parker and Becker 1998), which inform the theoretical basis of the study. Aspects of the investigation and the methodological trajectory that involves mapping HLE assets are presented. In conclusion, I suggest that the traditional role of HL communities in language maintenance can expand from organising and delivering language programmes, to establishing networks through research partnerships that locate and develop existing community resources.

The field

HLE is an emerging field of bilingual education (Brinton, Kagan and Bauckus 2008) that focuses on the teaching and learning of minority languages. Extra (2007) underlines the difference between immigrant minority (IM) languages and regional minority (RM) languages. RM languages are rooted in specific areas and are entitled to support based on internationally recognised minority linguistic rights (European Charter for Regional or Minority Languages 1992; UNESCO 1996; Skutnab-Kangas 2006). In contrast, IM languages have no minority status and, as they travel along with their speakers, are harder to locate, study and sustain. The term 'heritage language' was introduced in Canada in the 1970s in order to refer to the nation's non-official, immigrant languages (Cummins 2005). Indigenous languages are not included in the Canadian HL definition, unlike in other parts of the world and principally in the US, where the term is broadly used to define both immigrant and native tongues. In educational environments, HL is understood as 'a language spoken in the home that is different from the main language spoken in the society' (Bilash 2011). Polinsky and Kagan (2007) define HL as the incompletely learned home language arising from the phenomenon of language shift and the switch to the dominant language that is characteristic in the case of immigrants and their descendants. For Cho, Shin and Krashen (2004), HL is a 'language spoken by the children of immigrants or by those who immigrated to a country when young'. Fishman (2001) and Wiley (2005) expand this definition by adding 'refugee, indigenous and former colonial languages' and note that a HL encompasses 'particular family relevance' even though it may or may not be a language regularly used in the home and in the community.

The discussion around HL terminology includes an ongoing debate regarding who the HL learners are, what their profile is (Valdés 2001), and why it is important to distinguish them from first, second or foreign language learners. Maria Carreira (2004) categorises the definitions of HL learners using three criteria: 1) their place in the HL community; 2) their personal connection to a HL and culture through their family background, and 3) their HL proficiency. Several studies have identified distinct language acquisition and development characteristics of HL learners who have the potential of developing their HL almost to the level of native speakers given that certain cultural, social, political and educational conditions are met (Montrul 2010; Polinsky 2008; 2007; Valdés 2005; Fishman 2006; Oh, Jun, Knightly and Au

2003). Identifying HL learners as a diverse group of language learners is essential to teachers but also to parents, school administrators, policy makers and those responsible for curriculum and teacher development. As Wang and Green (2001) observe, programmes that traditionally teach courses in non-official languages often include instruction to HL speakers. However, only a few programmes are designed specifically to serve HL learners' needs (Montrul 2009).

Community-based programmes and challenges

In 1999, Professor Russell Campbell, one of the protagonists in shaping the field of HLE (Brinton, et al. 2008), hosted the first Heritage Language Conference in the US at the University of California, Los Angeles, (UCLA), to be followed a year later by a forum dedicated to HL research priorities. The main consideration of experts at the forum, who subsequently worked collaboratively to prepare a report on defining important enquiries related to HLE based on international research and policy experiences, was the urgent need to conserve the important linguistic and cultural resources of language minority groups. Specific research questions were identified within seven domains: the community, the heritage speaker, the family, a language-specific focus, policies, programmes and assessment. For HL communities the suggested priorities included: gathering accurate information on their demographic profiles for research purposes; investigating the general attitude and motivation within HL communities for support towards the study or maintenance of their HL; building efforts within the community and establishing broad collaboration in policy and planning for HL programmes, and training community members to work in the field of HL education (University of California, Los Angeles 2001).

Communities have always played a central role in HLE (Garcia, et al. 2013). Corson (1999) describes community education as characteristic of meaningful school reform with participants negotiating the role of the school in relation to community needs. Although such schools are grass roots-based and have been developed with passion and enthusiasm, they seem to be ignored in national or local surveys. Fishman (1979) has extensively studied the 'Ethnic Community Mother Tongue Schools' (ECMTS), which he considered as a significant, yet unknown, aspect of bilingual education in America:

> Where can one turn to find out how many Xish mother tongue schools there are and where they can be found? In a nation that counts its non-English or limited English speaking population (because this population is the target of governmental programmes), we are relatively unconcerned with those learning ethnic mother tongues at their own expense! *(Fishman 1975, 45)*

His efforts to locate the HL community schools in the US produced a map of more than 6500 programmes in the 1980s representing 145 different languages (Fishman 2006; see also Fishman 1980; 1985a; 1985b; 2001). The lack of information about HL programmes in America emerged also from the campaign launched by the Heritage Language Initiative (Brecht, Ingold 1998) and the Alliance for the Advancement of Heritage Languages (2010), and resulted in the development of the Heritage Language Programs Database (2013). Hosted at the website of the Center for Applied Linguistics, the database provides information about language-specific programmes offered across the US by Higher Education Institutions, K-12 schools and various community-based organisations.[1]

HL researchers have identified several challenges that HL community programmes face including participation and community involvement, lack of funding, access to resources, trained teachers and suitable curricula along with other practical problems associated with infrastructure, space and time limitations (Compton 2001; Moore, Ingersoll 2011; Liu et al. 2011). Community HL programmes take place typically in non-official settings, after the regular school hours, on weekday evenings and weekends. Given this scheduling, these HL courses are 'competing' with other more attractive extra-curricular activities, such as sports, arts and entertainment. It has also been noted that students sometimes need to cover substantial distances to get to a HL class that might be held in the basement of a community centre, a church or a rented facility, with minimum equipment and resources available to them (Mercurio 2010). Their teachers are often volunteers or underpaid practitioners with limited target language skills and pedagogic background (Feuerverger 1997), and their books and curricula might be outdated or inappropriate for their level or their interests. Additionally, they frequently attend classes of mixed age and language ability groups and usually they have to deal with even more homework than in their day schools, given the nature of HL programmes and their limited hours of instruction (Bilash 2011).

On the other hand, HL educators serving in community schools receive no pre-service training since their profession is not officially recognised and does not always offer full-time employment opportunities (Anderson 2008). Some of the instructors who happen to be professional language teachers have been trained either in their countries of origin or in the countries of practice. Nevertheless, even in this case, pre-service language teacher education programmes do not normally include preparation for the reality of HLE (Petraki, K. 2003; Mercurio 2010). As most HL classes are heterogeneous, teachers must be prepared to engage their lessons with varied goals as well as with methodological and pedagogical strategies geared to multi-level classes. In addition to the restrained professional development and advancement prospects, and the overall marginalisation that they face as minority language instructors (Feuerverger 1997), HL educators have to teach students who are usually tired from their day-school load or unmotivated for various reasons that include peer pressure and lack of opportunities to use their HL in 'real life' contexts (Mercurio 2010). As per the programme administration, having to deal with issues such as lack of funding, teacher turnover, student retention and infrastructure limitations is frequently the norm rather than the exception in HL community settings (Compton 2001). Finally, parents and grandparents, the ones who encourage and support HLE despite distance, time or financial limitations, frequently face a dead end when programmes in their HL are not available in their region. This is typically the case for non-concentrated immigrant communities or for the less commonly taught languages (Gambhir 2001).

The context

In Canada, the 2011 census confirmed that the nation enjoys an enormous cultural and linguistic wealth, with the co-existence of approximately 200 languages (Statistics Canada 2012a). While 98% of Canadians indicate that they can communicate in either English or French, the two official languages, the percentage of bilinguals who are proficient in both official languages is approximately 17.5%, or 5.8 million people. In comparison, the percentage of Canadians who are bilingual in one of the two official languages and one HL exceeds 20%, which is equivalent to 6.4 million people. From the 198 unofficial languages in Canada, 65 are indigenous languages and 130 are immigrants' languages, 22 of which are reported as mother tongues by more than 100000 citizens.

Following the Official Languages Act of 1969, Canada declared itself multicultural and established policies that guaranteed the promotion of respect and support for all cultures. Retention of heritage language and culture has been one of the core values of Canadian multicultural education

(Fleras, Elliott 1992) for almost half a century. With the Cultural Enrichment Program of 1977, the federal government subsidised the teaching of non-official languages (Cummins, Danesi 1990), but the programme was discontinued a few years later due to a significant decline in federal funding towards HLE (Duff 2008). To the great disappointment of the HL communities, legislation that was intended to establish the Canadian Heritage Language Institute in accordance with the federal multiculturalism policy (Canadian Multiculturalism Act 1988) was repealed despite its purpose of:

> . . . facilitating the acquisition and retention of linguistic knowledge in each heritage language, promoting the use of these languages through language instruction and by developing programmes to improve the quality of heritage language instruction; producing and disseminating materials; conducting research; establishing scholarly links with universities, colleges and other organizations; and encouraging consultation amongst governments, educational institutions, organizations and individuals interested in heritage language issues. (Section 4, Canadian Heritage Languages Institute Act 1991)

Since the 1970s, the vast majority of Canadian HL learners at the K-12 level have access to instruction in their HL, either through provincially mandated courses that public school boards operate on-demand or through community-operated courses (Cummins 2005) that vary in terms of programme length, ages of students involved, organisation, resources, curriculum and overall quality. There is no single authority at either the federal or the provincial level to oversee HL programmes[2] which have never enjoyed academic recognition (Ashworth; Toohey 1992) as they continue to run on the edges of mainstream education (Cummins 1992; Duff 2008). Consequently, HLE is primarily a community concern.

My big fat Greek school[3]

'Migration' and 'Greeks' are two terms that have gone hand-in-hand throughout history. From the mythical, epic journey of Odysseus described by Homer 4000 years ago, to the colonisation of an ancient metropolitan Greek city (Orrieux, Schmitt-Pantel 1999), Greeks have travelled and migrated in search of safety, prosperity and adventure. Situated at the crossroads of three continents, Europe, Asia and Africa, Greece has often become a battlefield. Ongoing wars and political, social and economic pressures are amongst the most significant forces behind Greek migration which reached a peak between the 1950s and 1970s, when many Greeks moved to Canada. Peter Chimbos (1999), a specialist on the early Greek experience in Canada, reports that Greeks primarily settled in Montreal and Toronto. By concentrating in areas where their compatriots were established, newcomers overcame social barriers. Most did not speak English or French, thus first employment was conveniently found within the immediate Greek social environment. In many cases, more than one family shared the same house and participated in social activities such as extended family gatherings and attending churches and schools which paved the way for the establishment of community organisations. Between 1945 and 1971 almost 110000 Greek immigrants arrived, and in 1967 alone, the number of newcomers rose to a record 10650, as many fled Greece to avoid involvement in the political turmoil created by the tyranny of a military regime (1967–74). But by the 1980s, immigration to Canada had slowed down considerably. In fact, after democracy was restored, quite a number of Greek Canadians repatriated to enjoy the new era of prosperity and stability. They were encouraged by the country's participation in the European Union[4]. However, thirty years later, a severe economic crisis hit the country, creating a migration wave once again. Many of the Greeks who had the privilege of immigration status and roots in Canada crossed the Atlantic once more, offering new blood to the Hellenic-Canadian *paroikia* (Arvanitis 2000).

One of the peculiarities of the Greek community structure in Canada (Liodakis 1998) is the development of many different types of organisations: civic, religious, cultural, professional, political, athletic and more. They synthesize a polymorphic map that indicates the need of immigrants to establish networks in the new country while it sets a challenge for their next generations who are expected to maintain traditional ties to all those groups that do not necessarily reflect their interests (Constantinides 2004). Greeks are a group with strong national ties. They consider their language as one of the main aspects of their culture and identity along with the Christian Orthodox faith. Thus Greek school and the church have always been at the centre of community life.

The most recent study of Greek Language Education in Canada took place between 1997 and 2001. It was conducted by the Institute for Intercultural and Migration Studies of the University of Crete (EDIAMME), headed by Professor Damanakis, and undertaken in Canada by Professor Constantinides. This study, which was part of a large-scale European Union funded project entitled 'Paedia of the Homogenous' (Damanakis 2007),[5] profiles the Greek language institutions in Canada and other major Greek diasporic centres across the world. It provided the basis for the development of educational materials that have been used ever since in Greek HL programmes internationally. According to the EDIAMME study, the majority of Greek language students at the time were enrolled mainly in afternoon and weekday evening community-based programmes, with the exception of Montreal, where the local Greek community, funded partially by the province of Quebec (Duff 2008), has been successfully operating trilingual day schools (Georgiou 2008).[6] Most Greek HL students were the children of second generation Greek Canadian parents or of inter-ethnic marriages. At this point, accurate statistics were unavailable as to the exact number of students attending Greek language programmes across Canada, but they were estimated at 10–11000, a number significantly decreased since the 1980s (Constantinides 2001). In 2006–7 the EDIAMME estimated that as the third generation of learners joined Greek HL schools in Canada, the student population in community programmes remained stable (Constantinides 2007).

In recent years, Greek community school operators in Canada have observed an increasing number of students who join the HL programmes with no prior knowledge of the language, and even after a few years of weekly instruction, the norm for the majority of them is that they communicate in English all the time. Some learners admit that their only chance to use their HL is when they come to Greek school and that the language is not used at home at all. Many Greek Orthodox churches nowadays perform major parts of their liturgy, if not all, in English. Mixed marriages are exceeding by far the inter-community ones (Chimbos 1971, 1999; Constantinides 2004). Several officials of community organisations and associations complain about the lack of youth participation. The signs of language shift within the group are evident. Teachers, administrators and parents often share their concerns over the preservation of the language and culture and the survival of the Greek community and heritage in the 21st century.

Amongst the immigrant languages spoken in Canada today (Statistics Canada 2012b), Modern Greek is one of a few with a decreasing number of speakers in comparison to previous censuses (Statistics Canada 1996; 2001; 2006). With the majority of contemporary learners representing the third generation, and a diverse and challenging HL student population (Alba et al. 2002; Valdés 2001), questions of accessibility to and quality of HL programmes are of primary concern for the community group.

Ethnolinguistic vitality and HLE

According to Baker (2001), language maintenance is the relative stability of a language in terms of the number and distribution of speakers, the adequate use by children and adults and its use in specific domains (e.g. cultural or community events, home, school, etc.). The term language shift (Fishman 1966), refers to the behaviour of an entire community, a sub-group of the community or an individual. Weinrich (1964), defined language shift as the change from the normal use of a language toward another language, while De Vries (1987), sees language shift as the transition of an individual from one linguistic community to another one. Language shift and language maintenance are the two sides of a coin that mainly concerns small language groups or communities that replace their language with the language of the dominant group.

In search of theoretical bases for the role of HL education in ethno-linguistic vitality, as part of the community-based study that was conducted, several relevant frameworks were examined starting with the one developed by Giles, Bourhis and Taylor (1977). They suggest that the strengths and weaknesses of a cultural/linguistic community can be measured through the examination of three variable factors: language status, institutional support and community demographics. Given that the status of a language and demographics are two aspects that an immigrant community cannot control, it appears that institutional support, which includes provision for HLE, is the only ethnolinguistic vitality variable that depends on actions undertaken by community groups.

Conklin and Lourie's (1983) framework is broadly used to address issues of language maintenance or shift and identifies influencing factors under three categories: 1) political, social and demographic; 2) cultural, and 3) linguistic. The political, social and demographic category is affected by the number of speakers in a community, the immigration flow, distance to the homeland and by ethnic group identity that differs from the one representing the dominant language community. Major cultural factors include the existence of mother-tongue institutions; cultural and religious ceremonies in the home language; ethnic identity strongly tied to the home language; emotional attachment to the mother tongue as a source of self-identity and ethnicity; emphasis on family ties and community cohesion, and emphasis on education in mother tongue schools. In his investigation of language maintenance, Fishman (1985b) used three criteria to predict community language survival in the US context: 1) the number of mother tongue claimants; 2) the number of institutional resources (schools, media, religious units etc.), and 3) an index of the relationship between (1) and (2). UNESCO (2003) classifies six major evaluative factors of language vitality: 1) intergenerational language transmission; 2) absolute number of speakers; 3) proportion of speakers within the total population; 4) trends in existing language domains; 5) response to new domains and media; and 6) materials for language education and literacy. Jo Lo Bianco, (2008a; 2008b; 2013), investigating the necessary conditions for language vitality and revitalisation, articulated the framework of Francois Grin (1990) and developed the capacity development, opportunity creation and desire (COD) framework that proposes: 1) an increase of young people's linguistic capacity, 2) development of opportunities for use of the language, and 3) motivating community members to use the language.

Education in HL is consistent as one of the crucial language vitality and maintenance indicators in every single relevant theoretical model examined. The role of HL schools is decisive for HL retention. As a consequence, the obvious starting point for a community group that attempts to assess its vitality is to assess its HLE system.

Mapping the assets

Lynch (2008) encourages community groups to incorporate an asset-based method in designing and evaluating their HL programmes. Based on the work of Kretzmann and McKnight (1993), who used this approach for the development of financially marginalised communities, the asset-based model is also widely used in health-related research. A Glasgow Centre for Population Health briefing paper describes assets as 'the collective resources that individuals and communities have at their disposal which protect against negative health outcomes and promote health status. These assets can be social, financial, physical, environmental, or human resources, for example employment, education and supportive social networks (Glasgow Centre for Population Health 2011, 4; Harrison et al. 2004).'

From a language maintenance point of view, such resources are the ones that communities should identify and use to prevent language shift and promote their linguistic and cultural status. Some key features of an asset-based approach that should be considered by HL stakeholders include 'making visible and value the skills, knowledge, connections and potential in a community; promote capacity, connectedness and social capital; emphasise the need to restore the balance between meeting needs and nurturing the strengths and resources of people and communities' (Glasgow Centre for Population Health 2012).

An asset-based approach in HL community settings would be concerned with 1) identifying the factors that promote the teaching and use of the HL, such as social and cultural community events and HL schools, and 2) bringing members of community together to achieve positive change using their own knowledge, skills and experience. The asset-based approach is viewed by Lynch (2008) as the HL communities' alternative to the traditional needs-based model that depends upon outside experts. It does not, therefore, build community cohesiveness, and usually results in benefiting the service providers rather than the community members. With the asset-based approach, existing community resources are identified and utilised. One of the tools of the asset-based approach for HL community programmes is mapping.

As presented by Lynch (2008), the mapping scheme of Kretzmann and McKnight (1993) illustrates a process that starts with locating resources of immediate use to the HL programmes (e.g. schools, churches, community centres) and proceeds with the identification of secondary resources in local/community institutions, associations and individuals. Incorporation of the asset-based approach in community research for the assessment of HLE places more emphasis on positive attributes and community engagement, rather than accepting the fate of marginalisation and relying on external help to deal with challenges that predominantly concern the community and its members. The challenge is to determine how HL communities can be mobilised and what type of methodology should be applied in locating and developing their assets. According to Perkins (2008), community mapping means 'local mapping, produced collaboratively, by local people and often incorporating alternative local knowledge' (p. 154). In the case of HL communities, mapmaking is a process that members can use to make sense of their culture and identity which has no geographical limits.

From community needs to community research

Ethnic community groups concerned with the maintenance of their language see it inevitably weakened as speakers tend to replace it with the dominant language(s) that they consider more valuable to them and their children.

Since most HL communities are minority groups with limited mainstream political influence, their opportunities to resist cultural and linguistic assimilation rely largely on actions taken within the community boundaries. Such actions cannot be authorised without consensus which is not guaranteed when many organisations, sometimes competing with each other, are involved (Chimbos 1999). One effective way to bring stakeholders together in pursuing collaborative actions to the benefit of the community is through research that runs from within and for the community.

Community-Based Participatory Research, also known as Community-Based Research (CBR), aims at gathering knowledge about a phenomenon or a problem of significant value to a community. Knowledge that emerges from such research informs the design of actions that benefit the community. CBR relies on the cooperation of academics and members of a community in all phases of the research process. Israel, Schulz, Parker and Becker (1998) define CBR as a partnership that equitably involves community members, organisational representatives and academic experts who contribute their expertise and share responsibility and ownership. CBR is a bottom-up research approach, based on participatory action research (Tandon 2002; Fals Borda and Rahman 1991) influenced by the popular education movement and the work of Paulo Freire (1970, 1982).

CBR used to investigate linguistic issues is known as Community-based Language Research. The term was coined by Czaykowska-Higgins, (2009) following the work of Cameron et al. (1992) to describe research for the production of knowledge in a language that involves a community, starts from the community and takes place within the community with the participation of its members as research experts rather than research objects. CBR in HL settings can result in a series of continuing, planned steps that language communities are able to take to make sure that they effectively preserve and promote their culture and language in a dynamic political, economic, cultural and social environment. CBR participants are able to work within their communities, leading the way to establish specific language-related goals and developing realistic strategies to achieve those goals.

The project

During the academic year 2011–12, the Education Coordinator at the Consulate General of Greece in Toronto (referred to as 'Coordinator' from this point on) launched a campaign with the purpose of locating Greek language schools in Canada and investigating whether members of the community had access to HL programmes. I undertook the role of co-investigator in the project as part of my doctoral studies at the Department of Curriculum and Teacher Development of the Ontario Institute for Studies in Education, University of Toronto. Other parties involved in the project were the Office of Education of the Greek Orthodox Metropolis of Toronto-Canada, the Ontario Association of Greek Language Teachers, and volunteers and members of the Toronto's Greek community. In our preliminary discussions about the need to identify and address problems related to the teaching and learning of HL in Canada, none of the participants brought up the idea of conducting community research. However, throughout our notes, three terms were underlined: 'community', 'cooperation' and 'action'. As stated on the website of the Centre for Community-Based Research,[7] these three notions that coincidently emerged out of our first meetings, are at the core of CBR, which is:

1. Community-situated: it begins with a research topic of practical relevance to the community (as opposed to individual scholars) and is carried out in community settings.
2. Collaborative: community members and researchers equitably share control of the research agenda through active and reciprocal involvement in the research design, implementation and dissemination.
3. Action-orientated: the process and results are useful to community members in making positive social change and to promote social equity (Centre for Community-Based Research 2013).

Our initial research question concerned access to HL programmes for our community members. As such, the 'community-situated' criterion of CBR was met. The collaborative nature of our project was evident since no one assumed the role of the expert researcher and no one claimed ownership of the research findings, which were only to be used to serve community needs. Every stage of the research process was co-planned and co-designed. Moreover, the action orientation of our project was also obvious from our decision to develop a database, through which we hoped not only to locate but also to connect our community schools and resources, making them accessible to all community members.

One of the most significant challenges in the study of HLE, especially involving community-based programmes, pertains to the fact that they are not adequately recorded. Therefore, only limited information can be available to community outsiders about the exact dimensions of the educational activities that take place in relation to a particular HL. Subsequently, anything related to the preservation of a community language remains primarily a community responsibility. The problem is that since HL communities, especially in Canada, are scattered and their educational undertakings are mainly locally developed, information concerning HL programmes are not shared even amongst community members.

The purpose of our research was to study the current status of Greek language education in Canada and examine its state in order to ensure that the next generation of community members will have access to programmes for the retention of their language and culture. Our initial mission was to find all community organisations and any institutions that offer Greek HLE in Canada. Our next step would be the development of a searchable database to allow interested parents, students and other stakeholders to locate programmes in their city. Ultimately, the database could be used by practitioners such as teachers and administrators to connect, network, access resources and learn about community events of educational interest that take place in different parts of the country. To explore the current status of Greek HLE in Canada, we needed to examine certain quantitative and qualitative parameters of the existing system. They include the following:

- Number and type of institutions and organisations operating and/or supporting Greek HL programmes in Canada.
- Number of schools, courses and programmes where Greek language and culture are taught, per province and city.
- Addresses and contact information for all the above.
- Number of students per class and educational level.
- Amount of tuition fees.
- School year duration; days and hours of Greek HL schools operation.
- Number and profile of Greek HL teachers.
- Curriculum information, such as lessons (other than language) offered as part of Greek Heritage education, books and other resources used in Greek HL classes, access to new technologies and various teaching aides used in Greek HL classes.
- Main challenges faced by each institution and site in relation to the organisation and operation of Greek HL programmes.

Collecting, organising and analysing the above information from schools and community organisations throughout Canada entails a complex and multi-layered investigation but in return offers practical solutions to community members. Students and parents could find out what their options are in pursuing HLE in their area, along with information about the school operator and the possible days, hours and settings for HL instruction. At the same time, HL teachers could find out where employment opportunities exist. Operators could explore the competition and organise programmes in under-served areas. Community organisations could find out how similar institutions operate in different parts of the country and establish collaboration. This sharing of information is very important considering the large number of agencies involved in Greek language education (Constantinides 2001). Additionally our database would allow governmental authorities and decision makers in Canada to find out how many citizens are learners of a particular language and how HL community education systems function. As for the country of origin – Greece, in this case – our database would be valuable in collecting information about the number of Greek expatriates who retain or try to retain their ethnolinguistic and cultural connection and their educational needs.

Methodology

The starting point of our research initiative was to organise focus groups. Several members of the community with professional involvement in different aspects of Greek HLE were invited and shared their experiences on various issues concerning the organisation and operation of community schools as well as the general state of Greek schools and programmes in Canada. The Coordinator facilitated five meetings that were held every two months during the 2011–12 school year. What became clear from the beginning was that in order to implement any change in HLE practices within our community and before organising meetings and seminars to address various issues – such as the need for professional development – we had to hear the voices of more agencies and professionals who were actively involved in the field. To maximise community participation in our discussions we put together a list of institutions, associations, schools, educators, parents, and interested professionals and volunteers from the community. In the following school year, our focus groups progressed into work groups that gathered contact information of Greek HL stakeholders across Canada and designed a questionnaire for school operators.

The decision of the co-researchers to create a database for the existing Greek HL schools in Canada aimed at addressing a shortage. How would it be possible to have greater participation in any professional development or other initiative to support our HL system without knowing the participants? The idea of creating a database responds essentially to the need of mapping our community resources and finding out not only how many programmes are out there serving community learners but how these programmes operate and what their strengths and weaknesses are. Suddenly our objective to create a service for our community education started to look more like a research study. During meetings, participants raised several questions that shaped the course of our investigation:

> ... in how many cities is our community language taught across Canada? How many Greek schools are there today? How many were there ten years ago? How many students do we have? Are there communities that used to have schools in the past but had to close down and for what reasons? Do we have enough teachers? Are they trained to teach Greek HL learners, and if yes, who trains them and how? What type of books and resources are they using? Who is responsible for the quality of these books? Who is providing them? What are the problems of our HL programmes? What are the tuition fees? Are there families who can't afford to send their children to a HL programme ...?[8]

Considering these questions and several more that were recorded during our meetings, a questionnaire was designed and made available to Greek HLE providers using an online survey platform. Additionally, to validate our data we followed three steps as part of a triangulation method:

1. Collected information about exiting Greek HL schools in Canada through the archives of the participating organisations (Coordinator/Greek Consulate, Teacher Association and Metropolis) and conducted online research to locate schools that had websites or social media exposure.
2. Sent out questionnaires to school operators.
3. Conducted interviews via telephone or email to verify the data we were collecting (through questionnaires, archives and our online research).

From February to June 2013, we were able to collect enough data to get a first impression about the state of Greek language education in Canada. During this time, we held a workshop in Toronto to introduce our research initiative to local community stakeholders and participated at a conference in Ottawa where we presented the results of the first phase of the investigation at a federal level. Furthermore, we started working on our next phase, the creation of an electronic portal through which we would be able to map and access information on the whereabouts and the activities of Greek HL schools across Canada for those interested in learning, teaching or supporting our language.

HLE aim: access, innovation, motivation

The purpose of this chapter is not to present details of the study findings as to how many students and teachers participate in Greek HL programmes and where such programmes are situated, but to discuss a few interesting elements in support of the concluding remarks about how important it is, primarily for the communities themselves, to locate their resources and realise the dimensions of their capacity in empowering HLE without depending on external support.

In our quest to uncover the wealth of HLE in Canada through the lens of the Greek language community, we have so far been able to map more than 100 programmes, in preschool, primary, secondary, tertiary and continuing education settings. We have located programmes that operate daily and programmes that operate beyond the typical hours of the school day, or on weekends or weekend evenings. We have been able to acquire their addresses and contact information, their schedules, their curricula and an overview of their challenges. We have identified more than 10000 students enrolled in various Greek HL schools that we mapped in eight Canadian provinces and approximately 300 teachers who offer their voluntary or paid services to more than 60 operators that include boards of education, academic institutions, community organisations, cultural associations, parent groups and private schools. Furthermore, we have categorised our HL schools in three sizes based on their student population (small, medium, large), and designed a campaign to provide support through community resources to vulnerable programmes.

The vitality of any minority group relies greatly on the opportunity that its speakers have to use their language in various spheres, including their home, their local community and, of course, their school. In accordance with the number of HL speakers, which is one ethnolinguistic vitality factor, there have to be enough schools to guarantee that all community members, regardless of their demographic distribution (another vitality variable), have access to a programme equipped to address their learning needs. Our first findings indicate that as far as the Greek HL is concerned, community-based institutions are operating HL programmes in all regions across Canada, where there is a concentration of at least one hundred 'Greek' families, yet some of these programmes are not always viable and their operation is disrupted from time to time, mainly because of teacher shortages and infrastructure limitations, such as a lack of proper facilities.

On the other hand, larger community groups and academic institutions have an abundance of specialised instructors and the means to support qualitative programmes for HL learners. Once collaboration between all community organisations that serve the same HL is established, new technologies, such as synchronous and asynchronous communication media and online distance learning platforms, can allow access to flexible instruction even for the most remote families. HL school networks and partnerships such as sister class collaborations which are currently practiced in the context of Greek HLE, under the supervision of universities within or outside Canada (i.e., University of Crete, University of the Aegean), can foster innovation in traditional programmes that have fallen behind in satisfying the interests of the new generation of HL learners. The introduction of modern technology in the Greek HL classroom can stimulate the motivation of students, teachers and parents to participate in more fun and engaging language and culture learning activities. Making the HLE protagonists known to the community, empowering educators who set best practice examples, offering incentives for young teachers to work in the field of HLE and providing professional development opportunities, which are also available online, are all actions that community groups can organise, implement and sustain with little or no external support.

In the case of Greek HLE in Canada, our Community-Based Research initiative and our project to map and further develop our educational assets, have been embraced by the government of Greece through the country's diplomatic representatives in Ottawa, Toronto, Montreal and Vancouver. Our work has also been recognised by the Greek Orthodox Metropolis of Toronto and its network of approximately 80 churches and communities across Canada; by one major community funding agency; by two universities in Greece and two in Canada; by the Association of Greek Language Teachers of Ontario and, most significantly, by many community volunteers from different educational and professional backgrounds. Our study findings, to this point, confirm the status of Greeks amongst the groups with high rates of mother tongue maintenance internationally (Buda 1992). Also, despite the decreasing figures of Greek language speakers that the official censuses report in Canada, we find that our new generation – that is, the third generation HL learners – are not distancing themselves from the community and its linguistic and cultural heritage.

Conclusion

Canada classifies its community languages as non-official. As a consequence, the government has no official obligation for provisions pertaining to their maintenance. Any responsibility to offer support for community groups trying to preserve their HL derives from the Canadian Multiculturalism Act (1988), a policy that recognises Canada's multicultural heritage as a heritage that must be protected. Since education does not fall under federal jurisdiction, there is no systematic national documentation and reporting of HL programmes and other related information concerning the teaching and learning of non-official languages. In other words, in Canada, since we have no idea as to how many citizens are studying a HL, where they are doing so and how effectively, it is extremely difficult to conduct research and analysis of issues regarding HLE. Unquestionably, this situation hinders policy and programming, leaving language groups with the responsibility for safeguarding their resources and initiating bottom-up activities to foster HLE at the community level.

As HLE evolves to a distinct domain of bilingual education, researchers, linguists and instructors will continue to work on exploring further the particularities of teaching and learning HLs, developing strategies to address the needs of HL learners and building the field's theory. Communities, on the other hand, have their own role to play. In rethinking the responsibility of cultural groups for the promotion of HLE throughout the 21st century, the initiative presented in this chapter offers an example of community-initiated, action-orientated research. As technology changes the way that people communicate and learn, HL communities must adapt and make use of these new conditions. Unluckily, many HL community groups, even within the same country, are often isolated from each other. Mapping the assets, locating and assessing the community educational resources and forming HLE networks is a practice well-suited to the creation of collaborative learning environments and focused efforts to support and sustain minority language and culture programmes. Community members, educators and researchers who participate in CBR work in the community, with the community, for the community. Thus, they become community experts who can generate attention, mobilise participants and develop agendas in response to the real challenges of HLE.

REFERENCES

Alba, R., Logan, J., Lutz, A. and **Stults, B.** (2002). 'Only English by the Third Generation? Loss and Preservation of the Mother Tongue Amongst the Grandchildren of Contemporary Immigrants'. *Demography,* 39 (3), 467–84.

Alliance for the Advancement of Heritage Languages (2010). http://www.cal.org/heritage/pdfs/heritage-flyer-June-2010.pdf (retrieved June 2013).

Anderson, J. (2008). 'Pre- and In-Service Professional Development of Teachers of Community/Heritage Languages in the UK: Insider Perspectives'. *Language and Education* 22 (4), 283–97.

Arvanitis, E. (2000) *Greek Ethnic Schools in Transition: Policy and Practice in Australia in the Late 1990s.* PhD thesis, Melbourne, RMIT University.

Ashworth, M. (1992). 'Views and Visions' in B. Burnaby and A. Cumming, eds, *Socio-political Aspects of ESL in Canada.* OISE Press, Toronto, 35–49.

Bilash, O. (2011). 'Heritage Language Teaching'. www.educ.ualberta.ca/staff/olenka.bilash/best%20of%20bilash/heritage.html (retrieved September 2013).

Brecht, R.D. and **Ingold, C.W.** (1998). 'Tapping a National Resource: Heritage Languages in the United States'. *ERIC Digest.* EDO-FL-98-12.

Brinton, D., Kagan, O. and **Bauckus, S.**, eds (2008). *Heritage Language Education: A New Field Emerging.* New York: Routledge.

Buda, J. K. (1992). 'Language Shift in Australia and Canada: Otsuma Women's University Annual Report'. *Humanities and Social Sciences* xxiv.

Cameron, D., Frazer, E., Harvey, P., Rampton, M.B.H. and **Richardson, K.** (1992). *Researching Language: Issues of Power and Method.* London and New York: Routledge.

Canadian Heritage Languages Institute Act (1991) (repealed before coming into force, 2008). c.20, s.3 c.7. http://www.slmc.uottawa.ca/?q=leg_heritage_languages_act_sum (retrieved August 2013).

Campbell, R. and **Christian, D.** (2003). 'Directions in Research: Intergenerational Transmission of Heritage Languages'. *Heritage Language Journal.* http://www.international.ucla.edu/cms/files/russ_and_donna.pdf (retrieved May 2013).

Carreira, M. (2004). 'Seeking Explanatory Adequacy: A Dual Approach to Understanding the Term Heritage Language Learner'. *Heritage Language Journal* 2 (1).

Centre for Community-Based Research (2013). www.communitybasedresearch.ca/Page/View/CBR_definition (retrieved May 2013).

Chimbos, P. (1971). 'Immigrants' Attitudes Toward their Children's Interethnic Marriages in a Canadian Community'. *International Migration Review* 5, 5–17.

Chimbos, P. (1999). 'The Greeks in Canada: an Historical and Sociological Perspective'. In Clogg. R., ed., *The Greek Diaspora in the Twentieth Century*, 87–102. New York: St. Martin's Press, Inc.

Cho, G., Krashen, K. and Shin, F. (2004). 'What do we Know about Heritage Languages? What Do We Need to Know About Them?' *Multicultural Education* 11 (4), 23–26.

Compton, C.J. (2001). 'Heritage Language Communities and Schools: Challenges and Recommendations'. In J.K. Peyton, D.A. Ranard, and S. McGinnis, eds, *Heritage languages in America. Preserving a National Resource*, 145–66). McHenry, IL: Center for Applied Linguistics.

Conklin, N.F., Lourie, M.A. (1983). *A Host of Tongues*. New York: The Free Press.

Constantinides, S. (2001). *Greek Language Education in Canada* (Greek), Rethymno: University of Crete.

— (2004). *The presence of Greeks in Canada* (Greek). Rethimno: University of Crete.

— (2007). 'Greek Language Education in Canada, 1997–2006' (Greek). In Damanakis, ed., *Proceedings of the International Conference Globalization and Hellenic Diaspora*. University of Crete-IIMS (EDIAMME): Rethymno, Greece.

Corson, D. (1999). *Language Policy in Schools: A resource for Teachers and Administrators*. Mahwah, NJ: Lawrence Erlbaum Associates.

Cummins, J. (1992). 'Heritage Language Teaching in Canadian Schools'. *Journal of Curriculum Studies* 24 (3), 281–6.

— (2005). 'A Proposal for Action: Strategies for Recognizing Language Competence as a Learning Resource within the Mainstream Classroom. *Modern Language Journal* 89, 585–91.

Cummins, J. and Danesi, M. (1990). *Heritage Languages: The Development and Denial of Canada's Linguistic Resources*. Toronto: Our Schools/Our Selves Education Foundation.

Czaykowska-Higgins, E. (2009). 'Research Models, Community Engagement, and Linguistic Fieldwork: Reflections on Working within Canadian Indigenous Communities'. *Language Documentation and Conservation* 3 (1), 15–50.

Damanakis, M. (2007). *Paedia of the Homogenous* (Greek). Rethimno: University of Crete.

De Vries, J. (1987). 'Problems of Measurement in the Study of Linguistic Minorities. *Journal of Multilingual and Multicultural Development* 8 (1, 2), 23–31.

Duff, P. (2008). 'Heritage Language Education in Canada'. In D. Brinton, O. Kagen and S. Bauckos, eds, *Heritage Language Education: A New Field Emerging*, 71–90. New York: Routlege.

European Charter for Regional or Minority Languages (1992). Strasbourg, France: Council of Europe. http://www.coe.int/t/dg4/education/minlang/default_en.asp. (retrieved June 2013).

Extra, G. (2007). 'From Minority Programmes to Multilingual Education'. In P. Auer and L. Wei, eds, *Multilingualism and Multilingual Communication. Handbooks of Applied Linguistics* 5, 175–206. Berlin/New York: Mouton de Gruyter.

Fals Borda, O. and Rahman, M.A. (1991). *Action and Knowledge: Breaking the Monopoly with Participatory Action-Research*. New York: The Apex Press.

Feuerverger, G. (1997). 'On the Edges of the Map: A Study of Heritage Language Teachers in Toronto'. *Teaching and Teacher Education* 8 (3), 123–46.

Fishman, J.A. (1966). *Language Loyalty in the United States: The Maintenance and Perpetuation of non-English Mother Tongues by American Ethnic and Religious Groups.* The Hague: Mouton.

— (1979). 'Ethnic Mother Tongue Schools in the USA: Where, How Many, What Kind?' In J.A. Fishman and Barbara Markman, *The Ethnic Mother Tongue School in the United States: Assumptions, Findings and Directory.* New York: Yeshiva University.

— (1980). 'Ethnic Community Mother Tongue Schools in the USA: Dynamics and Distributions'. *International Migration Review* 14 (2), 235–47.

— (1985a). 'Mother-Tongue Claiming in the United States since 1960: Trends and Correlates'. In Fishman, J. Gertner, M.H., Lowy, E.G. and Milan, W.G., *The Rise and Fall of the Ethnic Revival.* Berlin: Mouton Publishers, 107–94.

— (1985b). 'The Significance of the Ethnic-Community Mother-Tongue School'. In *The Rise and the Fall of the Ethnic Revival: Perspectives on Language and Ethnicity.* Berlin: Mouton Publishers.

— (2001). '300-plus Years of Heritage Language Education in the United States'. In J.K. Peyton, D.A. Ranard, and S. McGinnis, eds, *Heritage Languages in America. Preserving a National Resource*, 81–9. McHenry, IL: Center for Applied Linguistics.

— (2006). 'Acquisition, Maintenance and Recovery of Heritage Languages'. In G. Valdés, J. Fishman, R. Chavez, and W. Perez, eds, *Developing Minority Language Resources: The Case of Spanish in California*, 12–22. Clevedon: Multilingual Matters.

Fleras, A. and **Elliott, J.** (1992). *Multiculturalism in Canada.* Scarborough: Nelson Canada.

Freire, P. (1970). *Pedagogy of the Oppressed.* New York: Herder and Herder.

— (1982). 'Creating Alternative Research Methods. Learning to Do it by Doing it'. In Hall, B., Gillette, A. and Tandon R., eds, *Creating Knowledge: A Monopoly.* , New Delhi: Society for Participatory Research in Asia, 29–37.

Gambhir, S. (2001). Truly Less Commonly Taught Languages and Heritage Language Learners in the United States. In J.K. Peyton, D.A. Ranard and S. McGinnis, eds, *Heritage Languages in America: Preserving a National Resource*, 207–28. McHenry, IL: Center for Applied Linguistics.

Garcia, O., Zakharia, Z. and **Otcu, B.**, eds (2013). *Bilingual Community Education and Multilingualism. Beyond Heritage Languages in a Global City.* (2013). Clevedon: Multilingual Matters.

Georgiou, T. (2008). *The Contribution of Socrates School to the Identity Formation and Academic-Professional Evolution of its Graduates.* Rethimno: University of Crete.

Giles, H., Bourhis, R. and **Taylor, D.** (1977). 'Towards a Theory in Ethnic Group Relations'. In H. Giles, ed., *Language, Ethnicity and Intergroup Relations*, 307–49. London: Academic Press.

Glasgow Centre for Population Health (2011). 'Asset-based Approaches for Health Improvement: Redressing the Balance'. Briefing Paper 9 Concept Series. Glasgow Centre for Population Health. http://www.gcph.co.uk/assets/0000/2627/GCPH_Briefing_Paper_CS9web.pdf (retrieved October 2013).

— (2012). 'Asset-Based Approaches for Health Improvement: Redressing the Balance'. Briefing Paper 10 Concept Series. Glasgow Centre for Population Health. http://www.gcph.co.uk/assets/0000/3433GCPHCS10forweb_1_.pdf (retrieved October 2013).

Government of Canada (1988). Canadian Multicultural Act. http://laws.justice.gc.ca/eng/acts/C-18.7/page-1.html (retrieved July 2013).

Grin, F. (1990). The Economic Approach to Minority Languages. *Journal of Multilingual and Multicultural Development* 11 (1–2), 153–73.

Harrison D, Ziglio E, Levin L. and **Morgan A.** (2004). *Assets for Health and Development: Developing a Conceptual Framework.* Venice: European Office for Investment for Health and Development, World Health Organisation.

Heritage Language Programs Database (2013). The Center for Applied Linguistics. www.cal.org/heritage/profiles/index.html (retrieved August 2013).

Israel, B.A., Schulz, A.J., Parker, E.A., Becker, A.B., Allen, A. and **Guzman, J.R.** (2003). 'Critical Issues in Developing and Following Community-Based Participatory Research Principles'. In M. Minkler and N. Wallerstein, eds, *Community-Based Participatory Research for Health,* 56–73. San Francisco: Jossey-Bass.

Kretzmann, J.P. and **McKnight, J.L.** (1993). *Building Communities from the Inside Out: A Path Toward Finding and Mobilizing a Community's Assets.* Evanston, IL: Northwestern University Center for Urban Affairs and Policy Research, Neighborhood Innovations Network.

Liodakis, N. (1998). 'The Activities of Hellenic-Canadian Secular Organizations in the Context of Canadian Multiculturalism'. *Etudes Helleniques/Hellenic Studies* 6 (1), 37–58.

Liu, N., Musica, A., Koscak, S., Vinogradova, P. and **López, J.** (2011). 'Challenges and Needs of Community-based Heritage Language Programs and How They Are Addressed'. *Heritage Briefs.* Washington, DC: Center for Applied Linguistics (CAL). http://www.cal.org/heritage/pdfs/briefs/challenges-and%20needs-of-community-based-heritage-language-programmes.pdf (retrieved November 2013).

Lo Bianco, J. (2008a). 'Organizing for Multilingualism: Ecological and Sociological Perspectives'. In *Keeping Language Diversity Alive: A TESOL Symposium,* 1–18. Alexandria, VA: Teachers of English to Speakers of Other Languages.

— (2008b). 'Policy Activity for Heritage Languages: Connections with Representation and Citizenship'. In D.M. Brinton, O. Kagan and S. Bauckus, eds, *Heritage Language Education: A New Field Emerging,* 53–69. New York, NY: Routledge.

Lo Bianco, J. and **Peyton, J.K.** (2013). 'Vitality of Heritage Languages in the United States: The Role of Capacity, Opportunity and Desire'. *Heritage Language Journal* 10 (3).Winter 2013.

Lynch, B.K. (2008). 'Locating and Utilizing Heritage Language Resources in the Community: An Asset-Based Approach to Program Design and Evaluation'. In Brinton, D., Kagan, O. and Bauckus S., eds, *Heritage Language Education: A New Field Emerging,* 321–33. New York: Routledge.

Mercurio, B.M. (2010) 'A Vicious Circle of Struggle and Survival: the Italian International Languages Program Stakeholders' Accounts and Practices'. PhD Dissertation. https://tspace.library.utoronto.ca/handle/1807/19124 (retrieved November 2011).

Montrul, S. (2010). 'How Similar are L2 Learners and Heritage Speakers? Spanish Clitics and Word Order'. *Applied Psycholinguistics* 31, 167–207.

— (2009). 'Heritage Language Programs'. In, Long, M.H., Doughty, C.J., eds, *The Handbook of Language Teaching*, 182–200. Chichester: Wiley-Blackwell.

Moore S.C.K. and Ingersoll, G. (2011). 'Where do Community-Based Heritage Language Programs find Funding?' *Heritage Briefs*. Washington, DC: Center for Applied Linguistics. www.cal.org/heritage/ (retrieved June 2013).

Oh, J., Jun, S., Knightly, L. and Au, T. (2003). 'Holding onto Childhood Language Memory'. *Cognition* 86, B53–B64.

Orrieux, C. and Schmitt-Pantel, P. (1999). *A History of Ancient Greece*. Malden, MA, USA: Wiley-Blackwell.

Petraki, K. (2003).*Greek Language Education in the Diaspora: The Training of Greek Educators of the Diaspora in Hellenic Univerities – Their Social and Professional Profile* (Greek). Rethimno: University of Crete.

Perkins, C. (2008). 'Cultures of Map Use'. *The Cartographic Journal* 45 (2), 150–58.

Peyton, J.K, Ranard, D.A. and McGinnis, S., eds (2001). *Heritage Languages in America: Preserving a National Resource*. Washington, DC: Center for Applied Linguistics.

Phillipson, R. and Skutnabb-Kangas, T. (1996). 'English Only Worldwide or Language Ecology?' In *TESOL Quarterly* 30 (3).

Polinsky, M. (2007). 'Incomplete acquisition: American Russian'. *Journal of Slavic Linguistics* 14, 191–262.

— (2008). 'Russian Gender under Incomplete Acquisition'. *Heritage Language Journal* 5, 2007.

Polinsky, M. and Kagan, O. (2007). 'Heritage Languages: In the "Wild" and in the Classroom'. *Language and Linguistics*. Compass, 1/5: 368–95.

Skutnabb-Kangas, T. (2006). 'Language Policy and Linguistic Human Rights. *An Introduction to Language Policy: Theory and Method*, 273–91.

Statistics Canada (1996; 2001; 2006). Ottawa, Canada: Statistics Canada and Department of Canadian Heritage Ethnic Diversity Survey.

— (2012a). '2011 Census of Population: Linguistic Characteristics of Canadians'. www12.statcan.gc.ca/census-recensement/2011/as-sa/98-314-x/98-314-x2011001-eng.cfm (retrieved April 2013).

— (2012b). 'Census in brief: Immigrant languages in Canada'. *Language, Census of Population*, 2011. http://www12.statcan.gc.ca/census-recensement/2011/as-sa/98-314-x/98-314-x2011003_2-eng.pdf (retrieved October 2013).

Tandon, R., ed. (2002) *Participatory Research: Revisiting the Roots*, New Delhi: Mosaic.

Tamis, A. and Gavaki, E. (2002). *From Migrants to Citizens: Greek Migration in Australia and Canada*. Melbourne: National Centre for Hellenic Studies and Research.

Toohey, K. (1992). 'We Teach English as a Second Language to Bilingual Students', in B. Burnaby and A. Cumming, eds, *Socio-political Aspects of ESL in Canada*. Toronto: OISE Press, 87–96.

UNESCO (1996). 'Universal Declaration on Linguistic Rights: Articles 3, 7'. World Conference on Linguistic Rights, Barcelona, Spain. www.unesco.org/cpp/uk/declarations/linguistic.pdf (retrieved March 2013).

— (2003). 'Language Vitality and Endangerment. Ad Hoc Expert Group on Endangered Languages Document submitted to the International Expert Meeting on UNESCO Programme Safeguarding of Endangered Languages Paris, 10–12 March 2003'. http://www.unesco.org/culture/ich/doc/src/00120-EN.pdf (retrieved July 2013).

University of California Los Angeles (2001). 'Heritage Language Research Priorities Conference Report'. Los Angeles, CA: Author. www.cal.org/heritage (retrieved November 2013).

Valdés, G. (2001). 'Heritage Language Students: Profiles and Possibilities'. In J.K. Peyton, D.A. Ranard and S. McGinnis, eds, Heritage *languages in America. Preserving a national resource*, 37–80. McHenry, IL: Center for Applied Linguistics.

— (2005). 'Bilingualism, Heritage Language Learners, and SLA Research: Opportunities Lost or Seized?' *The Modern Language Journal* 89 (3), 410–26.

Wang, S.C. and **Green, N.** (2001). 'Heritage Language Students in the K-12 Education System'. In J.K. Peyton, D.A., Ranard and S. McGinnis, eds, *Heritage Languages in America. Preserving a National Resource*, 167–96. McHenry, IL: Center for Applied Linguistics.

Weinrich, U. (1964). Languages in Contact. Hague: Mouton Publishers.

Wiley, T. (2005). 'The Reemergence of Heritage and Community Language Policy in the U.S. National Spotlight'. *The Modern Language Journal* 89 (4), 594–601.

Zwick, J., Wilson, R., Hanks, T., Goetzman, G.,Vardalos, N., Corbett, J., Kazan, L. et al. (2003). *My Big Fat Greek Wedding*. New York, NY: HBO Home Video.

NOTES

1   As of 1 December 2014, the Heritage Language Programs Database (www.cal.org/heritage/profiles/) contained information for programmes offered in more than fifty languages. In the case of most communities, though, only sporadic programmes have been registered (e.g. only 18 Greek language schools have submitted their profile, from the hundreds of estimated Greek language programmes that operate across the US according to the office of the Greek Education Counsel in Toronto who provides support to Greek HL programmes in Canada and several US regions). In part this attests to the need for HL communities to realize the importance of mapping their assets.

2   Provincial governments in Canada provide funding and general guidelines to the public Boards of Education for the operation of the International Language Programs and in some case (e.g. Quebec, Alberta and Saskatchewan) funding is also available to community organizations that operate HL programmes (Duff 2008; Cummins 2005). Nevertheless, no single state authority has the mandate to oversee HLE as an educational system since a great part of it functions at a community level.

3   The 'big fat Greek school' term is used here in connection with the motion picture 'My Big Fat Greek Wedding' (Zwick, et al. 2003). The film became a huge box office success unveiling the story of a second generation Greek woman in North America who falls in love with a non-Greek. As she tries to get her family to accept him she is negotiating her heritage and cultural identity.

4   Greece joined the EU in 1981.
5   The programme is also known as Education of the Expatriates (in Greek: ΠΑΙΔΕΙΑ ΟΜΟΓΕΝΩΝ) and refers to Greek language education programmes offered worldwide to Greek immigrants and their descendants.
6   Metamorphosis Greek Orthodox private school in Toronto, is the only day school outside Quebec offering a Greek language programme.
7   www.communitybasedresearch.ca/Page/View/CBR_definition.
8   Anecdotal, unedited notes from the focus group discussions held in Toronto's Greek Orthodox Metropolis education office during the 2011–12 school year.

8 OVERCOMING CHALLENGES OF LANGUAGE CHOICE IN HERITAGE LANGUAGE DEVELOPMENT AMONGST MULTILINGUAL IMMIGRANT FAMILIES

James C. Kigamwa (Indiana University – Purdue University Indeanapolis)

Introduction

Immigrant families are not generally able to sustain their heritage languages (HLs) beyond the third generation (Portes and Schauffler 1994). Different factors have been attributed to this loss of HLs and the predictable shift to the use of dominant languages across generations. Amongst African immigrants, language practices that could be precursors of a language shift are observed in the language practices of first generation immigrant families. This chapter highlights some of the challenges faced by speakers of minority languages in their quest to transmit and maintain their HLs and surfaces some issues that may need rethinking as immigrant families consider strategies for reinvigorating efforts at maintenance of minority languages. Observations from a case study of three families that included parents, children and a grandparent are shared in this chapter. The observations depict some of the linguistic practices of immigrant families that influence HL development which expose a paradox associated with private and public use of HLs by parents and adult speakers. Besides highlighting the language practices of the three families, this chapter also reviews some of the existent literature relating to language shift and language. The chapter ends with some suggestions on how to reinvigorate HL development in the homes of language minorities by engaging stories, songs and dance in language learning.

Multilingualism and heritage languages

Immigrant families face numerous challenges associated with the mainten-ance of their HLs, including the inability to create environments that sup-port the easy development of HLs for children. Numerous reasons have been given to explain the shift from HLs to dominant languages such as English. Despite the trend of loss in HLs, few studies have focused on HL develop-ment amongst African immigrants (Obeng 2009), and on how children from language minority families learn to use language (Heath 1986). This is des-pite the fact that adult immigrants from Africa are generally multilingual, and utilise a 'repertoire' of languages in their communication, based on the linguistic abilities of African adults. It has been noted that individuals generally use up to three languages in different settings of everyday life in Africa (Laitin 1992). Commonly indigenous languages, national languages and colonial languages are used in linguistic settings in Africa, with indi-genous languages situated at the base of a language pyramid while colonial languages such as English and French, which are also referred to as official languages, hold higher linguistic status (Benson 2003; Muthwii 2004).[1] This multilayered language hierarchy, evident amongst adult African immigrant discourses, has been discussed by various authors, with the term 'triglossia' being used (Abdulaziz-Mkilifi 1978) to describe the relationship between dif-ferent languages used in multilingual settings.

This use of and proficiency in multiple languages amongst adult Africans makes HLs difficult to define, leaving it to individual families to assign. This is in contrast with the notion of HLs[2] in the US, which is tied to cultural identities, with the languages being distinguished from colonial languages and English as the dominant language. A HL is, in essence, the first language (L1) for most adult African immigrants, but this can get complicated when two parents have different L1s, leading to a situation where parents have to mutually agree to designate a specific language as their HL. The Second Language (L2) is usually a regional language, such as Kiswahili in eastern Africa. Languages such as Pidgin English also fit into this category. The third language is a colonial language, which, in many cases is English, French or Portuguese (Pawlíková-Vilhanová 1996; Anchimbe 2006). In Africa, the col-onisation history of the country often determines the official language, with most countries having adopted the language of their coloniser country as their official language of communication. These languages are embedded in the education systems of African countries (Rasool 2007; Anchimbe 2006).

The language acquisition process in home countries seems to ensure that residents will learn multiple languages easily; however in the diasporas, immigrant families have to contend with environments that make it difficult to sustain the development of HLs for their children since opportunities to experience the languages in different contexts is lacking. Social factors associated with language assimilation and limited opportunities for the use of HLs, combined with the language practices of immigrant families, can be attributed to the low transmission of HLs.

Language and assimilation

There are varying attitudes towards languages spoken by minorities and the coexistence of HLs with dominant languages such as English. While there are those who are concerned that English may be threatened by immigrant and minority languages, studies have shown that immigrant languages can generally not withstand shifts related to the influence of dominant languages and are lost easily since dominant languages such as English are acquired quickly amongst immigrant families (Krashen 1998; Fishman 1991; Brown 2008; Crawford 1996; Cho and Krashen 1998; Fillmore 2000). The maintenance of minority HLs in the diasporas is not an easy affair and requires that speakers of the languages put in place deliberate strategies for their transmission and maintenance. This is because societal structures including language use seem to favour the assimilation of immigrants and the replacement of their languages with dominant languages such as English.

Although educators espouse the virtues of bilingualism and express support for multilingualism in the US, one paradox of the language situation in the US is how quickly immigrant languages are abandoned in favour of English, with the limit for an absolute language shift being the third generation (Portes and Schauffler 1994). Related to this shift seems to be the covert value associated with the use of English amongst immigrant communities, which is seen by the dominant society as the 'litmus test of citizenship' (Portes and Schauffler 1994, 642). In the US the high value placed on English is manifested by immigrants' attitudes to their HLs *vis-à-vis* English. A study of more than 5000 immigrants of different nationalities found that knowledge of English as well as its preference in communication seemed almost universal and that only a minority of immigrants remained fluent in their HLs (Portes and Hao 1998). In the US, immigrants focus on societal cues and seem to strive to speak English without a 'foreign' accent, which seems to be the ultimate image of linguistic assimilation.

Despite many immigrants arriving in the US as bilinguals and multilinguals, it has been argued that immigrant bilingualism is temporary, as well as unstable and transitional, amongst immigrant communities (Hakuta and D'Andrea 1992; Baker 2006). In the absence of well-established linguistic practices that support the transmission of minority languages, the rapid shift from the minority language can be expected once immigrant children are fluent in English (Fishman 1991; Grosjean 1982). While previously bilingualism seemed to have been assured in the second generation of immigrants, recent trends show that language shift begins to take root in the first generation and that only a few second generation immigrants are bilingual (Fillmore 2000; Lopez 1982). Further, it has been argued that it is unlikely that bilingually educated children could pass minority languages on to their children if the languages are not 'embedded in the family-neighborhood-community experience and the economics of the family' (Baker 2006, 62). It therefore seems that for immigrant languages to be transmitted across generations, they would need to be incorporated into the community practices of the dominant society, which is unlikely. This chapter therefore offers suggestions for providing more intentional opportunities and the creation of spaces for HL use by immigrants in the home.

Opportunities to experience heritage language

Opportunities to experience varied uses of HLs in different domains of speech are limited in spaces that are occupied by a dominant language such as English. This limits the language experience of immigrant children learning to speak HLs in settings where the HLs are a minority, as it has been noted that experiencing language use across multiple contexts leads to development of a rich language repertoire (Heath 1986). Occasions to engage and be immersed in a HL seem to abound in home countries of immigrants as these languages are commonly spoken in homes, market places, churches and playgrounds for children (Muthwii 2004). In some cases the use of HLs is embedded within teaching and learning, since language policy permits space for the languages to be used in school curricula, as the policies of language of instruction in some African countries require school instruction in lower primary levels to be provided in local languages (Ongechi 2009; Obondo 2007). While it is difficult or nearly impossible for opportunities to experience HLs in the diasporas to mirror the home country contexts, there are ways that can be used to improve access to HLs especially in the homes of immigrant families. The lack of equivalent linguistic opportunities that support HL development in the diasporas, compared to the home countries, widely limits possibilities for children to experience their HLs across multiple contexts. In the diasporas adults seem to set the limit for HL usage since they are, in many cases, the only source of HL exposure to children. The amount of time assigned to the use of HLs is therefore an important consideration for immigrant parents who seek to transmit HLs to their children. Instances when adults switch from English to HLs should therefore be treated as important opportunities for learning the languages.

Language choice and code-switching

Adult immigrants who are fluent speakers may have to consider what language to designate as their HL for purposes of transmission to their children. While many bilinguals and multilinguals make choices regarding what language(s) to use during different communicative events, sometimes these choices lead to changes in the language in mid-sentence, while in other cases specific languages are used with different persons. These choices have far-reaching implications for the maintenance of HLs, and are regulated both by broad societal factors and personal factors (Baker 2006; Coronel-Molina 2009). The switching between languages, or 'code-switching', is a manifestation of language choice and is usually based on personal ability as well as the deliberate choice of a preferred language(s) during conversations. Code-switching is the practice of deliberately changing from one language to another, the code being a language or dialect of a language (Muysken 2000; Fasold 1984). Covert language attitudes exist that underlie code-switching and code-mixing linguistic practices, which may not have been carefully interrogated by speakers of a language (Baker 2006). Linguistic choices and overall behaviour can be viewed as 'acts of identity in which people reveal both their personal identity and their search for social roles' (LePage and Tabouret-Keller 1985, 14).

Two possible explanations have been advanced for the moment at which participants in a conversation switch from one language to another. The switches have been found to be regulated either by preference or by competence or linguistic ability (Shin 2003). Sometimes, when bilinguals have a problem finding an appropriate word or expression in a second language they could end up using words from a different language. Word choices that are based on difficulty in finding the right words are in the domain of competence or ability in the second language, or the language being spoken. On the other hand, by their own preference, some bilinguals may choose to speak in one language rather than another or to insert words or phrases from their HL into their conversations in order to obscure the meaning to those around them. These notions of choice-related and competence-related switching are important in determining the intentions of bilinguals, especially when they switch from one language to another in the presence of would-be language learners such as their children. Where competent speakers of a HL are also equally proficient in the dominant language, it can be assumed that code switches between the two languages are regulated by considerations that are not based on linguistic competence, but rather on personal factors related to the nature of the conversation.

The notion of choice of language can be extended further to considerations regarding decisions that families may have made regarding their home language policies. This may not necessarily be the case for all families as some literature suggests that many families have not deliberately agreed upon language policies, and may therefore have never implemented specific action regarding what languages to use for the family. Choices related to what language(s) children will be raised in have been referred to as 'private language planning' (Piller 2001). It has been noted that many immigrant parents generally do not engage in deliberate or conscious decisions regarding language use at home, and that such choices are derived from language habits that can be traced back to initial interactions between the married couples (Baker 2006). In essence, what this means is that couples will maintain the use and patterns of the language or languages they were speaking before they began raising their children, without giving due consideration to the influence their practices will have on the transmission of the HL to their children.

The need for adequate and authentic linguistic input from competent speakers of a language has been discussed extensively in language acquisition research (Ellis 1999; Krashen 1998; Heath 1986), leading to a general consensus that a basic requirement for effective language acquisition is the availing of adequate linguistic input to learners of a new language. These learners of new languages seem to thrive when conversations and general communication in a language they are learning is intended to be understood. Creating an environment that is rich in the use of a HL creates space for learners to be immersed in the language, which helps in learning any language. However, the new language must be used in a way that specifically supports the sustenance of this environment in order for it to be successfully transmitted to learners and to develop.

Code-switching and private conversations

This section highlights some findings from a case study of three African families that are currently residing in the US who took part in an ethnographic study that sought to determine ways in which their home language practices influenced HL acquisition. The families were drawn from East, Central and West Africa, representing Kenya, Rwanda and Cameroon respectively. Unlike the Cameroonian family, where the parents fluently spoke different indigenous languages, the Kenyan and Rwandan families had common indigenous languages between spouses which they could describe as their HLs. The adults in each of the families were fluent speakers of at least three common languages, with the Kenyan family having competence in English, Kiswahili and Ekigusii. In the Cameroonian family, adults were fluent speakers of English, French and Cameroonian Pidgin[3] English, while the Rwandan family adults were fluent in English, French and Kinyarwanda. Adults in this study spoke additional languages with varying proficiencies. For example, in the Rwandan family one of the parents was also fluent in Kiswahili; in the Kenyan family one of the parents was a fluent speaker of Spanish and French, and in the Cameroonian family one of the parents spoke Ngwe while the other spoke Ngaemba as indigenous languages.

Parents in the Kenyan family communicated between themselves mostly in English with occasional switches to Ekigusii. The Rwandan parents, on the other hand, spoke mainly in Kinyarwanda to each other and directed all communication to their children in English. The Cameroonian parents spoke English at all times when conversing between themselves and when conversing with their children. Therefore, conversations between all the children in the three families were exclusively in English. In the Kenyan family, occasionally the children would respond to their parents in short phrases in Ekigusii. All the families indicated that the choice of languages spoken in their homes seemed to have evolved naturally and that no private language policy (Piller 2001) guided the languages they spoke. The languages used facilitated easy communication between the different family members. Portrayals of code-switching were common in the Kenyan and Rwandan families. In the case of the Kenyan family, code-switching was generally from English to Ekigusii and, on a few occasions, into Kiswahili. For the Rwandan family, most code-switching was between English and Kinyarwanda and on very rare occasions, some French would be used. The fact that they had a live-in grandmother who spoke only Kinyarwanda created a language situation different from that of the other families in the study. The Cameroonian family did not seem to switch languages much, as most of their communication in their household was in English. The parents communicated in English between themselves and when they wanted to communicate with their children. However, there were few times when the father would speak to a cousin in their indigenous language, in which the mother had indicated she was not entirely proficient. The children confirmed that sometimes their parents would switch to their indigenous language or the Cameroonian Pidgin English with the father noting that there were times when the children would wonder if their uncle was telling on them.

In all three families, code-switching seemed to be a privilege of the parents as they were the only multilinguals in their homes. Private language around the researcher was consistent before a drink or meal was served. These switches from English to the HLs seemed to be necessary communicative events in the family domain. This kind of hospitality-related code-switch was common, but there were also moments when the parents seemed to code-switch during private conversations to the exclusion of everyone else. It appears that these instances of code-switching in the homes, by parents, were intended to create some 'private' space for conversation which would leave out visitors and children alike.

Children from the three families indicated that they thought their parents engaged in private conversations using their HL so that the children would not fully understand what they (their parents) were talking about. This switching, as reported by children, included the use of French, Spanish and Kiswahili for the Kenyan family, while for the Cameroonian family it was Pidgin English, which the children referred to as 'the dialect'. The children from the Rwandan family reported that their parents switched to the Kinyarwanda and sometimes on very rare occasions French when they wanted to have private conversations. The children reported that their parents' tendencies to engage in private conversation in HLs were associated with certain events, noting that parents tended to make the switch when they wanted to consult privately about specific issues and possible corrective action. Generally this switch elicited suspicion on the part of the children, who said that during such instances they wished they could understand what their parents were saying.

With parents and other competent speakers of a language sometimes being the only speakers of the HLs for their children, parental language use is a critical factor in HL development. Given also that parents were the only ones able to exercise language choice, because they were proficient in multiple languages, there were slight tensions associated with the switch to HLs during communication by parents. Children were inclined to think that parents were either unhappy about something that they had done or were discussing something that was really important or of consequence to them and therefore were not sure if they should know about it. It has been noted that sometimes bilingual parents code-switch in order to emphasise certain points or to make the children understand that they really mean what they are saying, which may have led to HLs being associated with rebuking and correction (Pavlenko 2004). The practice of code-switching as discussed in this chapter seems to curtail and limit the use of HLs within the family, which in essence seems to infringe on the time that could be allocated to communication that could develop the HLs.

Rethinking heritage language development at home

The large number of minority languages in the US makes it improbable and impractical for there to be considerations for their usage in school curricula. This leaves parents of minority languages with one option for the development of their HLs, which is the home front. In re-envisioning HL development, this chapter makes some suggestions about how to improve home language use in order to ensure the acquisition and maintenance of HLs. Given that language acquisition is logically predicated upon the quality and quantity of linguistic input, it follows that a home environment rich in the use of the HL is bound to be more useful for its transmission than an environment with less usage of the language. While opportunities to engage with HLs abound in countries where the languages are used widely, spaces for HL use have to be intentionally created by parents mainly in the home, because in the diasporas there are limited opportunities outside it.

Determining what language parents want children to inherit as their HL is a good place to start the conversation amongst parents who are speakers of multiple languages. A rational choice needs to be made which would make parents more intentional in transmitting their HLs. This choice could be based on a number of factors, including the proficiency of both parents in the language they choose. Families should also consider whether there is a pool of speakers available for their children to practice using their HL and what kinds of digital and non-digital resources are available. In cases where parents speak different languages, a decision to embrace a language of wider communication may be reasonable, much like the Cameroonian family in the study. Despite being individually proficient in their own HLs, the Cameroonian family opted to designate Cameroonian Pidgin English as their HL for many reasons, including the fact that it was the only non-Western language in which they were both proficient. Although the Kenyan and Rwandan families have common native languages in Ekigusii and Kinyarwanda, the choice of what languages they would want to associate as 'heritage' for their children is still complex because the parents may be interested in languages of wide communication, such as Kiswahili, which is spoken in both countries. The Kenyan family faced the dilemma that they had many family friends who did not speak their indigenous language of Ekigusii. There was a large pool of Kiswahili language speakers where they lived in the US, which made the language more accessible and capable of a utilitarian role amongst immigrant families. Similarly, the Rwandan family may have found that there were more Kiswahili language speakers as well as a summer school programme that taught it. All these were important factors to consider when assigning a HL.

It is difficult to determine the extent to which code-switching by adults works in favour of language shift amongst these families, but it is obvious that in seeking to develop HL abilities, families must be discouraged from linguistic events that obscure meaning in communication during private conversations amongst adults. Some of the reasons stated for code-switching are tied to functions of speech that include a desire to communicate more effectively and to connect more easily with other persons, and the need to clarify misunderstood concepts (Gumperz 1982; Kow 2003). The reasons for code-switching observed in this study were associated mainly with private communication between parents which seemed to restrict understanding by children during times when parents felt that information was privileged. Besides avoiding switches that keep conversation in the HL between adults, parents should also be encouraged to use their HLs in ways that would include their children. One of the families had a practice of consistently greeting their children in the HL. Taking this practice a step further by having discussion around themes of the day would create additional opportunities for engagement in HLs in the home. The use of one language by one parent when communicating with children has been explored and recommended

(Dopke 1992). Such a practice could be extended to other routine interactive family conversational events and times, such as during meal times.

Reinvigorating heritage language in the home with stories, songs and dances

The final section of this chapter confers some of the possible opportunities to experience HL in the diasporas through the use of digital media in the use of HL development. These opportunities are also grounded in the need for parents to be intentional about the use of HLs when they are around their children. This chapter recommends the pursuit of opportunities around engaging various genres of language use by speakers of the minority languages. Besides being valued as useful tools for language learning in schools, these genres and many others are commonly used forms of communication amongst language minorities, with examples of usage amongst Chinese-American families and Mexican-American families provided by Heath (1986), who lists: label quests, meaning quests, recounts, accounts, eventcasts and stories. Given that children in many immigrant families are at different levels of language development, parents would have to determine what would be useful for the purpose of language learning and maintenance of their HLs. This section focuses on how stories, songs and dances in HLs, which are now widely available online, could be used to reinvigorate learning of HLs by language minorities who wish to provide additional learning and engagement opportunities for their children at home.

Using digital media to spur interest and secure content for HL could go a long way towards arousing interest in and motivating the development of HLs. Stories offer a powerful avenue for language exchange in families. In order for stories to provide the necessary leverage in language learning, parents should strive to always tell stories in their HLs. There are various possibilities for storytelling that include the use of both fictional and non-fictional stories. Children love listening to stories; children of immigrants are generally keen on learning about children in other parts of the world and would be interested in learning about experiences of children as well as their parents' childhood stories. When narrated in the HL, parents could assign another adult who is fluent in the language to be the translator if need be. Depending upon the ages of children, stories could also be read to them. Since there are many online texts in HLs, parents could identify what would be of interest and appropriate for their children. As is the case of many tales and stories, there is always a moral lesson tied to a story. Parents should therefore not lose track of the lessons that the stories carry, and could use lessons learnt as possible points of discussion and practice of using the HLs to strengthen language development.

Songs, movies and other videos could also be used to engage children and youth in discussion using the HLs. Websites such as YouTube are an invaluable resource for viewing these, many of which promote African values, both in English and in HLs. Some tend to switch between the languages and transmit both traditional and contemporary cultures in home countries. The stories carried in these videos could provide rich discussion by families if viewed as part of weekly family events such as family nights.

The use of song and dance in language learning actitivities has not yet been fully exploited. There are currently hundreds of music videos available on the internet. The music is in different HLs and in various genres that appeal to all ages, including traditional songs, gospel music and other contemporary forms such as hip-hop. Such music could provide important content for discussion within families seeking to observe authentic language use in local contexts. Parents and children could listen to HL music together and could practice some of the cultural dances as part of language learning.

Conclusion

This chapter has highlighted some of the challenges of HL development for immigrant families and factors that seem to encourage language shifts towards English. The challenges faced by families that seek to transmit their HLs to their children will always play out in contexts where there are dominant languages that occupy a high status, and in places where dominant languages pervade most of the public spheres of communication, including schools. How speakers of minority languages choose to contend with challenges of language assimilation will influence their language practices in the home. Speakers of minority languages must not lose sight of the fact that the home front may be the only domain of language use that they may be capable of regulating, and the need for families to be intentional about the languages they choose to use in their home therefore cannot be over-emphasised. In being deliberate about the languages that are employed in homes, adult speakers of HLs must continue to be creative about their use, and must continue to seek ways to afford opportunities for their children to experience them in varied genres and other domains of language use. This chapter has recommended the use of stories, songs and dances to reinvigorate HL development amongst African immigrants. There are certainly other strategies that could be added to create new excitement about HL learning in the home. The resolve to strengthen the use of HLs in homes should be founded upon the realisation that, if speakers of minority languages fail to fortify such use at home, then there will be no basis for trying to preserve the languages in other domains. It must all start at home!

REFERENCES

Abdulaziz-Mkilifi, M. (1978). 'Triglossia and Swahili-English Bilingualism in Tanzania'. In J.A. Fishman, ed., *Advances in the Study of Societal Multilingualism*. Hague: Mouton Publishers.

Anchimbe, E. (2006). 'Functional Seclusion and the Future of Indigenous Languages in Africa: The Case of Cameroon'. *Proceedings from the 35th Annual Conference on African Linguistics*. Sommerville, MA: Cascadilla Proceedings Project.

Baker, C. (2006). *Foundations of Bilingual Education and Bilingualism*, 4th ed. Clevedon: Multilingual Matters.

Benson, C. (2003). 'Trilingualism in Guinea-Bissau and the Question of Instructional Language'. In C. Hoffmann and J. Ytsma, eds, *Trilingualism in Family, School and Community*, 166–84. Clevedon: Multilingual Matters.

Brown, A. (2008). Language Shift or Maintenance? An Examination of Language Usage across Four Generations as Self-Reported by University Age Students in Belarus'. *Journal of Multilingual and Multicultural Development* 29 (1), 1–15.

Cho, G. and Krashen, S. (1998). The Negative Consequences of Heritage Language Loss and Why We Should Care'. In S. Krashen, L. Tse and J. McQuillan, *Heritage Language Development*, 31–9. Culver City, Ca: Language Education Associates.

Coronel-Molina, S. (2009). 'Definitions and Critical Literature Review of Language Attitude, Language Choice and Language Shift: Samples of Languge Attitude Surveys'. Unpublished Monograph.

Crawford, J. (1996). 'Seven Hypotheses on Language Loss Causes and Cures'. *Stabilizing Indigenous Languages*. Paper adapted from a speech given on May 4, 1995, at the second Symposium on Stabilizing Indigenous Language, North Arizona University, AZ. (ERICED39573).

Dopke, S. (1992). *One Parent, One Language: An Interactional Approach*. Philadelphia, PA: John Benjamins Publishers.

Echu, G. (2004). 'The Language Question in Cameroon'. *Linguistik Online* 18 (1), 19–33.

Ellis, R. (1999). *The Study of Second Language Acquisition*. Oxford: Oxford University Press.

Fasold, R. (1984). *The Sociolinguistics of Society*. Oxford: Blackwell Publishers.

Fillmore, L. (2000) 'Loss of Family Languages: Should Educators be Concerned?' *Theory into Practice* 39 (4), 203–10.

Fishman, J.A. (1991). *Reversing Language Shift*. Clevedon: Multilingual Matters.

— (2000). 'Reversing Language Shift: RLS Theory and Practice Revisited'. In G. Kindle and M.P. Lewis, eds, 'Assessing Ethnolinguistic Vitality: Theory and Practice'. Dallas, TX: SIL International.

— (2001). '300-Plus Years of Heritage Language Education in the United States'. In J. Peyton, D. Ranard and S. McGinnis, eds, *Heritate Languages in America: Preserving a National Heritage*, 81–98. Long Beach, CA: Center for Applied Linguistics.

Gumperz, J. (1982). *Discourse Strategies*. Cambridge: Cambridge University Press.

Hakuta, K. and D'Andrea, D. (1992). 'Some Properties of Bilingual Maintenance and Loss in Mexican Background High-School Students'. *Applied Linguistics* 13 (1), 72–99.

Heath, S. (1986). 'Sociocultural Contexts of Language Development. Beyond language: Social and Cultural Factors in Schooling Language Minority Students'. Los Angeles, CA: Evaluation, Dissemination and Assessment Center, 144–86.

Kelleher, A. (2008). 'What is Heritage Language?' In J. K. Peyton, ed., *Frequently Asked Questions about Heritage Languages in the United States*, 3–4. Washington, DC: Center for Applied Linguistics.

Kow, K. (2003). 'Codeswitching for a Purpose: Focus on Preschool Malaysian Children'. *Multilingua* 22, 59–77.

Krashen, S. (1998). 'Language Shyness and Heritage Language Development'. In S. Krashen, L. Tse and J. McQuillan, eds, *Heritage Language Development*, 41–9. Culver City, CA: Language Education Associates.

Laitin, D. (1992). *Language Repertoires and State Construction in Africa: Cambridge studies in Comparative Politics*. Cambridge: Cambridge University Press.

LePage, R.B. and Tabouret-Keller, A. (1985). *Acts of Identity – Creole-Based Approaches to Language and Ethnicity*. Cambridge: Cambridge University Press.

Muthwii, M. (2004). Language Planning and Literacy in Kenya: Living with Unresolved Paradoxes'. *Current Issues in Language Planning* 5 (1), 34–50.

Muysken, P. (2000). *Bilingual Speech: A Typology of Code-Mixing*. Cambridge: Cambridge University Press.

Obeng, S. (2009). 'Language Maintenance and Shift amongst Akan Immigrant College Students in the United States'. In J. Anderson, C. Green and S. Obeng, eds, *African linguistics across the discipline* (pp. 1-10). Bloomington, IN: IULC Publications.

Obondo, M.A. (2007). 'Tensions Between English and Mother Tongue Teaching in Post-Colonial Africa'. In J. Cummins and C. Davidson, eds, *International Handbook of English Language Teaching*. New York, NY: Springer Science and Business Media, LLC, 1, 37–50.

Ongechi, Nathan (2009) *The Role of Foreign and Indigenous Languages in Primary Schools: The Case of Kenya*. Stellenbosch: Stellenbosch Papers in Linguistics. Plus. 39, 143–58.

Pavlenko, A. (2004). 'Stop Doing That, Ia Komu Skazala: Language Choice and Emotions in Parent-Child Communication'. *Journal of Multilingual and Multicultural Development* 25 (2, 3), 179–203.

Pawliková-Vilhanová, V. (1996). 'Swahili and the Dilemma of Ugandan Language Policy'. *Asian and African Studies* 2 (5), 158–70.

Piller, I. (2001). 'Private Language Planning: The Best of Both Worlds?' *Estudios de Sociolinguistica* 2 (1), 61–80.

— (2002). *Bilingual Couples Talk: The Discursive Construction of Hybridity*. Amsterdam, Netherlands: John Benjamins.

Portes, A. and Hao, L. (1998). 'Bilingualism and Language Loss in the Second Generation'. *Sociology of Education* 71 (4), 269–94.

Portes, A. and Schauffler, R. (1994). 'Language and the Second Generation: Bilingualism Yesterday and Today'. *International Migration Review* 28 (4), 640–61.

Rasool, N. (2007). *Global Issues in Languages, Education and Development: Perspectives from Postcolonial Countries*. New Delhi: Orient Longman.

Shin, S. (2003). *Role of Parents' Knowledge about Bilingualism in the Transmission of Heritage Languages*. UCLA, CA: Centre for World Languages.

Valdés, G. (2001). 'Heritage Language Students: Profiles and Possibilities'. In D.R. Joy Kreeft Pyeton, ed., *Heritage Languages in America*, 37–80. McHenry, IL: Delta Systems.

Vygotsky, L. (1978). *Mind and Society: The Development of Higher Psychological Processes*. Cambridge, MA: Harvard University Press.

NOTES

1   Indigenous languages are local languages spoken by different ethnic groups in Africa. National languages are more widely spoken than ethnic languages, and in some cases are used for school instruction in lower grades; an example is the Kiswahili language in Kenya.

2   HLs are generally viewed against a backdrop of dominant languages and are therefore always viewed as 'other' languages wherever there is a dominant language (Fishman 2001; Valdés 2001). Different terms have been used to describe HLs, including immigrant languages, home languages, minority languages, ethnic languages and community languages (Kelleher 2008). Valdés (2001) noted that in the US context, HLs refer to 'all non-English languages, including those spoken by Native American peoples' (39). Fishman (2001) placed HLs into three categories (immigrant, indigenous, and colonial) and defined immigrant HLs as those spoken by immigrants who came to the US after it became independent, thus distinguishing them from the indigenous HLs spoken by Native Americans. This study adopts the term 'heritage language' to refer to national or indigenous languages from Africa spoken by adult African immigrants in the US.

3   There are various forms of pidgins spoken globally. Cameroonian Pidgin English is one of the most widely used languages of wider communication in Cameroon (Echu 2004).

9 THE IMPACT OF THE CEFR ON CANADA'S LINGUISTIC PLURALITY: A Space for Heritage Languages?

Enrica Piccardo (University of Toronto)

Introduction

In recent years Canada has shown a growing interest in the *Common European Framework of Languages* (CEFR), published by the Council of Europe in 2001 and widely used across the European continent and beyond. This interest has moved from academic discussion and feasibility studies (Vandergrift 2006) to the publication of institutional documents informing language education policies (CMEC 2010). In spite of this, so far the CEFR is primarily implemented as a standard setting tool, with a real risk of overlooking its conceptual density and its pedagogical value. In particular, the groundbreaking notion of plurilingual competence it presents, where languages are interrelated and not just juxtaposed, still appears to be undervalued.

The rich and diverse linguistic landscape of Canada is in fact the ideal setting for the implementation of effective plurilingualism and for a reconsideration of language education scope and practices. What is at stake is the linguistic capital of Canada's future generations. The adoption of the CEFR has a great potential for increasing real and effective plurilingualism, provided we go beyond paying lip service to the idea of the plurality of languages and become aware that the (bio)diversity of languages needs to be nurtured and protected in order to avoid running the risk of uniformity and language loss in the time span of a couple of generations.

After a short introduction to the linguistic landscape of Canada and the interest of the country in the CEFR, this chapter will present the notion of plurilingualism in contrast with the myth of 'pureness of languages'. It will then analyse in what way the adoption of a plurilingual and pluricultural perspective may foster a paradigm shift in language education. Finally, it will underline how heritage languages (HLs) can potentially benefit from this paradigm shift.

The CEFR in Canada: a milestone?

The linguistic situation

The Canadian demographic context is very dynamic. According to the data published by the national statistics agency (www.statcan.gc.ca/) in the last census of 2011, the country had nearly 33.5 million inhabitants, 5.9% more than in 2006. Two thirds of them were immigrants. The Canadian linguistic landscape is very diverse as it includes the two official languages, English and French, the wealth of Aboriginal languages (First Nations, Méetis and Inuit communities), and the numerous HLs of the populations who immigrated into the country, particularly from the 20th century onwards. Nearly 1.2 million individuals belong to aboriginal communities and almost 6.6 million Canadians speak a first language other than English or French: over 200 different first languages are spoken by 20% of the population. One fifth of the inhabitants of Canada were born in another country (data from the Government of Canada for 2006).[1] From the analysis of the most recent census data (1996, 2001, 2006, 2011), the emerging tendency shows an increasing linguistic diversity, as the number of inhabitants declaring one language other than English and French has increasd by nearly 2% every five years. This wealth of languages is paired with an even higher number of cultures as each language conveys a mosaic of cultures.

In spite of such linguistic wealth, 'non-dominant' languages are frequently not recognised and undervalued in both mainstream society and education (Hornberger 2001; Wiley and Lukes 1996). While there is an active contingent of educators and academics who advocate for multilingual language polices that support cultural and linguistic diversity (Cummins 2001; García, Skutnabb-Kangas, and Torres-Guzmán 2006; Lo Bianco 2010), homogenising and assimilationist language policies still prevail in North America (Connelly 2008; Hornberger 2001, Cantoni 1997). The risk of these policies is that of perpetuating, amongst many educators, a negative perception of bilingualism – unless bilingualism is restricted to official languages – and of contributing to the decline of the languages spoken at home (Cantoni 1997; Crawford 2000).

Interestingly, in the Canadian context, various policy and curricula documents from provincial ministries of education appear to support the use of multiple languages in classrooms and first language maintenance for minority language students (Alberta Education 2010; British Columbia Ministry of Education 2009; Ontario Ministry of Education 2005; Ontario Ministry of Education 2006). These documents advise teachers to encourage first language use in certain situations and provide theoretical justification for multiple language use by citing research that has illustrated the social and academic benefits of first language (L1)/HL maintenance and bilingualism (Cook 2001; Cummins 2007; Cummins, Bismilla, Chow, Cohen, Giampapa, Leoni, Sandhu and Sastri 2005; Taylor, Bernhard, Garg and Cummins 2008). Nevertheless, teachers are not provided with the tools and support that they need to achieve these aims, a fact which renders implementation of multiple language use in the classroom implicitly 'optional' or 'additional'.

In contrast with this rhetorical support for multiple language use, recent analyses of Canadian educators' discourse reveal a distinct lack of support for linguistic diversity in schools. Connelly (2008) notes that schools typically mirror Canadian society, where despite the official policy of multiculturalism, 'the homogeneous society has often been invoked as the emblem of success' (Connelly 2008, 166). Similarly, homogenous schools are 'considered apt to success, while a school with a high proportion of 'underperforming' recent immigrants is seen as having a handicap' (ibid., 166–7). As (linguistic minority) students realise that, since perceived difference may be classified as inadequate performance (ibid.; Flecha 1999), they frequently cease to use their L1/HL in (and even outside of) the classroom. This trend is a contributing factor to widespread language attrition which affects students, their families, their associated linguistic or cultural communities and Canadian society as a whole.

The discrepancy between Canada's linguistic diversity and educational environments that recognise and reward only majority language speakers, coupled with the need to preserve the linguistic capital represented by HLs, suggests a dire need for ideological and pedagogical change in relation to language learning and use.

The CEFR in the Canadian context

On top of scholarly research and debate around the need to reconsider language education in the light of societal and demographic change, and in general around the consideration of the value and the potential of bilingual education, the CEFR caught the attention of Canadian stakeholders some years ago and is becoming more and more popular and increasingly implemented at institutional level. The CEFR is appropriately perceived as an effective guiding document for educational policies, particularly suitable for a bilingual country where education is under the jurisdiction of each province.

The growing interest of Canada in Council of Europe projects in the domain of language policies and education has seen, on one side, the active participation of researchers in the European Centre for Modern Languages (ECML)[2] projects and, on the other, the publication of studies and reports (Vandergrift 2006, 2008; Rehorick and Lafargue 2005) on the feasibility of adopting the CEFR in the Canadian context. More recently, the Council of Ministers of Education Canada (CMEC) has formally encouraged the use of the CEFR by the different provincial ministers of education with the publication in 2010 of *Working with the Common European Framework of Reference for Languages (CEFR) in the Canadian Context,* which is – as indicated in the subtitle – a *Guide for Policy-Makers and Curriculum Designers.* Consideration, and implementation, of the CEFR, which has started on a voluntary basis, is ongoing and is expected to be 'upscaled' to inform curricula and textbooks. This will potentially introduce effective innovation in language teaching if judged on the basis of the impact that the CEFR has had in the European context in the time span of a decade.

Nevertheless, even if the interest in the CEFR needs to be seen as positive and useful for increasing accountability and coherence in assessing language proficiency across the country, it is not in itself a guarantee that the innovation potential of the CEFR in the domain of language pedagogy will be exploited, or simply that the conceptual density of the document will be taken into consideration. In fact, if the message conveyed by official documents such as the CMEC *Guide* is considered, there is a real risk of underestimating the complexity of the CEFR and as such there is an urgent need for a real reflection on its methodological and conceptual depth (Piccardo 2013; forthcoming).

What seems to be predominant in the consideration of the CEFR is its potential to be a standard-setting tool, its ability to provide coherence and transparency in the definition of proficiency levels. In fact, the need for clear reference points is becoming stronger in every domain in our glo-balised societies, which are more and more complex, unstructured and 'li-quid' (Baumann 2007). Languages are no exception in this respect, since all countries are increasingly faced with a plurality of languages and cultures (Byrnes 2007a, 2007b; Bärenfänger and Tschirner 2008). There is a growing quest for visibility, exchange and comparison, and the CEFR seems able to respond to this with its clear use of scales and grid-based tools, which are both straightforward to understand and easy to apply. Nevertheless, several scholars (Coste 2007; Little 2011; Piccardo 2012) are worried about its partial implementation, an issue that can be observed at various degrees in almost all contexts where it has been introduced. This attitude is rather problematic as it overlooks the pedagogic dimension of the document inextricably linked to the standard-setting one. The CEFR is complex, conceptually dense and also extremely rich and innovative: the complexity of the CEFR prevents any linear, top-down implementation.

Of the two dimensions of the CEFR – the vertical one referring to the levels of proficiency organised in a scale and the horizontal one, which fo-cuses on the wealth of communicative activities and competences involved in the different tasks users accomplish (Little 2006; Hulstijn 2011; Huver and Springer 2011) – it is actually this second, more complex dimension, that can prove critical for preserving and fostering Canada's linguistic diversity and cultural wealth. In fact, while other assessment frameworks may also prove effective for setting proficiency standards (Tschirner 2012), the conceptual density of the CEFR provides a unique basis for powerful innovation in lan-guage pedagogy whose multidimensionality deserves to be fully exploited (Little 2006; 2007; Krumm 2007; Hulstijn 2011; Piccardo 2012).

The multidimensional nature and innovative concepts of the CEFR

One of the most important concepts adopted and systematised by the CEFR, and one of its main assets, is plurilingualism, a new term mirroring the French 'plurilinguisme' (Beacco and Byram 2007; Beacco 2005; Coste 2010; Piccardo, Berchoud, Cignatta, Mentz and Pamula 2011). This notion was first defined during the decade that preceded the CEFR publication (Coste, Moore and Zarate 1997, reprinted in 2009), and has been developed by the work of several researchers (Grosjean 1982, Ludi and Py 1986; Gajo and Mondada 2000), conducted mainly in the Francophone area and in bi/multilingual regions (Switzerland, Val d'Aosta, and so on), although not exclusively. The term has also recently been considered with interest in Anglophone research (Canagarajah and Liynage 2012). In fact, the vision underlying plurilingualism has a lot in common with the results of the studies concerning bilingualism (Garcia 2009a) conducted in non-European contexts, particularly in North American countries and, it may be assumed, some form of cross-fertilisation of research on both sides of the Atlantic. Garcia has identified 'a dynamic model of bilingualism that captures the complexity of bilingualism and multimodalities [and that] has much to do with the concept of plurilingualism that has been advanced in the European context' (ibid., 71). While we acknowledge the similarities between the two models, we nevertheless have a preference for the term 'plurilingualism', with its broader and more dynamic connotation, than other semantically related words such as 'bilingualism' or 'multilingualism'.

According to the CEFR, bilingualism is only one specific type of plurilingualism (ibid., 168), thus losing its aura of balanced proficiency of two languages. Also, linguistic diversity is not seen as a series of isolated languages, but is rather presented in a way that 'allows for the interaction and mutual influence of the languages in a more dynamic way' (Canagarajah and Liynage 2012, 50).

In paragraph 1.3, 'What is plurilingualism?', the CEFR makes the fundamental terminological distinction between plurilingualism and multilingualism by stressing the additive connotation of the latter term:

> Plurilingualism differs from multilingualism, which is the knowledge of a *number* of languages, or the *co-existence* of different languages in a given society. (CEFR 2001, 4, my emphasis)

And it implies a brand new vision:

> as an individual person's experience of language in its cultural contexts expands, from the language of the home to that of society at large and then to the languages of other peoples (whether learnt at school or college, or by direct experience), *he or she does not keep these languages and cultures in strictly separated mental compartments,* but rather builds up a communicative competence to which all knowledge and experience of language contributes and in which languages interrelate and interact. In different situations, a person can call flexibly upon different parts of this competence to achieve effective communication with a particular interlocutor'. (CEFR 2001, 4, my emhpasis)

There is here a double movement: from a rather socially orientated dimension to an individually orientated one, which includes the psycho/neurological aspect, from a paradigm of addition to one of synergic and flexible use of skills and knowledge.

To make things clearer, in the CEFR some examples follow these definitions, which stress the role of:

1. Partial competences, as productive and receptive skills may vary considerably.
2. Exploiting the wealth of languages one masters to make sense of a text in an 'unknown' language.
3. Using international words.
4. Mediating/making communication possible beyond linguistic barriers.
5. Using all linguistic or paralinguistic features to enable effective communication.

Thus, the notion of language competence has been rethought, restructured and recontextualised, becoming 'plurilingual and pluricultural competence' (CEFR 2001, 135), including multiplicity and recurrence at all levels, seemingly as a fractal, where the whole contains every part and every part contains the image of the whole object.

Such a dynamic vision of the language implies a great deal of initiative and agency from the language learners/users, who are in fact defined by the CEFR as 'social agent[s]' (p. 9). These social agents are expected to be fully involved in their own learning process and to actively participate in it, thus developing awareness and consequently autonomy. In order to help them in this process of (self-)discovery and of construction of competence, another tool has been conceived by the Council of Europe, the European Language Portfolio (ELP),[3] which supports language learners/users in their own journey towards awareness, autonomy and eventually construction of plurilingual competence. The ELP particularly provides space for all languages, including HLs, but also dialects and language variations, which have been learned at some point, whether formally or not.

Why then is the ELP still not extensively known and used, and why is the CEFR's main impact on standard definition? Why is the notion of plurilingualism, which appears to be so much in tune with today's global village, and in particular with such a linguistically and culturally diverse country as Canada, not really openly – even institutionally – supported? Above all, why is language diversity still not seen as an individual and social asset whatever combination of languages individuals may have?

I will try to answer these questions by presenting and discussing some major obstacles to the paradigm shift represented by plurilingualism. To pursue this aim, I will provide a historical overview first and then question the individual and social levels of the issue.

Plurilingualism versus the myth of language pureness

Plurilingualism: an effect of globalisation?

The widespread reductionist and nationalistic perspective towards language we are so familiar with contrasts with several realities witnessed in the world over the centuries and in different geographical areas. Despite the fact that plurilingualism appears as a fundamental trait of our world characterised by mobility and by the presence of minorities, migrant workers and refugees, it is not a new phenomenon: the identity of the old continent has been plurilingual for centuries (Krumm 2003, 41), and in several other areas of the planet plurilingualism has been, and still is, a distinctive societal characteristic (Canagarajah and Lyinage 2012).

In the Western world, the Hellenistic and Roman empires were not really concerned with imposing a single, standardised language. Language was not seen as the symbol of the nation, but rather as a common means for communicating, writing and creating. The universalistic ideal of Alexander the Great was at the basis of the birth and diffusion of Hellenistic κοινή (koiné), a *lingua franca* of the Mediterranean able to merge and express different cultures. This koiné was not a straightjacket of coded political imposition, but rather a melting pot of different linguistic and cultural contributions. It was also the vehicle for integrating different ideas and for the diffusion of a wealth of philosophical schools.

In Roman society, standard classical Latin used by scholars – the official language of the empire and the only written language – always coexisted with vulgar, or everyday, Latin, the unofficial second language of the empire. This language was composed of several languages and dialects, and reflected a wealth of local cultures. Multilingualism and multiculturalism also characterised much of the Middle Ages and the Renaissance. The elite of Europe were in fact multilingual and multicultural as they needed to exchange and collaborate despite their linguistic diversity. This very mobile elite saw acquisition of another language as normal. The common, supranational language, the Latin of the Church, was reserved for academia, law, religion and political treaties, but commercial and business-orientated exchanges were conducted in different languages. Several artistic and literary forms were also quite mobile and interrelated beyond linguistic barriers. Furthermore, the majority of the population, even if fundamentally monolingual, situated themselves along continua of language groups and were able to understand other vernacular languages of their neighbouring villages despite linguistic differences (Wright 2000, 2001).

Three key phenomena contributed to fundamentally changing this landscape, setting the first basis for later linguistic conceptions (and misconceptions): the consolidation of national kingdoms, the reformation of the church and the invention of printing. The shaping of national identities, seen as a means for exercising power away from the Vatican, implied the need for a standardised language for translating the Bible, and consequently grammars and other norm-defining books started to be published (Ruiz Vieytez 2001).

This movement reached its highest point in the nineteenth century with the final definition of nation-states and their nationalistic ideology. As nation-states systematically attempted to assimilate minorities and minority languages, they played a fundamental role in the creation of the monolingual myth (Edwards 2004, 5), that is, the idea that one language is the ordinary situation of individuals and nations. The inevitable consequence of this relatively recent historical phenomenon is 'the establishment of an ethnically exclusive and culturally and linguistically homogeneous nation-state' (May 2008, 6). In fact, the ideology permeating the nation-state, political nationalism, requires speaking a common language as well as complete congruence between the boundaries of political and national identity.

With the myth of 'one state – one language' consolidated, the nation was seen as a unified ethnocultural and ethnolinguistic group (Singh 1998), despite the fact that most nations witnessed the presence of regional languages or languages of minority groups. Furthermore, the ideology of the nation-state and its view on languages was a pivotal feature of colonisation, as the monolingual myth was perpetuated in the colonies (Edwards 2004, 5).

The birth of Saussurian linguistics reinforced the vision of 'langue' as separate from 'parole', that is, its users. Later, Chomsky's theory based on the possibility of separating competence and performance further reinforced this dualism. But, as Makoni and Pennicook (2007) argue, the concepts of 'language' and of discrete 'languages' are products of Western imagination. They are historically situated Western inventions and not natural objects. Scholarly discourse on languages, together with its metalanguage, further reinforced the process of reification and actually invented what it was claiming to study. This process and the simplistic vision of the 'linguistic' world that it implied lasted well beyond the golden age of the nation-states, setting the basis of the common vision of language speaking and language learning we are still facing today. (Carrasco and Piccardo 2009; Crystal 2011). Even the bilingual or multilingual states were thus conceived as an addition of linguistically defined areas and their citizens.

Considering the shift that nation-states imposed on thought, culture and world vision, it is not surprising that the cosmopolitan attitude, which had been favoured by the Romans in the context of their tolerance towards ethnic and cultural diversities and by the development of philosophy, was very much pushed to the background. Yet, this attitude continued to exist: a 'cosmopolitan lineage' (Hansen 2011, 22) can be traced in the history of thought and culture throughout the centuries in the Western world and beyond, despite the persistent influence of the nation-states and their linguistic policies. Cosmopolitanism implies much more than tolerance of difference. It is real openness to and interest in other peoples' perspectives, in different tastes and customs, seen as indices of new views and visions characterising human nature; it is the capacity that humans have not only to build barriers but to open doors (Hansen 2011, 24–25). The cosmopolitan idea is naturally linked to openness to other languages, exactly as it is to openness to other cultures (Gadamer 1989). Nowadays, multilingualism remains the norm on a global scale and permeates even the apparent homogeneity of monolingual states.

Plurlingualism: good, bad or simply invisible

The myth of homogeneity and pureness, of unified ethnolinguistic cultures, extends from the social to the individual level. The 'monolingual disposition' (Gogolin 1994) that permeates our *Weltanschauung* prevents us to fully perceive the variability of language in each individual, including the so-called 'monolinguals'. Chomsky's 'ideal speaker-listener, in a completely homogeneous speech community, who knows its language perfectly' (1965, 3), does not really exist, as language itself is a dynamic and ever changing phenomenon, incompatible with the idea of perfection and stability. Individuals live in their own mother tongue in several languages, as Wandruszka articulated many years ago (1979). In fact, human languages are unique, complex, flexible dynamic 'polysystems' (Wandruszka 1979, 39); they are open systems, which constantly change internally as well as externally. We think that the notion of 'monolingual individual' needs to be revisited in the same way as the notion of language has started to be: monolinguals do not exist; they are at least as invented as languages are. Each individual has a specific linguistic profile which is not static but which modulates itself according to contexts, interlocutors, communicative aims, and also to the specific feelings and emotions of the language users, his/her own greater or lesser awareness of word origins, semantic implications, metaphorical connotations, paralinguistic features, and so on – not to mention the fact that receptive and productive skills are unbalanced even in what is generally referred to as 'the mother tongue(s)'. Such variety makes it difficult to define what our own personal language is. 'No matter how monolingual we consider ourselves to be, we are fundamentally plurilingual, albeit unconsciously so. No matter how *standard* and *pure* we consider each language, it is inevitable that all languages are ensembles of different elements in a dynamic and constantly changing relationship' (Piccardo 2013, 605).

The issue is precisely our 'monolingual disposition' (Gogolin 1994), which has grown throughout the centuries to the extent that it prevents people from noticing and acknowledging the different expressions of plurilingualism. This 'disposition' was so pervasive even in the 20th century that 'for decades bilingual speakers were largely regarded as linguistic exceptions rather than as the rule. Emphasis in the language lab and in the classroom was placed on seeking out and eliminating the damaging cognitive influence of being bilingual' (Franceschini 2009, 31). From the early 19th century until approximately 1960, in fact, educational researchers considered bilingualism as having a detrimental effect on intelligence, predicting that the intellectual and spiritual growth of a bilingual child would be not doubled but halved (Laurie 1890, 15; cited in Baker 1988, 9). In general, the superiority of monolinguals over bilinguals was unquestioned, as shown by several reviews (Darcy 1953, 1963; Jensen 1962, Peal and Lambert 1962). After the turn of the century, research seemed to confirm that 'a facility in two languages reduces the amount of room or power available for other intellectual pursuits' (Baker 1988, 10), a view that, according to the author, was still very common at the time he wrote his book. The publication of Peal and Lambert's research (1962) is considered a starting point not only in acknowledging the beneficial effects of bilingualism, but also in overcoming the narrow concept of IQ and opening to the wider concept of cognitive abilities (Lambert 1962, 16). Baker points out how Peal and Lambert's conclusions about assets of bilingualism (i.e. 1) Greater mental flexibility; 2) The ability to think more abstractly and independently of words resulting in superiority in concept formation; 3) A more enriched bicultural environment benefitting IQ; 4) Positive transfer between languages benefitting verbal IQ; p. 17) anticipated later research. Again as in the case of Wandruszka, we are faced with a visionary position, which would be confirmed several years later by research and would need even more time to be widely accepted. In fact, the monolingual disposition to which we referred earlier still prevents many people from considering plurilingualism as a personal asset and multilingualism as an essential feature of our contemporary society.

Plurilingualism or a collection of monolingualisms

This unawareness, lack of consideration and sometimes even contempt of plurilingualism, which has built up over time, sits alongside deep change in the linguistic landscape due to the complexification of social spaces and personal trajectories. The wealth of languages and cultures mentioned earlier in relation to the Canadian situation as a global phenomenon, and the policies for facing such changes, still very vary widely from one country to the next, including Europe, despite the efforts of the Council of Europe to promote and foster plurilingualism. The situation is more delicate in countries whose official languages are strong international ones, but it is also dependent on the attitudes towards cultural diversity that each country adopts. These attitudes can be situated along a continuum, going from assimilation to identification and isolation of minorities and ethnic communities. At the risk of generalising, we can say that the first attitude more accurately characterises the Francophone world, and the second the English-speaking countries. The reasons are again to be found in the historical policies of France and the United Kingdom and their respective underlying notions of state and of its role. This fundamental difference was particularly visible in the colonisation and subsequent decolonisation process and in its socio-political consequences (Benrabah 2009). Even if this can appear as a paradox, both extremes of the continuum are equally dangerous from a plurilingual perspective. While at one end of the coninuum, assimilation is clearly opposing plurilingual values and ideals, at the opposite end the danger is more subtle: the idea of community certainly implies notions such as respect and support, but 'community-ism' – that is, the fact of keeping well identified communities living side by side (*communautarisme*, as the phenomenon is called in France) – implies a high risk of ghettoisation, of creating 'enclaves,' both linguistic and cultural, which hardly communicate with each other beyond the practical, functional level. As far as languages are concerned, this second scenario is in line with what the CEFR refers to as 'multilingual societies'

(2001, 4), where different languages and cultures live side by side without significant interaction.

This situation is quite common in Canada, and is actually not restricted to the English-speaking area of the country. HLs are often confined to the respective communities, and preserved and transmitted at various degrees according to the value that each community attributes to language and culture vitalisation. In any case, the idea of multilingual societies composed of different well-defined communities reproduces on a different scale – and in a sense multiplies – the monolingual definition of nation-states explained above, thus representing an obstacle to the development of a plurilingual society.

A paradigm shift: the plurilingual/pluricultural perspective

Plurilingualism as philosophy

It is evident from the previous discussion that adopting a plurilingual perspective is not an easy step as it implies a deep change both at the level of the individual and at the level of the society. The simple existence of a wealth of languages and cultures is not *per se* a guarantee that some form of plurilingualism is being implemented; on the contrary, considering the conceptual and historical importance attributed to pureness, to the norm and to categorisation in all domains, all phenomena of hybridity, of mixing, of syncretism are considered with a suspicious or, worse, with a despising attitude. What the CEFR advocates is not therefore a straightforward change: it is a real paradigm shift which reveals itself as challenging to implement.

As we saw above, in a plurilingual perspective the different languages an individual comes into contact with during his/her language trajectory are not kept in separate mental compartments, but interrelate and interact to allow a larger communicative competence (CEFR 2001, 4). This idea is aptly exemplified:

> For instance, partners may switch from one language or dialect to another, exploiting the ability of each to express themselves in one language and to understand the other; or a person may call upon the knowledge of a number of languages to make sense of a text, written or even spoken, in a previously 'unknown' language, recognising words from a common international store in a new guise. Those with some knowledge, even slight, may use it to help those with none to communicate by mediating between individuals with no common language. In

the absence of a mediator, such individuals may nevertheless achieve some degree of communication by bringing the whole of their linguistic equipment into play, experimenting with alternative forms of expression in different languages or dialects, exploiting paralinguistics (mime, gesture, facial expression, etc.) and radically simplifying their use of language.' (CEFR 2001, 4–5)

Stressing a constant movement from one language to the other, and from one partial competence to the other, embracing dialects, paralinguistics and all forms of linguistic creativity and *métissage*, this vision is fundamentally different from any traditional vision of language learning and linguistic competence, which insists on the separation of languages and pureness, but is consistent with practices that are actually being observed in multilingual environments (Garcia 2009a, 304–5), where individuals come to terms with their language diversity by using all possible ways of conveying a message. It is also consistent with the way in which the brain of a plurilingual individual works where connectionist models are most frequently used (Rumelhart and McClelland 1986; Antonietti 1996), and where languages are constantly interacting and even somehow competing when it comes to producing utterances (Bialystok 2001). The plurilingual vision stresses movement and flexible construction, dynamic development and mediation, thus proving coherent with two key concepts that are becoming increasingly central to language acquisition research and discourse: languaging and translanguaging.

'Languaging' refers to 'the fluid ways in which languages are used in the twenty-first century' (Garcia 2009a, 22–3), more specifically to 'the process of making meaning and shaping knowledge and experience through language' (Swain 2006, 98). 'Translanguaging' refers to 'the act performed by bilinguals of accessing different features of various modes of what are described as autonomous languages, in order to maximise communicative potential' (Garcia 2009b, 128). Languaging and translanguaging are complementary. Languaging implies reflection as it stresses the ability of constructing linguistic knowledge through, and by means of, the very act of producing language; translanguaging extends it to plurality as it is the process through which the brain accesses different linguistic features to maximise communication, to create a meaningful tapestry of words and sentences. The importance of constructing and shaping knowledge, and specifically linguistic knowledge, in a mediated form is central to both processes and provides further support to the paradigm shift advocated by plurilingualism. This mediation exists both at the level of the individual, who is mediating between his/her already existing knowledge and the new input in order to make sense of new acquisitions, and at the social level where individuals use mediation to co-construct knowledge (Piccardo 2012b). What should be noticed here is again the normality and inevitability of languaging and translanguaging: as Swain and Garcia point out, the two processes take place in any case, even when they are not supported or when they are 'forbidden'. But once again the question is to see to what extent language users are aware that they are languaging and/or translanguaging. Exactly as we saw earlier with reference to plurilingual competence, many people are unaware of these processes and are therefore unable to capitalise on them, as we will also see later.

Languages are not interchangeable

The CEFR does not limit itself to seeing plurilingualism as a pure linguistic phenomenon completely disconnected from any cultural dimension, but connects it from the beginning with the cultural dimension. Plurilingualism and pluriculturalism go hand in hand, in a complex configuration, as cultures are also 'composita' – much as languages are. They also share with languages the same dynamic nature. But in stressing the link between languages and cultures, and the interactive and integrated configuration of individuals' pluricultural competence, the CEFR opens a space for reconsidering an aspect that has been neglected or controversial in SLA research: the link between the structure of a language and the culture(s) it conveys. This link has been the basis of linguistic relativity theory, according to which the structure of a language affects the ways in which speakers of that language conceptualise the world, i.e. their *Weltanschauung*, and/or influences their cognitive processes. This principle was formulated and popularised by scholars in the first half of the 20th century and is popularly known as the 'Sapir-Whorf hypothesis' (Hoijer 1954). Researchers in linguistic relativity examine the interface between cognition, language and culture, and describe the degree and kind of interrelatedness or influence (Niemeier and Dirven 2000; Kramsch 2004). Unfortunately, after the first definitions by Boas and then by Sapir and Whorf, the hypothesis continued to be deeply reworked to introduce the notion of 'linguistic determinism' as opposed to 'linguistic relativity' (Brown 1958). Whereas the latter acknowledges that the structure of a language affects its speakers' world view and influences their cognitive processes, the former considers that language entirely determines the range of possible cognitive processes of an individual. This has cast a shadow over the whole area of study, preventing an objective analysis for a long time. Pavlenko (2011, 19) shows how the work of Brown and his pupil Lenneberg have considerably deviated from the concepts presented by Sapir and Whorf and before them by Boas, who 'argued that cultures are reflected in the language of their speakers [even though] humans [...] are unaware of the ways in which their languages classify experience differently because of the automatic nature of language use' (Pavlenko 2011, 15). Even though the original theory does not openly express a multilingual disposition, we may hypothesise that it was, in a sense, taken for granted as linked as it certainly is to the cosmopolitan vision of the German Enlightment (*Aufklärung*). Only later scholars began to see openness to other languages as keys to acquiring new visions of the world, thus enriching and enlarging *Bildung*[4] into linguistic determinism: separation of languages appears critical in a deterministic vision, whereas the coexistence – and possible synergies – of different world-views is fully compatible with linguistic relativity.

The monolingual myth and the deeply rooted monolingual mindset of the Western world and academia did not allow for an open reception of ideas of openness and linguistic relativity. It has only been recently that an interest in the real message of Sapir and Whorf could be observed (Pavlenko 2011, 23), and it is still a work in progress to pair the renewed interest in these theories with the emerging scientific area of research represented by the study of multilingual phenomena (Athanasopoulos 2011).

In a plurilingual perspective, the study of different languages goes beyond the functional-communicative vision. It overcomes the idea that everything can be thoroughly translated into a different language, that languages are only different ways of saying exactly the same thing. Connotation becomes as strong as – if not more than – denotation as the learner/user comes to terms with the idea of embracing the new language on one side and maintaining the possibility of making a step back, of seeing things from a distance, on the other.

In such a perspective, all aspects of the language, not just the semantic one, acquire a specific, well-defined, personal meaning and a powerful connotation. Let us consider some examples to clarify this point.

In grammar, the passive includes two forms in English and only one in French or in Italian. The sentence 'Mary offered a book to John' becomes in the passive either 'A book was offered to John by Mary' (less frequent), or 'John was offered a book by Mary' (more frequent). In French or in Italian only the former is possible, thus, in these languages, the possibility for the person – in this case John – to maintain the grammatically central place in the sentence, to be the grammatical subject even if he receives the action of the verb instead of accomplishing it, does not exist. The passive marks the loss of agency in the subject more strongly than in English. In French, in some specific cases, another form assigns a grammatically central place to the subject of a passive action. I am referring for example to expressions such as 'Jean s'est fait voler son porte-monnaie'. Interestingly, the addition of 's'est fait' bears no agency meaning for a French speaker (Jean is still perceived as the victim of the theft), whereas it implies a real shift when read/heard by an Italian speaker, who cannot avoid perceiving an agency connotation, where Jean would be in a sense responsible for being the victim of a theft.

In vocabulary, for example, different types of small fruit all contain the word 'berry' in English, or 'Beeren' in German, whereas each of them has an entirely different name in other languages (like French or Italian). In the first case the meaning is certainly more transparent and visually orientated, we may not know exactly what each fruit looks like but we know that, if the word berry/Beeren is there, they are small fruits growing on bushes or small plants. In another case, different verbs can convey very specific, and some-times very different, meanings through a simple change in the prefix (for instance, in German, *schlafen/verschlafen/sich ausschlafen*, where the second means to sleep too long, and the third means to sleep really well so that you are completely rested), another language may need an entire sentence to ex-press precisely the same meaning.

In pragmatics, not addressing unknown people with greetings and leave-taking expressions in an elevator, which is acceptable in North America, is perceived as impolite by a French or an Italian person. Along the same lines, the restricted possibility of modulating discourse by using either diminu-tive forms (in Italian) or the addition of 'petit' in French makes the English discourse sound sometimes too harsh or too direct to French and Italian listeners.

In phonetics, the different frequency bands[5] – that is, the different ranges of sound frequencies used by each language – may have a great impact on other speakers' perception and therefore of interpretation of messages and speakers' attitude and intentions. The volume is also culturally and lin-guistically specific, which can explain for instance why English and French speakers may perceive Italians as often shouting.

All these little examples aim to demonstrate the relationship between lin-guistic forms and related cultures, between different ways of describing the world and dealing with making meaning of it through language. But they are not 'little' if seen as examples of linguistic relativity. Kramsch warns us against 'the traditional distrust of words, images, and other symbolic forms' (Kramsch 2009, 44) that we can find everywhere, even in traditional folk sayings, and reminds us that 'linguistic structures are seen as separate from psychic states, words as distinct from thoughts, form as quite different from emotion. These [traditional folk sayings] and other ways of scorning "mere" words and of minimising their effects have led to a misunderstanding of the relation of language and thought' (ibid.). Drawing upon what the anthropologist Deacon says (1997), Kramsch underlines how important symbolic forms such as words are: 'For we can apprehend ourselves and others only through the symbolic forms we have created' (ibid.).

In a plurilingual perspective, the differences between languages and symbolic ways in which languages codify the world are not neglected; on the contrary they represent a starting point for developing awareness amongst learners, a space of liberty and creativity that helps them cope with the tension between the conventional meaning of the new terms and their own subjective and even imaginary meaning. In this respect, HLs are called upon to play an important role as they provide a secure basis for new explorations.

Language awareness

Language and communication awareness are defined by the CEFR as:

> Sensitivity to language and language use [which] enables new experience to be assimilated into an ordered framework and welcomed as an enrichment . . . [T]he associated new language may then be more readily learnt and used, rather than resisted as a threat to the learner's already established linguistic system, which is often believed to be normal and 'natural'. (CEFR 2001, 107)

Language awareness begets real openness to 'other', as a way of questioning one's own beliefs and frameworks.

The notion of language awareness is pivotal in plurilingualism and its implementation. Language awareness in a plurilingual perspective is not limited though to an awareness of linguistic forms of each language taken in isolation, but is also an awareness of similarities and differences between languages, cultures and the ways in which different languages express and symbolically represent a variety of cultures. Through awareness, both linguistic and cultural, the still dominant linear vision of language learning is being questioned, i.e. that learning a new language is putting new labels onto real world objects, events and ideas that exist independently from their linguistic denotation, that: 'the language is . . . a transparent conduit for the practice of conventional meaning-making and the expression of standard meaning' (Kramsch 2009, 28). What is also being questioned is the fact that the presence of at least one developed language system represented by the first language/L1 (if not more in the case of an already plurilingual trajectory of the learner) may be irrelevant, or even detrimental, to the acquisition of a new language. At last, a space between the two languages and cultures is opened, where each individual can go back and forth, as many times as s/he wants, to learn something different each time and to make sense of the context:

> Knowledge, awareness and understanding of the relation (similarities and distinctive differences) between the 'world of origin' and the 'world of the target community' produce an intercultural awareness. It is, of course, important to note that intercultural awareness includes an awareness of regional and social diversity in both worlds. It is also enriched by awareness of a wider range of cultures than those carried by the learner's L1 and L2. This wider awareness helps to place both in context. In addition to objective knowledge, intercultural awareness covers an awareness of how each community appears from the perspective of the other, often in the form of national stereotypes. (CEFR 2001, 103)

Through language and intercultural awareness, instead of seeking meaning apart from context, learners seek meaning as embedded in, and dependent on, the context. They are potentially able to see beyond the conventional meanings of the monolingual vision of the world and can distinguish between 'glossodiversity' and 'semiodiversity' (Halliday 2002). In other words, they understand that diversity of languages and diversity of meanings are not the same thing and are not interchangeable. Valuing semiodiversity protects language relativity. Using and occupying the space in-between is not a straightforward process: 'making other people's words one's own while retaining their 'otherness' requires distance, reflexivity, irony and a certain dose of humour' (Kramsch 2009, 115). As the philosopher Derrida reminds us, there is not just one appropriate way of realising speech acts or one fixed meaning (Derrida 1972a; 1988). His deconstruction is all but destruction: 'It is simply a question of being alert to the implications, to the historical sedimentation of the language we use' (Derrida 1972b, 271). In this space and openness between languages and cultures, the possibility exists for the esthetic appreciation of language, for exploring possible and invented meanings, for play, for creativity.

In a plurilingual vision, these possibilities are potentially multiplied as a learner allows him/herself to venture into different paths which are not only shaped around one centre but are polycentric and multidirectional. Awareness of languages represents Ariadne's thread that helps individuals navigate the labyrinth of paths. '[M]ultilingual subjects, rather than being condemned to some original division against themselves, can draw strength from the flexibility and versatility afforded by their various languages' (Kramsch 2009, 195).

Heritage languages and plurilingualism: opening perspectives

Acknowledging the complexification of our globalised society, Kramsch proposes to replace her notion of 'third place' with the notion of 'symbolic competence' (Kramsch 1993, 200), which she defines as 'an ability that is both theoretical and practical, and that emerges from the need to find appropriate subject positions within and across the languages at hand' (ibid.). The plurilingual and pluricultural perspective opens doors to developing such symbolic competence as it offers a wealth of possibilities to individuals who navigate different languages and cultures.

The notion of plurilingualism is certainly one of the most innovative ideas of the CEFR and is potentially able to favour a paradigm shift in language education and beyond. As stated at the beginning of the chapter, Canada's linguistic diversity appears to be the perfect context for the implementation of a plurilingual agenda aimed at acknowledging the presence and the potential of heritage and aboriginal languages, and eventually at reconsidering scope and practice of language education.

Historically speaking, Canada is moving from what Stuart Hall called 'modernist globalisation' (1997) – which characterised colonisation and implied hierarchical relationships between different communities where 'the dominant communities assumed the superiority of their cultural and social systems, even that of their language, and attempted to spread their influence at the cost of local traditions' (Canagarajah 2006, 230) – to postmodern globalisation, characterised by hybridity and complexity, and by enhanced interaction and flow between communities and their languages and cultures. Even in the so-called dominant language, the ability to navigate between different varieties and to negotiate communication within different contexts and conditions becomes crucial. The recognition that dominant languages share the nature of what we earlier referred to as 'composita' has become increasingly evident and is supported by several scholars, even those in opposition to widespread normative discourse. As a result, the need to focus on language awareness has become more urgent.

As we have seen, language awareness is at the core of plurilingualism. The ability to navigate linguistic trajectories and to acquire the capacity to use different languages for the creation of different symbolic systems (Kramsch 2009, 188) cannot be reached without the reflexive involvement of the language user; without the development of a form of Socratic irony, able to help the individual remain both within and outside the new languages and cultures with which s/he is faced. But in the case of HLs, another awareness is also crucial: awareness of possessing an asset, a potential, a capital.

Now, as Bourdieu (1991) explained, the notion of capital, including that of linguistic capital, is linked to the idea of power: not all languages are equal when it comes to measuring the value of linguistic capital. Dominant languages' power and value are in a direct relationship; thus HLs as well as aboriginal languages (possibly in an even more acute way) can suffer from this 'banking' metaphor of language capital value. Now, if we stay with that metaphor, the HLs see their value diminished when they are not recognised at all: it is like coming to a foreign country with a considerable amount of money in a different currency and being obliged to accept an extremely low exchange rate in the local currency, if any, in both cases ending up by being severely/dangerously impoverished.

Whereas the idea that bilingualism or plurilingualism have a detrimental effect on cognition has mostly been overcome, and the plurality and diversity of languages are starting at least in principle to be seen in a positive way, as a good byproduct of our globalised society, the predominant view of knowledge of languages is still turned towards a banking model where languages would cumulate in the same way as other forms of investment. Knowledge of several languages would mean acquisition of capital and power, and in this perspective certain languages are more profitable than others. This vision is linked though to the issue of what Halliday (2002) calls 'glossodiversity'; that is, using different languages to say the same things. This is like the fast-food chain McDonald's idea of slightly changing their menu in order to make it more 'contextualised' or contextually appropriate, but essentially serving the same standardised food all over the world. The vision that emphasises functional use of the language, the idea that languages have mainly practical communicative goals for helping people dealing with everyday aspects of life, and that words are merely different labels for the same objects and concepts, is in opposition to the idea of language as symbolic competence.

In our globalised societies, as mentioned earlier, there is great risk – a risk of the folklorisation of HLs; a risk of community-ism, of creating well defined, non-threatening spaces where these languages would continue to live, maybe for a couple for generations, before being irreversibly diluted in the official languages, the languages of schooling, the language of the workplace – the dominant languages. With HLs, we risk seeing something happening that is similar to what we have unfortunately seen with heritage cultures, which sometimes survive only in an invented, folkloric form, such as in the mythos of a name or the menu of a restaurant.

The paradigm shift represented by plurilingualism indicates a possible path for avoiding this risk. Adopting the plurilingual vision that the CEFR proposes would enhance awareness of the real value of language diversity; it would mean understanding that knowledge of different languages – any language – has a deeper and more subtle value than the utilitarian one proposed by the banking metaphor, one which touches at identity, at the history of each individual and at the world vision that each language conveys. It would eventually bring a new attitude towards the language phenomenon as a whole, from awareness of own plurilingualism and language relativity to demystification of monolingualism and the ideal of the native speaker.

It is clear that HLs could greatly benefit from the paradigm shift represented by the notion of plurilingualism included in the CEFR and that Canada, with its unique language and cultural diversity, would benefit from realising the potential of such notion for its sociopolitical context. Why then, we should ask, does this important notion remain in the background of all official discourse concerning the CEFR? What are the pitfalls and the problems? Why are there so many obstacles to the adoption of a plurilingual vision?

Towards a new vision: a space for heritage languages

The expression 'paradigm shift' has been used deliberately here when referring to plurilingualism. As the CEFR underlines:

> From this perspective, the aim of language education is profoundly modified. It is no longer seen as simply to achieve 'mastery' of one or two, or even three languages, each taken in isolation, with the 'ideal native speaker' as the ultimate model. Instead, the aim is to develop a linguistic repertory, in which all linguistic abilities have a place. (CEFR 2001, 5)

In everyday class practice, the notion of pureness and perfection is still the dominant one. This implies preserving the language class as pure and un-contaminated as possible, while every 'other' language and culture is seen as some dirty pair of shoes that people would take off when entering some-body's house. A plurilingual vision not only allows contamination but it val-ues and fosters it. In such a vision the concept of language is expanded from the language of the home to that of the different communities with which any individual has come into contact, to the language of the school and of the different surrounding socio-economic contexts. Languages are seen as being in a dynamic relationship and being learnt from a comparative per-spective. We used a spatial metaphor, that of a path between the languages that an individual learns and uses. From a plurilingual perspective we would enlarge this metaphor to see the different paths as nonlinear, not all depart-ing from the same centre, traditionally identified with the first language, but as a weft of different paths, sometimes even a maze, connecting the different languages, be they heritage, school, second or foreign languages, in several, sometimes unexpected, ways. The two notions of languaging and translan-guaging discussed earlier deploy all their potential provided that learners are supported in their metacognitive process, in their reflective journey. It is a constant movement in and out: done with and through the language, and observing and reflecting on what has been done.

From this perspective, the concept of partial competences presented by the CEFR appears very appropriate, as the learner constructs and refines his/her own languages through explorations of the different paths. Partial competences can for instance be linguistic in nature or general, can refer to a specific mode, like production or reception, or to a particular nuance of language use. It is clear that they carry more than a utilitarian value, one for example that focuses on what is most needed in a certain job, and that they acquire a more general synergic and structuring sense.

In the same way, the notion of imbalance that the CEFR evokes when it comes to the description of plurilingualism (CEFR 2001, 133) acquires all its meaning and loses its negative connotation (Piccardo and Puozzo 2012); it is in fact perfectly compatible, even unavoidable, in the construction of (par-tial) competences, in the languaging and translanguaging process.

Opening up all these barriers, showing that languages, and parts of them, are in a constantly changing relationship both at the individual and at the social level, breaking down rooted and long-lasting myths such as those of native speakers, neat definitions of the object language, separation of lan-guages and the power of the norm, interchangeability of languages when it comes to expressing meaning, constitutes a real paradigm shift, seemingly a 'revolution' in the field of second-language acquisition. This can be an explanation for resistance to embracing a plurilingual vision. But there is more: as we have seen, language has a symbolic value, but further, language is a symbolic system (Kramsch 2009, 6), which is inseparable from a symbolic power (Bourdieu 1991) when used.

Learning new languages means coping with their symbolic nature. Plurilinguals have to come to terms with a wealth of different symbolic systems and symbolic powers. This symbolic dimension of the language is what constitutes the basis for identity construction. The different information and symbolic meanings that individuals accumulate through mind and body experience constitute a sort of map that eventually informs the world view of each of those individuals and structures their identity. What learners of a new language lack is that map, something that can be seen as puzzling, but which can also be seen as a new start, opening up the possibility of exploring potential worlds and constructing new identities. It is precisely in this symbolic dimension that HLs have a role to play and in turn can find their space.

REFERENCES

Alberta Education. (2010). *Making a Difference: Meeting Diverse Learning Needs with Differentiated Instruction*. http://education.alberta.ca/teachers/resources/cross/making-a-difference.aspx.

Antonietti A. (1996). *Il luogo della mente*. Milano: Franco Angeli Editore.

Athanasopoulos, P. (2011). 'Cognitive Restructuring in Bilingualism'. In A. Pavlenko, ed., *Thinking and Speaking in Two Languages*. Clevedon: Multilingual Matters. 29–65.

Baker, C. (1988) *Key Issues in Bilingualism and Bilingual Education*. Clevedon: Multilingual Matters.

Bärenfänger, O. and **Tschirner, E.** (2008). 'Language Educational Policy and Language Learning Quality Management: The Common European Framework of Reference'. *Foreign Language Annals* 41 (1), 81–100.

Baumann, Z. (2007). *Liquid Times: Living in an Age of Uncertainty*. Cambridge, MA: Polity.

Beacco, J-C. (2005). 'Langues et répertoire de langues: le plurilinguisme comme 'manière d'être' en Europe. Étude de référence, Division des politiques linguistiques'. Strasbourg: Éditions du Conseil de l'Europe.

Beacco, J.-C. and **Byram, M.** (2007). *From Linguistic Diversity to Plurilingual Education: Guide for the Development of Language Education Policies in Europe*, Strasbourg: Council of Europe Publishing. www.coe.int/t/dg4/linguistic/Publications_en.asp (retrieved July 2012).

Benrabah, M. (2009) *Devenir langue dominante mondiale: un défi pour l'arabe*. Genève: Librairie Droz.

Bialystok, E. (2001). *Bilingualism in Development: Language, Literacy and Cognition*, Cambridge: Cambridge University Press.

Bourdieu, P. (1991). *Language and Symbolic Power*. Cambridge, MA: Harvard University Press.

British Columbia Ministry of Education (2009). *English as a Second Language and Francisation: Langue seconde in the Conseil scolaire: Policy and Guidelines*. www.bced.gov.bc.ca/esl/policy/guidelines.pdf.

— (2010). *Curriculum of Additional Languages*. www.bced.gov.bc.ca/irp/pdfs/drafts/additional_languages_draft.pdf .

Brown, R. (1958). *Words and Things*. Glencoe, IL: The Free Press.

Brown, R. and Lenneberg, E. (1954). 'A Study in Language and Cognition'. *Journal of Abnormal and Social Psychology* 49, 454–62.

Byrnes, H. (2007a). 'Perspectives'. *The Modern Language Journal* 91 (4), 641–45.

— (2007b). 'Developing National Language Education Policies: Reflections on the CEFR'. *The Modern Language Journal* 91 (4), 679–85.

Canagarajah, S. (2006). 'Changing Communicative Needs, Revised Assessment Objectives: Testing English as an International Language'. *Language Assessment Quarterly* 3 (3), 229–42.

Canagarajah, S. and Liynage, I. (2012). 'Lessons from Pre-Colonial Multilingualism. In M. Martin-Jones, A. Blackledge and A. Creese, eds, *The Routledge Handbook of Multilingualism*, 49–65. New York, NY: Routledge.

Cantoni, G. (1997). Keeping Minority Languages Alive: The School's Responsibility. In J. Reyhner, ed., *Teaching Indigenous Languages* 1–9. Northern Arizona University Press.

Carrasco Perea, E. and Enrica Piccardo (2009). 'Plurilinguisme, cultures et identités: la construction du savoir-être chez l'enseignant'. *LIDIL* 39, 19–41.

Connelly, C. (2008). 'Marking Bodies: Inhabiting the Discursive Production of Outstanding "Canadian Education" within Globalization'. In D. Gérin-Lajoie, ed., *Educators' Discourses on Student Diversity in Canada: Context, Policy and Practice*, 163–82. Toronto: Canadian Scholar's Press Inc.

Cook, V. (2001). 'Using the First Language in the Classroom'. *Canadian Modern Language Review/La Revue canadienne des langues vivantes* 57 (3), 402–23.

Coste, D. (2010). 'Diversité des plurilinguismes et formes de l'éducation plurilingue et interculturelle'. *Les Cahiers de l'Acedle* 7 (1), 141–65.

— (2007). *Contextualising uses of the Common European Framework of Reference for Languages*, Paper presented at Council of Europe Policy Forum on use of the CEFR, Strasbourg.

Coste, D., Moore, D. and Zarate, G. (2009). 'Plurilingual and Pluricultural Competence' (with a Foreword and Complementary Bibliography French version originally published in 1997). *Studies towards a Common European Framework of Reference for Language Learning and Teaching*. Strasbourg: Council of Europe Publishing.

Council of Europe (2001). *Common European Framework of Reference for Languages: Learning, teaching, assessment*. Cambridge: Cambridge University Press.

Council of Europe (2005). 'Survey on the Use of the Common European Framework of Reference for Language (CEFR): Synthesis of Results'. www.coe.int/t/dg4/linguistic/Source/Surveyresults.pdf.

Council of Ministers of Education, Canada. (2010). 'Working with the Common European Framework of Reference for Language (CEFR) in the Canadian Context: Guide for policy-makers and curriculum designers'. www.cmec.ca/Programs/assessment/Documents/CEFR-canadian-context.pdf.

Crawford, J. (2000). At War With Diversity: US Language Policy in an Age of Anxiety. Clevedon: Multilingual Matters.

Crystal, D. (2000). Language Death. Cambridge: Cambridge University Press.

— (2011). 'From the World to the Word – and Back Again'. Plenary Lecture given to the CILT Primary Languages Show 'From the Word to the World', Liverpool, 4 March 2011. www.davidcrystal.com/DC_articles/Education27.pdf (retrieved July 2012).

Cummins, J. (2001). Negotiating Identities: Education for Empowerment in a Diverse Society (2nd ed.). Los Angeles, CA: California Association for Bilingual Education.

— (2007). 'Rethinking Monolingual Instructional Strategies in Multilingual Classrooms'. Canadian Journal of Applied Linguistics (CJAL)/Revue canadienne de linguistique appliquée (RCLA) 10 (2), 221–40.

Cummins, J., Bismilla, V., Chow, P., Cohen, S., Giampapa, F., Leoni, L., Snadhu, P. and Sastri, P. (2005). 'Affirming Identity in Multilingual Classrooms'. Educational Leadership 63 (1), 38–43.

Darcy. N.T. (1953). 'A Review of the Literature on the Effects of Bilingualism upon the Measurement of Intelligence'. Journal of Genetic psychology 82, 21–57.

— (1963). 'Bilingualism and the Measurement of Intelligence: Review of a Decade of Research'. Journal of Genetic Psychology 103, 259–82.

Deacon, T. (1997). The Symbolic Species. New York, NY: W. W. Norton.

Derrida, J. (1972a). 'La différance'. In J. Derrida. Marges de la philosophie, 1–29. Paris: Les éditions de minuit.

— (1972b). 'Discussion: Structure, Sign and Play in the Discourse of the Human Sciences'. In R. Macksey and E. Donate, eds, The Structuralist Controversy, 247–72. Baltimore: Johns Hopkins University Press.

— (1988). Limited, Inc. Evanston, IL: Northwestern University Press.

Edwards, V. (2004). Multilingualism in the English-speaking World. Oxford: Blackwell Publishing.

Flecha, R. (1999). 'New Educational Inequalities'. In M. Castells, R. Flecha, P. Freire, H. Giroux, D. Macedo and P. Willis, eds, Critical education in the new information age, 65–82. Lanham, MD: Rowman and Littlefield.

Fleming, M. and Little, D. (2010). 'Languages in and for Education: A Role for Portfolio Approaches?' Plurilingualism and Intercultural Education: Languages In and For Education. Strasbourg: Council of Europe, Language Policy Division.

Franceschini, R. (2009). 'The Genesis and Development of Research on Multilingualism: Perspectives for Future Research'. In L. Aronin, B. Hufeisen, eds, The Exploration of Multilingualism: Development of Research on L3, Multilingualism, and Multiple Language Acquisition, 27–62. Amsterdam/Philadelphia: John Benjamins.

Gadamer H-G. (1989). *Das Erbe Europas* (*The Heritage of Europe*). Frankfurt: Suhrkamp.

Gajo, L. and Mondada, L. (2000). *Interactions et acquisitions en contexte. Modes d'appropriation de compétences discursives plurilingues par de jeunes immigrés.* Fribourg: Editions universitaires.

Garcia, O. (2009a). *Bilingual Education in the 21st Century: A Global Perspective.* Malden, MA: Wiley-Blackwell.

— (2009b). 'Education, Multilingualism and Translanguaging in the 21st century'. in A.K. Mohanty, M. Panda, R. Phillipson and T. Skutnabb-Kangas, eds, *Multilingual Education for Social Justice: Globalising the local,* 128–46. New Delhi: Orient BlackSwan.

García, O., Skutnabb-Kangas, T. and Torres-Guzmán, M., eds (2006). *Imagining Multilingual Schools: Languages in Education and Globalisation.* Clevedon: Multilingual Matters.

Gogolin, I. (1994). *Der monolinguale Habitus der multilingualen Schule* (*The Monolingual Habitus of Multilingual School*). Münster: Waxmann.

Grosjean, F. (1982). *Life with Two Languages: An Introduction to Bilingualism.* Cambridge MA: Harvard University Press.

Hall, S. (1997). 'The Local and the Global: Globalization and Ethnicity'. In A.D. King, ed., *Culture, globalization and the world system,* 19–40. Minneapolis: University of Minnesota Press.

Halliday, M. (2002). 'Applied Linguistics as an Evolving Theme'. Plenary address to the Association Internationale de Linguistique Applique. Singapore, December.

Hansen, D. (2011). *The Teacher and the World. A Study of Cosmopolitanism as Education.* New York: Routledge.

Hoijer, H. (1954). 'The Sapir-Whorf Hypothesis'. In H. Hoijer, ed., *Language in Culture: Conference on the interrelations of Languages and Other Aspects of Culture,* 92–105. Chicago, IL: University of Chicago Press.

Hornberger, N. (2001). 'Multilingual Language Policies and the Continua of Biliteracy: An Ecological Approach'. *Language Policy* 1 (1), 27–51.

Hulstijn, J.H. (2011). 'Language Proficiency in Native and Nonnative Speakers: An Agenda for Research and Suggestions for Second-language Assessment'. *Language Assessment Quarterly* 8, 229–49.

Huver, E. and Springer, C. (2011). *L'évaluation en langues.* Paris: Didier.

Jensen, J.V. (1962). 'Effects of Childhood Bilingualism. *Elementary English* 39, 132–43.

Kramsch, C. (2004). 'Language, Thought, and Culture'. In A. Davies and C. Elder, eds, *Handbook of Applied Linguistics,* 235–61. Oxford: Oxford University Press.

— (2009). *The Multilingual Subject.* Oxford: Oxford University Press.

Krumm, H-J. (2003). 'Sprachenpolitik und Mehrsprachigkeit'. ('Linguistic policy and Plurilingualism'). In Hufeisen, B. and Neuner, G. *Mehrsprachigkeitskonzept – Tertiärsprachenlernen – Deutsch nach Englisch.* ('*The Plurilingualism Project: Tertiary Language Learning – German after English*'). Strasbourg : Council of Europe Publishing, 35–49.

Krumm, H-J. (2007). 'Profiles Instead of Levels: The CEFR and its (Ab)uses in the Context of Migration'. *The Modern Language Journal* 91 (4), 667–69.

Little, D. (2006). 'The Common European Framework of Reference for Languages: Content, Purpose, Origin, Reception and Impact'. *Language Teaching* 39, 167–90.

— (2007). 'The Common European Framework of Reference for Languages: Perspectives on the Making of Supranational Language Education Policy'. *The Modern Language Journal* 91 (4), 645–55.

— (2011). 'The Common European Framework of Reference for Languages: A Research agenda'. *Language Teaching* 44 (3), 381–93.

Lo Bianco, J. (2010). 'The Importance of Language Policies and Multilingualism for Cultural Diversity'. *International Social Science Journal* 61 (199), 37–67.

Lüdi, G. and Py, B. (1986). *Être bilingue*. Bern: Peter Lang.

Makoni, S. and Pennycook, A. (2007) *Disinventing and Reconstituting Languages*. Clevedon: Multilingual Matters.

May, S. (2008). *Language and Minority Rights: Ethnicity, Nationalism and the Politics of Language*. New York: Routledge.

Multilingual Schools: Languages in Education and Globalization. Clevedon: Multilingual Matters.

Niemeier, S. and Dirven, R. (2000). *Evidence of Linguistic Relativity*. Amsterdam: John Benjamins.

Ontario Ministry of Education (2005). *Many Roots, Many Voices: Supporting English Language Learners in Every Classroom*. www.edu.gov.on.ca/eng/document/manyroots/manyroots.pdf.

— (2006). *The Ontario Curriculum, The Kindergarten Program*. www.edu.gov.on.ca/eng/curriculum/elementary/kindercurrb.pdf.

Pavlenko, A. (2011). *Thinking and Speaking in Two Languages*. Clevedon: Multilingual Matters.

Peal, E. and Lambert. W.E. (1962). 'The Relation of Bilingualism to Intelligence'. *Psychological Monographs* 76 (27), 1–23.

Piccardo E. (2013). '(Re)conceptualiser l'enseignement des langues en contexte canadien: la formation des enseignants au Cadre européen commun de référence (CECR)'. *The Canadian Modern Language Review/La Revue Canadienne des langues* vivantes 69 (4), 386–414.

— (2013). 'Plurilingualism and Curriculum Design: Towards a Synergic Vision'. *TESOL Quarterly* 47 (3), 600–14.

— (forthcoming). 'Le CECR au Canada: entre réalité et représentation'. In V. Bigot, A. Bretegnier and M. Vasseur, eds, *Actes du colloque Vers le plurilinguisme: 20 ans après Université d'Angers*.

— (2012a). 'Multidimensionality of Assessment in the Common European Framework of References for languages'. (CEFR). *Les Cahiers de l'ILOB/OLBI Working Papers* 4, 37–54.

— (2012b). 'Médiation et apprentissage des langues: Pourquoi est-il temps de réfléchir à cette notion?' *Études de linguistique appliquée* 167, 285–94.

Piccardo, E. and Puozzo, I. (2012). 'La créativité pour développer la compétence plurilingue déséquilibrée'. In G. Alao, M. Derivry-Plard, E. Suzuki and S. Yun-Roger, eds, *Didactique plurilingue et pluriculturelle: L'acteur en contexte mondialisé*, 23–38. Paris: Editions des archives contemporains.

Piccardo E., Berchoud, M., Cignatta, T., Mentz, O. and Pamula, M. (2011). *Pathways through Assessing, Learning and Teaching in the CEFR.* Strasbourg: Council of Europe.

Rehorick, S. and Lafargue, C. (2005). 'The European Language Portfolio and its Potential for Canada: National Workshop Report on Proceedings'. Fredericton: University of New Brunswick, Second Language Education Centre. www.unbf.ca/L2/Resources/PDFs/ELP/UNB_ELP_fullreport.pdf.

Ruiz Vieytez, E.J. (2001). 'The Protection of Linguistic Minorities: A Historical Approach'. *IJMS: International Journal on Multicultural Societies.* 3 (1), 5–14. www.unesco.org/shs/ijms/vol3/issue1/art1 (retrieved July 2012).

Rumelhart, D.E., McClelland, J.L. and the PDP Research Group (1986). 'Parallel Distributed Processing: Explorations in the Microstructure of Cognition. Volume 1: Foundations'. Cambridge, MA: MIT Press.

Swain, M. (2006). 'Languaging, Agency and Collaboration in Advanced Language Proficiency'. In H. Byrnes, ed., *Advanced Language Learning: The Contribution of Halliday and Vygotsky,* 95–108. London: Continuum.

Taylor, L.K., Bernhard, J.K., Garg, S. and Cummins, J. (2008). 'Affirming Plural Belonging: Building on Students' Family-based Cultural and Linguistic Capital through Multiliteracies Pedagogy. *Journal of Early Childhood Literacy* 8 (3), 269–94.

Tschirner, E., ed. (2012). *Aligning Framworks of Reference in Language Testing. The ACTFL Proficiency Guidelines and the Common European Framework of Reference for languages.* Tübingen: Stauffenburg Verlag.

Vandergrift, L. (2006). *New Canadian Perspectives: Proposal for a Common Framework of Reference for Languages for Canada.* Ottawa: Canadian Heritage. http://elp.ecml.at/Home/IMPEL/Documents/Canada/ProposalofaCFRforCanada/tabid/122/language/fr-FR/Default.aspx.

— (2008). 'Commentary: A Common Framework for Languages in Canada: In Canadian Parents for French'. *The State of French-Second-Language Education in Canada* 10–11. Ottawa: CPF.

Wandruska, M. (1979). *Die Mehrsprachigkeit des Menschen. (The plurilingualism of the human being)* Stuttgart: Kohlhammer.

Wiley, T.G. and Lukes, M. (1996). 'English-only and Standard English ideologies in the US'. *TESOL Quarterly* 30 (3), 511–35.

Wright, S. (2000). *Community and Communication: The Role of Language in Nation Building and European Integration,* Clevedon: Multilingual Matters.

— (2001). 'Language and Power: Background to the Debate on Linguistic Rights'.*IJMS: International Journal on Multicultural Societies* 3 (1), 44–54. www.unesco.org/shs/ijms/vol3/issue1/art5 (retrieved July 2012).

NOTES

1   www.canada.gc.ca/.
2   Website of the European Centre for Modern Languages: www.ecml.at.

3   www.coe.int/t/dg4/education/elp/.

4   The German term *Bildung* encompasses and overcomes the concept of education, referring rather to the German tradition of self-cultivation. In this process of personal and
cultural growth, philosophy and education are linked. This results in harmonious development of the individual's mind and heart and of the individual identity within the
broader society.

5   'Frequency bands' are the oscillations that the human ear can theoretically capture. These range from frequencies of 16–16000 Hz and include an infinite number of
rhythms. As we get older our ears tend to settle into a habit, and remain efficient only in
those frequencies and rhythms that we use for our mother tongue. French mainly uses
frequencies from 1000 to 2000 Hz, while British English use frequencies that range from
2000 to 12000 Hz.

STRENGTHENING OUR TEACHER COMMUNITY: Consolidating a 'Signature Pedagogy' for the Teaching of Spanish as Heritage Language

María Luisa Parra (Harvard University)

Introduction

During the final session of a recent annual national conference on heritage languages (HLs), one of the attendees asked how a teacher could initiate a new course for heritage learners. The conference organisers – all of them experts in the field of HL instruction and research – offered her some advice: she should make sure there are enough heritage students to form a group, define her goals for the course and put together relevant course materials. They also mentioned several textbooks designed for heritage learners that could serve as support for the course curriculum. As a member of the audience, I suggested that she also seek financial and human resources within her institution and build upon others' support and experience.

As the teacher listened attentively to our answers, I thought about my own situation several years ago, when I had wished to start a new course for Spanish HL learners at my institution. My own experience and my conversations with other teachers had taught me that the question 'Where to start?' – which the others in the conference room and I had apparently answered quickly and with ease – was not, in fact, a simple one. As I became part of the community invested in and committed to promoting respect for linguistic diversity as a major national resource in the US, I also became increasingly aware of the monumental size of the task of maintaining and developing HL amongst our students.

A fundamental part of this task lies in familiarising oneselves with the 'wealth of knowledge' about HLs available today (Peyton 2001, 5) – the result of over four decades of work and research in the field. This wealth includes knowledge of the linguistic and socio-cultural characteristics of heritage students (Carreira 2004; Parra 2013; Polinsky and Kagan 2007), the most effective pedagogical practices (Peyton, Ranard and McGinnis 2001; Potowski and Carreira; 2004; Scalera 2004) for expanding oral bilingual range (Valdés 1997), biliteracy skills (Hornberger 2003; Hornberger and Wang 2008), a critical language awareness of students in heritage classrooms (Aparicio 1997; Correa 2011; Ducar 2008; Irwin 1996; Leeman 2005; Leemand and Rabin 2001; Martínez and Schwartz 2012), and the challenges of placement and assessment (Fairclough 2012; Polinsky and Kagan 2007). Yet as Roca (2001) has emphasised, the most important task is not that of accumulating information about HLs but that of integrating 'the knowledge we have accumulated and better [coordinating] our educational, planning, and policy efforts in the fields of foreign, bilingual, and HL education and research' (p. 307). How then to support the many efforts made by teachers who wish to initiate or update HL courses around the country? How can we provide them with the theoretical and practical tools for becoming experts in the pedagogy of the field and for engaging their students in meaningful linguistic and cultural experiences that they, in turn, can bring back to benefit their own communities?

Upholding the purpose of this book and responding to the urgent call by authors who advocate professional development programmes for Spanish HL teachers (Carreira and Kagan 2011; Fairclough 2006; Potowski 2003 Potowski and Carreira 2004; Roca 2001), I propose that our priority as a community of practitioners, language programme directors and administrators should be that of consolidating a notion of 'signature pedagogy' (hereafter SP), that is, specific forms of teaching and learning (Shulman 2005) for teaching Spanish as a HL. I believe that reflection on what makes our field and teaching mission unique will strengthen current professional development programmes and provide a model for encouraging the design of new ones that may help future and current teachers and assist them in: 1) integrating the most updated advances on HL pedagogy into their practice, and 2) creating pedagogical spaces that would nurture and enhance the linguistic and cultural abilities of heritage speakers in the 21st century.

This chapter is divided into three parts. In the first, I elaborate on the concept of SP and make a case for its relevance to teaching Spanish HL. In the second, I present theoretical and pedagogical frameworks that are emerging as scaffolds for an SP of Spanish HL. In the third and final part, I elaborate on the importance of strengthening the two main relations that sustain our profession: the relationship with our students and the relationship with researchers within our field and other disciplines. I believe these relationships to be a fundamental component for the development and advancement of a SP for Spanish HL in the twenty-first century.

The concept of 'signature pedagogy' and its relevance to teaching Spanish as a heritage language

Programs for Spanish HL learners (hereafter Spanish HL learners) are on the rise across the US, especially at institutions of higher education (see Beaudrie 2012 for an overview). However, the creation of these pedagogical spaces implies an enormous amount of work, effort and commitment on the part of many teachers, language programme directors and administrators. All openly acknowledge the fact that a regular Spanish-as-a-foreign-language classroom cannot fully serve the needs and interests of Spanish HL learners students looking to expand their knowledge of their home language and culture into more formal contexts.

Given this rise in opportunities for Spanish HL learners, I believe that now is the time to consolidate the already existing pieces and principles of Spanish HL instruction into a solid SP framework for teaching Spanish HL – a theoretical and pedagogical scaffold upon which both novice and experienced teachers as well as researchers can build in order to meet the goals of 21st-century Latino students.

In 2005, as part of the Carnegie Project on the Doctorate in Education, Lee S. Schulman proposed the term 'signature pedagogy' to designate 'characteristic forms of teaching and learning' (Schulman 2005, 52) within a professional field. These pedagogies 'organize the fundamental ways in which future practitioners are educated for their new professions' (p. 52), and play a critical role 'in shaping the character of future practice and in symbolizing the values and hopes of the professions' (p. 53).

Within this SP framework, novice teachers are trained beyond the specific content of their field. They are 'instructed to *think*, to *perform*, and to *act with integrity*' (Schulman 2005, 52). SPs form what Schulman calls 'habits of the mind, heart, and hand' (p. 59), along with a 'disposition', since SPs are ways of socialising novice teachers into the culture of our profession, its practices and values (p. 59).

This SP framework is relevant to teaching Spanish HL because conceptualising an SP for the profession demands a deep exercise in reflection on the goals and means not only of teaching a subject, but also on our role, hopes and values as HL teachers serving a specific population and community.

What is our role as teachers when Spanish HL learners come to us to reconnect with and expand their linguistic and cultural knowledge? Can we identify the 'habits of the mind, heart, and hand' of the type of teaching that we want to develop in novice teachers of Spanish HL? 'What kind of disposition do we wish to encourage in novice teachers and in more experienced teachers in other fields or subfields (i.e. literature or Spanish as a foreign language) who will be teaching Spanish HL?' What are the theoretical assumptions and beliefs that sustain our pedagogical practices? For Chick, Haynie and Gurung (2012, xi), *any* pedagogy 'grounded in the development of the entire person' is a good model for an SP. Are we thus aiming to develop the 'entire person' in our current HL programmes? What advances have been made and what challenges remain to be addressed in terms of teaching Spanish HL in the twenty-first century?

A proposal for a signature pedagogy of Spanish as a heritage language

Spanish HL instruction has a unique feature that distinguishes it from the teaching of other disciplines and makes it both fascinating and challenging: a complex relationship between the learner and the Spanish language to which the learner relates as both tool of communication (with family) and object of academic study at school. Both the familiar and academic relations that the students have with their HL is complex and intertwined with many individual, social, cultural and affective factors.

What are the theoretical and pedagogical frameworks that can provide teachers with a conceptualisation of the nature of such relationships – between Spanish HL learners and the Spanish they learn at home, and academic Spanish – in the most comprehensive way possible? And what are the pedagogical frameworks that can transform such conceptualisations into meaningful learning experiences for Spanish HL learners? Most current theoretical and pedagogical initiatives in Spanish HL are based on two main assumptions: 1) students develop their language abilities within a system of social, cultural and linguistic interrelations or ecology and 2) language – in its oral and written modality – is a social practice.

Theoretical frameworks for a signature pedagogy of Spanish HL

An ecological conception of Spanish HL learners

One of the major challenges facing Spanish HL teachers in the classroom is the broad range of 'functional proficiencies' (Valdés 2005) – both oral and written – that Spanish HL learners bring into the classroom as a result of their different immigration, family and educational experiences in Spanish and English. Spanish HL learners include people with ties to different countries in Latin America, who have different historical and cultural backgrounds and practices, and who speak different variants and registers of Spanish, depending on the specific region from which they are from and their family's socio-economic status and educational level.[1] Spanish HL learners also include different generations: newcomers of various ages, children of immigrant parents born in the US, and second- and third-generation students who maintain a cultural and community bond with their Latino ancestry. Another central source of diversity lies in their educational experience, which plays a central role in shaping their linguistic abilities in both Spanish and English.

These various degrees of functional proficiency and the unique social circumstances in which each one of our students has developed are the focus of our pedagogical efforts.[2] In Carreira's words, 'Distilling good HL teaching to its essence: It is all about the learner' (2012, 235).

Teachers thus need a tool to help them capture and understand in a comprehensive way the nature and history of each of their students' linguistic abilities (in both Spanish and English), cultural identity and educational outcome. In particular, they need a tool that can shed light on how home and school have come into play in the lives, language and cultural development of their students.

The ecological model (first proposed in the field of child development by Uri Bronfenbrenner, 1979) is one that can serve our purpose. Two of the chief premises of this model are: 1) children/students develop in different contexts (mainly family and school), and 2) the members of these contexts (i.e. parents and teachers) continuously interact while shaping the linguistic, social, emotional and academic development of children.

The ecological model can be particularly useful for conceptualising different kinds of relations between immigrant families and mainstream educational institutions (Brizuela and García-Sellers 1999; Garcia-Sellers 1996; Parra and García-Sellers 2005). Important questions in this respect are ones such as: How much linguistic and cultural continuity has the student had between their home and school environment? How much of an emotional struggle did the student experience in transitioning between the values of home and school? Did their teachers value and support the maintenance of their heritage language and culture? Did their parents support the heritage language? Or did they decide to speak to the student only in English to avoid possible discrimination or academic confusion? Were relations with family members affected by the student's linguistic changes (i.e. acquisition of English and possible loss of Spanish)?

The role of teachers is particularly important because they value or stigmatise the Spanish language (and its different variants) along with the student's family culture (Brizuela and García-Sellers 1999; Trueba and Bartolomé 2000).[3] Teachers' values reflect the status they grant to the HL *vis-à-vis* the dominant language (Beaudrie 2012, 7), and, more importantly, *vis-à-vis* the standard or prestigious variants of Spanish usually spoken by teachers. This imbalance in values and status regarding heritage and prestigious variants of Spanish brings into the relationship between Spanish HL teachers and their students a dimension of power that teachers need to recognise in order to minimise negative effects on the classroom environment (Potowski 2001, 2002). I will return to this point later on. The ecological model therefore conceives the interactions amongst teachers, parents and students as crucial to the maintenance of Spanish (or any other language) as a HL, and on any educational level.

The main point of bringing in the ecological model to the teaching of Spanish HL is to understand that the linguistic and cultural identities of Spanish HL learners (or of any student) do not develop in isolation. On the contrary, they are shaped by a complex system of interrelations (Bronfenbrenner 1979). And when these interrelations develop 'in Spanish and English amongst the student, her family, and the educational institutions and opportunities they have had throughout their life, the result is no single profile of [HL learners]' (Hornberger and Wang 2008, 6).

The various profiles of Spanish HL learners can be organised in a continuum of Spanish language proficiencies that range from students who are fairly fluent speakers (capable of sounding almost like competent native speakers) to students who can barely speak their home language (Carreira 2004; Polinsky and Kagan 2007). Spanish HL learners also have a range of mastery over the written modality and academic register of the language (see Valdés 1997 for a description of four possible literacy profiles).

Linguistic profiles, however, give us a 'narrow' definition of the Spanish heritage speaker or learner (Carreira 2004; Polinsky and Kagan 2007) since they exclude non-Spanish speaking Latino students (Carreira 2012) who are indistinguishable from foreign language learners but 'have familial or ancestral ties to a particular language that is not English [Spanish] and who exert their agency in determining whether or not they are HLLs (heritage language learners) of that HL (heritage language) and HC (heritage community)' (Hornberger and Wang 2008, 27). A broad conception of Spanish HL learners is therefore needed in order to include not only the student's linguistic profile but also her/his ties to the culture and the affective factors behind her motivation to study it (Carreira 2004; Polinsky and Kagan 2007).

It is beneficial, then, to work from an ecological perspective that captures students' complex history and the interplay of factors such as immigration, family history and educational opportunities, as these provide us with key information about their ethnolinguistic and cultural identity, their self esteem and their motivation for studying the language. In fact, many of the current proposals for initial interviews with Spanish HL learners are designed to obtain this information (Carreira and Kagan 2011; Schwartz 2001, amongst others) in order to help us understand affective and motivational issues that the students bring into the classroom.

A functional approach to Spanish HL

Two principal advances in the field of foreign language teaching as well as in Spanish HL have been: 1) the adoption of National Standards (ACTFL, 1996), which have moved both fields towards a broader conception of communication that goes beyond the traditional teaching of grammar and the four language skills to incorporate not only 'interpersonal' but also 'interpretive' and 'presentational' modes, and 2) the adoption of a functional approach to language in which its oral and written modalities are understood as social practices anchored to specific social contexts (Byrnes 2011; Kern 2004, Achugar and Colombi 2008; Colombi 1994, 2003).

The functional theory of language has initiated a broader understanding of bilingual development in which the existing language abilities and strategies of heritage students can be conceptualised within a 'biliteracy continuum' (Hornbeger 2003) that incorporates the relation between oral and written abilities in both languages (Colombi 1994, 2003). This comprehensive framework aims to provide language students with an 'opportunity to grow in their mother tongue, and the opportunity to use it in meaningful communication and creative expression' (Valdés, Lozano, and García-Moya 1981, 14).

This approach is principally beneficial to Spanish HL learners who are looking to expand their 'bilingual range', which Valdés (1997) defines as 'the continuum of linguistic abilities and communicative strategies that these individuals may access in one or the other of two languages at a specific moment' (p. 30). Such a range includes not only grammatical and textual competencies, but also illocutionary and sociolinguistic competencies (Bachman, 1990), all of which are in continuous interaction (Valdés, 1997).

Contrary to the prescriptive approach and its tendency to view the less prestigious variants of Spanish as problematic and full of 'errors,' the functional approach to language conceptualises the dialects used by students and prestigious or standard Spanish as two variants to be used in different social situations. Such an approach focuses not on 'correcting errors' but on teaching the different communicative and social functions of Spanish in different social contexts, including the academic one (Achugar and Colombi 2008; Colombi 1994, 2003).

When taking this comprehensive and functional approach, it is important to remember that the problem is not that of teaching grammar or the norms of a standard or prestigious variant of Spanish. Students do want to learn the register that will allow them to perform in academic and social contexts. The problem is valuing this norm and standard *over* students' own language use and linguistic home practices.

The teaching of literacy

The same approach has been incorporated into the teaching of Spanish literacy. It is well known that due to the lack of schooling opportunities for developing Spanish reading and writing skills, literacy is the area in which most Spanish HL learners need the most support (Valdés, Lozano, and García-Moya 1981; Colombi and Alarcón 1997). As with teachers' conception of oral modality, so too their conception of what constitutes written language and how it functions in society plays a central role in the pedagogical approaches they use to develop Spanish writing skills. For example, traditional approaches to literacy presuppose that reading and writing are about mechanically decoding and reproducing information; reading and writing are conceived as independent of any cultural or social contexts.

However, some scholars in the field of foreign and HL teaching have proposed a literacy-based framework combined with a genre-based approach (Byrnes 2011; Byrnes and Sprang 2004; Kern 2004, Achugar and Colombi 2008; Colombi 1994, 2003) that considers literacy and *bi*literacy (Hornberger 2003) as anchored in the cultural and social contexts of their use. A principal goal is to make students learn the specific linguistic features of different types of texts and genres that are needed for different specific contexts, such as the academic one.

Drawing from genre and register theory (Martin 2010) as well as Systemic Functional Linguistics (SFL) (Halliday 2007), scholars in the HL (as well as the foreign language) field are making important headway in the research of biliteracy development, particularly at the high school and college level (see Colombi 2012 for a review). Most current research has focused on two main areas: 1) the development of academic Spanish where oral and written modalities are considered as 'two different language resources to fulfill different functions in different social contexts' (Colombi 2012, 248), and 2) the transference of skills from previous literacy knowledge in English into Spanish academic writing (Martínez 2007; Schleppegrell and Colombi, 1997).

Although its detailed analysis lies outside the scope of this chapter, it is important to highlight that a framework that conceptualises this use of Spanish and English from an ecological perspective is being developed by scholars such as Hornberger and Wang (2008). The concept of biliteracy is thus multidimensional and considers the different contexts and sociocultural dimensions that promote or inhibit it (Hornberger and Wang 2008).

Pedagogical frameworks for a signature pedagogy for Spanish HL

Many professionals in the field of teaching Spanish HL have already taken steps towards incorporating an ecological understanding of Spanish HL learners as well as a functional approach to language into their classrooms, as an alternative to traditional and prescriptive approaches to language teaching. This shift is reflected in the goals they have for their students, the curriculum they design, the materials they choose, and the discussions they promote with their students. This is a major step towards consolidating an SP for Spanish HL, since, as Chick, Haynie, Gurung (2012) propose, 'the most important question' we can ask ourselves as academic professionals is precisely that of the '*alignment* [emphasis mine] between the knowledge, skills, and dispositions we want to develop in our students and the pedagogy we currently use' (Chick, Haynie, Gurung 2012, xiii).

The pedagogical frameworks that have proven to be effective and meaningful for teaching Spanish HL and which I find aligned with some of the main principles of the ecological model and the functional approach to language are: critical pedagogy (Freire 2005; Giroux 1991) and language awareness, multiliteracies (New London Group, 1996; Parra, forthcoming), and community service (Carreira and Kagan 2011, Verona 1999).

The common ground that these approaches share is the understanding that given their familial and cultural ties with the Spanish language, the content we choose and the curriculum we design for Spanish HL learners has to include relevant and meaningful topics for students (Webb and Miller 2000; Scalera 2004).

Different immigrant experiences, social, cultural and language topics related to the community to which the speakers belong, family traditions, cross-generation relations, race, gender and identity are some of the many themes that could be covered in the curriculum for Spanish HL learners.

Critical pedagogy and the multiliteracies approach

These topics, however, introduce the challenge of disentangling the complexity of the Latino experience represented in our classrooms. As I have asked elsewhere (Parra, forthcoming), how can we present to students the heterogeneous yet shared experiences of the migration and settlement, marginalisation and creativity of Latinos in the US? In the multiliteracy approach (New London Group 1996) I have found a creative and productive way to analyse the different media – literary texts, films and documentaries, newspaper and academic articles about and by Latino authors, music and printed art materials by Latino artists – through which the Latino community has represented its history and various cultural and linguistic identities (Parra, forthcoming).

The New London Group proposes that:

- Multiliteracies create a different kind of pedagogy, one in which language and other modes of meaning are dynamic representational resources, constantly being remade by their users as they work to achieve their various cultural purposes (New London Group 1996, 5).

- The multiliteracies approach proposes four pedagogical principles for guiding productive tasks in the classroom (p. 6): situated practice, overt instruction, critical framing and transformed practice.

- Situated practice refers to the importance of organising teaching contexts and learning opportunities around concrete goals that relate directly to the community, allowing students to draw on the experience of meaning-making in life worlds, the public realm, and the workplace.

- Overt instruction consists of providing explicit instruction about the language as well as the goals of the course, what is being taught, and the methodology used in class. Overt instruction also demands that students be provided with a 'metalanguage' that will promote awareness of and control over what they are learning (New London Group, 1996) 'so that the teacher and students can identify, talk about and learn the various elements that contribute to particular meanings in communication' (Kern 2004).

- Critical framing encourages reflection and analysis through language in order to facilitate a 'theoretical and personal distance' from what has been learned (New London Group 1996, 87). This distance allows students to 'constructively critique [their new knowledge], account for its cultural location, creatively extend and apply it, and eventually innovate on their own, within old communities and in new ones' (p. 87).

Topics related to the family immigrant experience and the communities of speakers to which students belong necessarily incite discussions in and about the Spanish language in a US context. When aligned with the functional approach, a critical pedagogy (Freire 2005; Giroux 1991) – and more specifically a critical language awareness approach – offers students a possibility to reflect on the complex sociopolitical aspects of the Spanish language in the US, its variants and dialects (Martínez 2003; Leeman 2005) *vis-à-vis* a common discourse that privileges a standard Spanish, which is more a construct than a reality (Villa 1996; Rodriguez Pino and Villa 1994). It also allows for a comprehensive understanding of language contact phenomena (e.g. code-switching, transfers, calques, and interferences) that typically occur when Spanish is in contact with English (Carvalho 2012; Correa 2011; Potowski and Carreira 2004; Leslie 2012) and helps make students aware of the range of registers in the Spanish language that it would benefit them to acquire (Carreira 2000; Valdés and Geoffrion-Vinci 1998). Such reflections validate the linguistic practices that students have acquired from the characteristics of the Spanish they have learned at home (Valdés 2001).

A critical pedagogy framework also follows the call of authors such as Leeman (2005) and Leeman and Rabin (2007), who emphasise the connection between the Spanish language and key issues in politics, ideology, culture, race, ethnicity, gender and class.

The goal of such reflections is to empower Spanish HL learners and provide them with the questions, space and 'voice' to become aware of and to problematise their surroundings, namely, the power structures in which they live and are educated (Aparicio 1997; Correa 2011; Ducar 2008; Irwin 1996; Leeman 2005; Leemand and Rabin 2001; Martínez and Schwartz 2012). Teachers who work within this critical framework add the possibility of learning a new discourse that, in Giroux's words, 'provide[s] students with a range of pedagogical options in which they can invest, act, and speak in order to affirm their capacities for critical, social agency' (2000, 84). The main goal is to develop their social consciousness and voice so that they can take constructive action towards constructive change (Freire 2005). The fourth principle of the multiliteracies approach – transformed practice – concurs with this conclusion.

 In what the New London Group (1996) called 'transformed practice', students need *to apply* what they have learned from the process of critical reflection to a meaning-making action at a different level from where they started. Teachers thus need to provide students with opportunities to focus on this process. As some authors have argued, art and images can play an effective role in language classes as a 'point of entry into a web of other texts and images whose analysis starts to sensitise students to and socialise them into the broader cultural narratives' (Barnes-Karol and Broner 2010) of the foreign and HL. Parra (forthcoming) has proposed that teachers use images and art as productive and creative options (for both FLLs and HSLLs) in order to engage students in transformed practice. Art-making is an effective meaning-making activity through which students can express and capture their reflections on their family journey, ethno-linguistic identity and various aspects of their cultures (Parra, forthcoming).

Community service

There is probably no better place to learn and reflect critically on linguistic and cultural issues that matter to Spanish HL learners and to bring in constructive action than within their community. Community Service Learning (CSL) experiences have long been advocated for making the language class experience for FLLs more meaningful (Hellebrandt and Verona 1999; Lear and Abbot 2008; Thompson, 2013; Wurr and Hellebrandt 2007). CSL has been viewed as a powerful model and effective pedagogical resource for providing students with experiences and tools that broaden their learning experience. As Varona (1999) states, CSL 'actively engages students in the learning process and bridges the gap between theory and practice while connecting students with the community (and vice versa) to accomplish worthwhile and meaningful goals' (p. 69).

CSL experiences are even more powerful for Spanish HL learners since, as Carreira and Kagan (2011) propose, they provide highly effective pathways by which to 'harness the wealth of knowledge and experiences these students bring to the classroom' (Carreira and Kagan 2011, 62). Leeman, Rabin and Román Mendoza (2011) suggest that CSL 'foster students' development of identities as 'legitimate' (as opposed to deficient) speakers of Spanish.' (Leeman, Rabin, and Román Mendoza 2011, 2). And as Martínez and Schwartz (2012) state, 'Community engagement provides students with a level of motivation and investment in language learning that would be difficult to achieve in a classroom setting alone' (p. 46).

Furthermore, student involvement with the community demands a step beyond 'learning by doing' to emphasise *the process* of learning through critical reflection (Freire 2005; Martínez and Schwartz 2012; Leeman 2005; Samaniego and Pino 2000, Trujillo 2009). Students engage in a back-and-forth process of reflection between classroom and community work. The result is a continuous reinterpretation of the readings and the community that generates new understandings and questions in students (Parra, Liander and Munoz 2011; Thomsen 2006).

In summary, the main purposes of pedagogical approaches such as multiliteracies, critical pedagogy, critical language awareness and community service is to provide students with the tools through which they can become designers of social futures. In the SP for Spanish HL these tools are meaningfully situated actions that generate a new sense of awareness of the language, culture and community that they belong to and are (re)signifying.

Differentiated teaching

The pedagogical frameworks outlined in the last section have one additional advantage for SP of Spanish HL; they facilitate differentiated teaching (Tomlinson, 1999). Potowski and Carreira (2004) and Carreira (2012) have proposed this approach as a pedagogical framework for addressing the different needs and strengths of Spanish HL learners in the classroom (particularly for mixed classes with Spanish HL learners and FLLs). This approach allows teachers to come up with 'specific ways for each individual to learn as deeply as possible and as quickly as possible, without assuming one student's roadmap for learning is identical to anyone else's' (Tomlinson 1999, 2). For Potowski and Carreira (2004), the chief advantages of differentiated teaching include the availability of multiple learning materials, variable pacing, varied grading criteria, work that is assigned to students based on their level of readiness, ongoing student assessment built into the curriculum and, most importantly, student participation in the setting of goals and standards.

Strengthening our relationships with students and researchers

Teacher-student relations

According to Schulman (2005), one of the main characteristics of SPs is their pervasiveness: '[SPs] implicitly define what counts as knowledge in a field and how things become known. They define how knowledge is analysed, criticised, accepted, or discarded' (p. 54). Current efforts in Spanish HL training programmes face the challenge of dealing with a pervasive old SP for teaching Spanish HL, which is rooted in a language ideology (Leeman 2012) that subscribes to a prestigious or standard variant of Spanish as the only learning goal for Spanish HL learners, and which embraces a prescriptive approach and normative view for teaching Spanish to Spanish HL learners. Such an SP tends to criticise and dismiss the language practices of Spanish HL learners as deficient.

As we work towards consolidating an SP for Spanish HL for our new century, I concur with other authors (Leeman 2012; Potowski 2001, 2002, Roca 2001) that teachers need to become aware of their own ideological positions *vis-à-vis* the Spanish variant that they and their students speak. As Potowski (2001) has stated, we need to move teachers beyond a framework of correction and beyond a 'language authority' (Potowski 2002, 39) position with the assumption that remediation 'would help undo the damage that had been done at home' (Valdés 1995, 9).

Different exercises, discussions and surveys for teachers can be done to serve this purpose (Potowski 2001; Parra 2013). The goal is for teachers to become facilitators and create a learning atmosphere in which students feel they are treated 'with respect for their linguistic and cultural knowledge' (Scalera 2004, 4), and thus become engaged in a more cooperative learning experience (Rodriguez Pino, 1997).

Schulman's proposal for SP also highlights the importance of the quality of the teacher-student relation when he proposes that:

> When the emotional content of learning is well sustained, we have the real possibility of pedagogies of formation–experiences of teaching and learning that can influence the values, dispositions, and characters of those who learn. And when these experiences are interactive rather than individual, when they embody the pervasive culture of learning within a field, they offer even more opportunity for character formation. (Schulman 2005, 57)

Strengthening the teacher-research dialogue

Without a doubt, important and definite advances in pedagogy for Spanish HL have been made since the National Foreign Language Center (NFLC) and the Center for Applied Linguistics (CAL) organised the HLs Initiative in 1998 (Brecht and Ingold 2002), the principal goal of which was to tap the linguistics resources of the country in order to 'strengthen the ability of the United States to participate effectively in an increasingly interdependent world [. . .] and build an education system that is responsive to the national language needs and the HL communities in this country' (Peyton 2001, 14).

Along with an impressive production of textbooks, dissertations, theses and articles for specialised journals such as the *Heritage Language Journal*, the increase in the number of programmes for Spanish HL across the country (Beaudrie 2012) and current efforts to develop professional training programmes for Spanish HL teachers (see Carreira 2012 for a review; Potowski 2005) shed promising light on our field and commitment to Latino youth.

Nevertheless, as each one of the chapters in Beaudrie and Fairclough's (2012) state-of-the-field book highlights, many questions regarding the learning processes of Spanish HL learners remain unanswered. Research plays a central role in this advance. However, besides annual conferences on HLs (for example, the summer institutes sponsored by the National Heritage Language Resource Center), there are few spaces in which teachers and researchers can engage in ongoing interaction and benefit from each others' work and practice.

In 2011 and 2012, in an effort to build such spaces and dialogue between teachers and researchers, I organised two public symposiums on Spanish HL. The first one, 'Sharing knowledge, finding pathways: Developing pedagogical resources for Spanish heritage speakers,' was structured around the main theoretical themes related to our conception of heritage language. The second one, 'Applying innovative and effective pedagogy for Spanish heritage speakers in the classroom,' was organised around the principal pedagogical issues of Spanish HL. In these symposiums, the gathering of experts in the field presented state-of-the-art research on Spanish HL pedagogy, as well as the ideological and cross-cultural dimensions of Spanish HL course curriculum design. Their presentations made it clear that though the field is rapidly expanding, more research and particularly more connections between teachers and researchers are needed to move the field forward. In addition to the theoretical and pedagogical richness of all the presentations, both symposiums had the unexpected outcome of bringing together a number of important teachers and administrators dealing with different educational levels (mainly high school and college) from various schools and universities in the area. The active participation of this group of researchers, practitioners and administrators demonstrated the need for, and broad interest in, Spanish HL, which needs to be fulfilled and encouraged.

An open and continuous dialogue between teachers and researchers will ensure the future of a solid SP for Spanish HL. In this regard, I have proposed elsewhere (Parra 2013) that professional development programmes for Spanish HL teachers should include a component of research methodology so that classrooms can be used as 'language laboratories' (Cross 1990). Teachers could benefit from concrete and systematic observation and assessment of student performance in the classroom, especially since the assessment of students' linguistic abilities and progress is one of the main areas that still needs development (See Fairclough 2012 for a review of the latest approaches and research on this matter). Teachers can also benefit from having concrete information about vulnerable areas in Spanish HL learners' linguistic systems affected by overgeneralisation and simplification (Benmamoun, et al. 2010; Silva-Corvlán 1994). This information can guide teachers in assessing the linguistic behaviour they observe in class, designing effective activities to target these vulnerable areas and formulating the right questions to move students' language performance forward (Leslie 2012). Finally, 'self-reflective' (Ham and Schueller 2012, 37) activities such as learning how to track teachers' own performance, successes and areas for improvement could also be part of this research component.

Conclusion

The unprecedented growth of the field of Spanish HL at the beginning of the century is the result of a continuous, sustained effort and commitment by many teachers and researchers to serving the growing population of Latino youth in the US. In this chapter I have outlined what I consider the already existing basis of an SP (Schulman 2005) for Spanish HL – the 'characteristic forms of teaching and learning' (Schulman 2005, 52) – for strengthening existing teacher programmes and workshops and for shaping future professional development efforts. The theoretical basis is comprised of the ecological model (for understanding the complex system of interrelations in which Spanish HL learners grow up and develop their language proficiencies in Spanish and English as well as their sense of identity) and a functional approach to language that conceptualises the oral and written language behaviour of Spanish HL learners as a social practice anchored in specific contexts of interaction. I have also proposed four pedagogical frameworks that are aligned with the assumptions of these ecological and functional theoretical models. A combination of these four approaches – critical pedagogy, multiliteracies, community service and differentiated teaching – will provide teachers and students with ample opportunities to reflect critically on the various facets of the 'Latino imaginary' (Flores 2000), and take meaningful, even if small, steps towards constructive action and change (Freire 2005).

However, as Schulman (2005) notes:

> Professional education is not education for understanding alone; it is preparation for accomplished and responsible practice in the service of others. It is preparation for 'good work.' Professionals must learn abundant amounts of theory and vast bodies of knowledge. They must come to understand in order to act, and they must act in order to serve. (Schuman 2005, 53)

I believe this quote highlights the importance of the teacher-student relationship in the teaching of any field but becomes even more meaningful in Spanish HL instruction. It is crucial for teachers to realise that their relationship with students is an essential part of the learning process (Potowski 2001, 2002; Parra 2013). In doing so, teachers need to acknowledge and validate the individual differences of their students, their different needs and strengths, affects and motivations. Therefore, in the field of Spanish HL, the concept of 'difference' can be considered 'an intrinsic point of theoretical validation' (Trifonas 2003, 1).

As actors in the students' current ecology, teachers play a central role in encouraging or discouraging students to pass Spanish on to subsequent generations. The main task of professional training programmes is to provide tools for making 'pedagogical choices designed to produce deep, personal change, the kind of transformation characteristic of all successful signature pedagogies' (Ham and Schueller 2012, 31), along with the 'habits of the mind, heart, and hand' (Shulman 2005, 52) so necessary to the development of teachers of Spanish HL learners.

An SP for Spanish HL must also have strong ties with ongoing research in the different areas of the field. The future of such SP lies not only in teacher-student relations, but also in continuous dialogue between teachers and researchers. An SP for Spanish HL needs to extend this dialogue and reach out to other disciplines beyond the subfields of language, such as psychology, education and the scholarship of teaching and learning (SoTL) which can provide teachers of Spanish HL with tools for 'systematic inquiry of both instructional methods and learning' and for 'enabling language practitioners with diverse backgrounds to explore, assess and improve students learning in their own classes' (Ham and Schueller 2012, 36). Such disciplines can contribute new tools and methodologies for strengthening and enriching teachers' classroom practices as well as ways in which to enquire about the development of Spanish HL learners.

Our ultimate goal is to develop a more productive, informed and interdisciplinary dialogue that provides teachers and researchers with the integrated view necessary to promote the maintenance of the Spanish language in a variety of contexts and in dialogue with the different actors of our society.

REFERENCES

Achugar, M. and Colombi M.C. (2008). 'Systemic Functional Linguistic Explorations into the Longitudinal Study of Advanced Capacities'. In L. Ortega and H. Byrnes, eds, *The Longitudinal Study of Advanced L2 Capacities*. New York: Routledge.

ACTFL (American Council on the Teaching of Foreign Languages) (1996). *Standards for Foreign Language Learning: Preparing for the Twenty-First Century (Executive Summary)*. Yonkers, NY: American Council on the Teaching of Foreign Languages.

Aparicio, F.R. (1997). 'La Enseñanza del Español para Hispanohablantes y la Pedagogía Multicultural'. In M.C. Colombi and F.X. Alarcón, eds, *La Enseñanza del Español a Hispanohablantes*. Boston: Houghton Mifflin.

Bachman, Lyle F. (1990). *Fundamental Considerations in Language Testing*. Oxford: Oxford University Press.

Barnes-Karol, G. and Broner, M.A. (2010). 'Using Images as Springboards to Teach Cultural Perspectives in Light of the Ideas of the MLA Report'. *Foreign Language Annals* 43 (3), 422–45.

Beaudrie, S.M. and Fairclough, M., eds (2012). *Spanish as a Heritage Language in the United States: The State of the Field*. Washington, DC: Georgetown University Press.

Beaudrie, S.M. (2012). 'Research on University-Based Spanish Heritage Language Programs in the United States: The Current State of Affairs'. In S.M. Beaudrie and M. Fairclough, eds, *Spanish as a Heritage Language in the United States. The State of the Field*. Washington, DC: Georgetown University Press.

Benmamoun, E., Montrul, S. and Polinsky, M. (2010). *Prolegomena to Heritage Linguistics. (White paper)*, University of Illinois and Harvard University. http://nhlrc.ucla.edu/pdf/HL-whitepaper.pdf (retrieved June 2013).

Brecht, R.D. and Ingold, C.W. (2002). *Tapping a National Resource: Heritage Languages in the United States. ERIC Digest*. Washington, DC: ERIC Clearinghouse on Languages and Linguistics. http://bern.library.nenu.edu.cn/upload/soft/0-article/+025/25141.pdf (retrieved July 2013).

Brizuela, B. and García-Sellers, M.J. (1999). 'School Adaptation: A Triangular Process'. *American Educatinal Research Journal*, Summer, 36 (2), 345–70.

Bronfenbrenner, U. (1979). *The Ecology of Human Development. Experiments by Nature and Design*. Cambridge, MA: Harvard University Press.

Byrnes, H. (2011). 'Reconsidering Graduate Students' Education as Scholar-Teachers: Mind Your Language!' In H.W. Allen and H.H. Maxim, eds, *Educating the Future Foreign Language Professoriate for the 21st Century: Issues in Language Program Direction: A Series of Annual Volumes*. Boston, MA: Heinle.

Byrnes, H. and Sprang, K. (2004). 'Fostering Advanced L2 Literacy: A Genre-Based, Cognitive Approach'. In H. Byrnes and K. Sprang, *Advanced Foreign Language Learning: A Challenge to College Programs*. Boston: Heinle.

Carreira, M. (2000). 'Validating and Promoting Spanish in the United States: Lessons from Linguistic Science'. *Bilingual Research Journal* 24 (4), 423–42.

— (2004). 'Seeking Explanatory Adequacy: A Dual Approach to Understanding the Term "Heritage Language Learner"'. Selected Articles from the *Heritage Language Journal* 2 (1).

— (2012). 'Meeting the Needs of Heritage Language Learners: Approaches, Strategies, and Research'. In S.M. Beaudrie and M. Fairclough, eds, *Spanish as a Heritage Language in the United States: The State of the Field*. Georgetown University Press.

Carreria, M. and Kagan, O. (2011). 'The Results of the National Heritage Language Survey: Implications for Teaching, Curriculum Design, and Professional Development'. *Foreign Language Annals* 44 (1), 40–64.

Carvalho, A.M. (2012). 'Code-Switching: From Theoretical to Pedagogical Considerations'. In S.M. Beaudrie and M. Fairclough, eds, *Spanish as a Heritage Language in the United States. The State of the Field*. Georgetown University Press.

Chick, N.L., Haynie, R.A.R. and Gurung, A.R., eds (2012). *Exploring More Signature Pedagogies: Approaches to Teaching Disciplinary Habits of Mind*. Sterling, VA: Stylus.

Colombi, M.C. (1994). 'Perfil del Discurso Escrito en Textos Hispanohablantes: Teoría y Práctica'. In M.C. Colombi and F.X. Alarcón, eds, *La Enseñanza del Español a Hispanohablantes*. Boston, MA: Houghton Mifflin.

— (2003). 'Un Enfoque Functional para la Enseñanza del Ensayo Expositivo'. In A. Roca and M.C. Colombi, eds, *Mi Lengua: Spanish as a Heritage Language in the United States*. Washington, DC: Georgetown University Press.

— (2012). 'Advanced Biliteracy Development in Spanish'. In S.M. Beaudrie and M. Fairclough, eds, *Spanish as a Heritage Language in the United States. The State of the Field*. Washington, DC: Georgetown University Press.

Colombi, M.C. and Alarcón, F.X., eds (1997). *La Enseñanza del Español a Hispanohablantes*. Boston: Houghton Mifflin.

Correa, M. (2011). 'Advocating for Critical Pedagogical Approaches to Teaching Spanish as a Heritage Language: Some Considerations'. *Foreign Language Annals* 44 (2), 308–20.

Ducar, C.M. (2008). 'Student Voices: The Missing Link in the Spanish Heritage Language Debate'. *Foreign Language Annals* 41, 415–33.

Fairclough, M. (2006). 'La Enseñanza del Español como Lengua de Herencia: Un Curso de Preparación para Docentes'. *Revista Iberoamericana de Ligüística* 1 (31), 50.

— (2012). 'Language Assessment: Key Theoretical Considerations in the Academic Placement of Spanish Heritage Language Learners'. In S.M. Beaudrie and M. Fairclough, eds, *Spanish as a Heritage Language in the United States. The State of the Field*. Washington, DC: Georgetown University Press.

Flores, J. (2000). *From Bomba to Hip-Hop*. New York: Columbia University Press.

Freire, P. (2005). *Pedagogy of the Oppressed* (30th anniversary edition, trans. Myra Bergman Ramos). http://www.msu.ac.zw/elearning/material/1335344125freire_pedagogy_of_the_oppresed.pdf (retrieved October 2012).

García-Sellers, M.J. (1996). *A Conceptual Model of School Adaptation Applied to Hispanic Immigrant Children*. Manuscript.

Giroux, H.A. (1991). 'Postmodernism as Border Pedagogy'. In H.A. Giroux, ed., *Postmodernism, Feminism, and Cultural Politics: Redrawing Educational Boundaries*. Albany, NY: State University of New York Press.

Halliday, M.A.K. (2007). *Language and Education. The Collected Work of M.A.K. Halliday* 9, ed. J. J. Webster. London/New York: Continuum.

Hellebrandt, J. and Varona, L.T., eds (1999). *Construyendo Puentes: Concepts and Models for Service-Learning in Spanish*. AAHE's Series on Service-Learning in the Disciplines 13. Washington, DC: American Association for Higher Education.

Hornberger, N. (2003). *Continua of Biliteracy: An Ecological Framework for Educational Policy, Research, and Practice in Multilingual Settings*. Clevedon: Multilingual Matters.

Hornberger, N. and **Wang, S.C.** (2008). 'Who Are our Heritage Language Learners? Identity and Biliteracy in Heritage Language Education in the United States'. In D.M. Brinton, O. Kagan, and S. Bauckus, eds, *Heritage Language Education: A New Field Emerging.* New York, NY: Routledge.

Irwin, J.W. (1996) *Empowering Ourselves and Transforming Schools: Educators Making a Difference.* New York: SUNY Press.

Kern, R. (2000). *Literacy and Language Teaching.* Oxford: Oxford University Press.

— (2004). 'Literacy and Advanced Foreign Language Learning: Rethinking the Curriculum'. In H. Byrnes and H.H. Maxim, eds, *Advanced Foreign Language Learning: A Challenge to College Programs.* Boston, MA: Heinle.

Lear, **D.W.** and **Abbot, A.R.** (2008). 'Foreign Language Professional Standards and CSL: Achieving the 5 Cs'. *Michigan Journal of Community Service Learning* 14 (2). http://www.freepatentsonline.com/article/Michigan-Journal-Community-Service-Learning/187695577.html (retrieved November 2012).

Leeman, J. (2012). 'Investigating Language Ideologies in Spanish as a Heritage Language'. In S.M. Beaudrie and M. Fairclough, eds, *Spanish as a Heritage Language in the United States. The State of the Field.* Washington, DC: Georgetown University Press.

— (2005). 'Engaging Critical Pedagogy: Spanish for Native Speakers'. *Foreign Language Annals* 38, 35–45.

Leeman, J. and **Rabin, L.** (2007). 'Reading Language: Critical Perspectives for the Literature Classroom', *Hispania* 90 (2), 304–15.

Leeman, J., **Rabin, L.** and **Román-Mendoza, E.** (2011). 'Critical Pedagogy Beyond the Classroom Walls: Community Service-Learning and Spanish Heritage Language Education', *Heritage Language Journal* 8 (3). http://www.heritagelanguages.org (retrieved May 2013).

Leslie, S.R. (2012). *The Use of Linguistics to Improve the Teaching of Heritage Language Spanish.* Unpublished bachelor's thesis. Department of Linguistics, Harvard University, MA. www.people.fas.harvard.edu/~herpro/site/Research_files/Leslie.pdf (retrieved July 2012).

Martin, J. (1984). 'Language, Register and Genre'. In F. Christie, ed., *Children Writing.* Geelong: Deakin University Press.

Martínez, G. (2003). 'Classroom Based Dialect Awareness in Heritage Language Instruction: A Critical Applied Linguistic Approach'. *Heritage Language Journal* 1 (1). http://www.heritagelanguages.org (retrieved September 2008).

— (2007). 'Writing Back and Forth: the Interplay of Form and Situation in Heritage Language Composition'. *Language Teaching Research* 11 (1), 31–4.

Martínez, G. and **Schwartz, A.** (2012). 'Elevating "Low" Language for High Sakes A Case for Critical, Community-Based Learning in a Medical Spanish for Heritage Learners Program'. *Heritage Language Journal* 9 (2). http://www.heritagelanguages.org (retrieved May 2013).

New London Group (1996). 'A Pedagogy of Multiliteracies: Designing Social Futures'. *Harvard Educational Review* 66 (1), 60–92.

Parra Velasco, M.L. (2013a). 'Exploring Individual Differences amongst Spanish Heritage Learners: Implications for TA Training and Program Development'. Forthcoming, in C. Sanz and B. Lado, eds, *Individual Differences, L2 Development and Language Program Administration: From Theory to Application.* Boston, MA: Cengage.

— (forthcoming). 'Expanding Language and Cultural Competence in Advanced Heritage- and Foreign-Language Learners Through Community Engagement and Work with the Arts'. *Heritage Language Journal.*

Parra Velasco, M.L., Liander, J. and Muñoz, C. (2011). 'Spanish in the Community: An Interactive Language Course'. (Presentation at the American Council on the Teaching of Foreign Languages). Denver, CO: Empowering Language Educators Through Collaboration.

Parra Velasco, M.L. and García-Sellers, M.J. (2005). *Comunicación Entre la Escuela y la Familia: Fortaleciendo las Bases para el Éxito Escolar (Home-School Communication: Strengthening the Basis for Academic Success)* Piadós Press, México.

Peyton, J.K., Ranard, D.A. and McGinnis, S. (2001). 'Charting a New Course: Heritage Language Education in the United States'. In J.K. Peyton, D.A. Ranard and S. McGinnis, eds, *Heritage Languages in America: Preserving a National Resource. Language in Education: Theory and Practice.* Washington, DC, and McHenry, IL: The Center for Applied Linguistics and Delta Systems.

Polinsky, M. and Kagan, O. (2007). 'Heritage Languages: In the "Wild" and in the Class- room'. *Language and Linguistics Compass* 1 (5), 368–95.

Potowski, K. (2001). 'Educating University Foreign Language Teachers to Work with Heritage Spanish Speakers'. In B. Johnston and S. Irujo, eds, *Research and Practice in Language Teacher Education: Voices from the Field. Selected Papers from the First International Conference on Language Teacher Education.* Minneapolis, MN: University of Minnesota, Center for Advanced Research in Language Acquisition.

— (2002). 'Experiences of Spanish Heritage Speakers in University Foreign Language Courses and Implications for Teacher Training'. *ADFL Bulletin* 33, 35–42.

— (2003). 'Chicago's "Heritage Language Teacher Corps": A Model for Improving Spanish Teacher Development'. *Hispania* 82 (20), 302–11.

— (2005). *Fundamentos de la Enseñanza del Español a los Hablantes Nativos en los Estados Unidos (Foundations in Teaching Spanish to Native Speakers in the United States).* Madrid: Arco/Libros.

Potowski, K. and Carreira, M. (2004). 'Towards Teacher Development and National Standards for Spanish as a Heritage Language'. *Foreign Language Annals* 37 (3), 427–37.

Roca, A. (2001). 'Heritage Language Maintenance and Development: An Agenda for Action'. In J.K. Peyton, D.A. Ranard and S. McGinnis, eds, *Heritage Languages in America: Preserving a National Resource. Language in Education: Theory and Practice.* Washington, DC, and McHenry, IL: The Center for Applied Linguistics and Delta Systems.

Rodríguez Pino, C. (1997). 'La Reconceptualización del Programa de Español para Hispanphablantes: Estrategias que Reflejan la Realidad Sociolingüística de la clase'. In M.C. Colombi and F. X. Alarcón, eds, *La Enseñanza del Español a Hispanohablantes.* Boston, MA: Houghton Mifflin.

Rodríguez Pino, C. and Villa, D. (1994). 'A Student-Centered Spanish for Native Speakers Program: Theory, Curriculum and Outcome Assessment'. In C. Klee, ed., 'Faces in a Crowd: Individual Learners in Multisection Programs'. *American Association of University Superisors and Coordinators and Directors of Foreign Language Programs: Issues in Language Program Direction.* Boston, MA: Heinle.

Samaniego, F. and **Pino, C.** (2000). 'Frequently Asked Questions about SNS Programs'. In American Association of Teachers of Spanish and Portuguese, ed., *Professional Development Series Handbook for Teachers K-16: Spanish for Native Speakers* 1, 29–63. Fort Worth, TX: Hartcourt College.

Scalera, D. (2004). 'The Invisible Learner: Unlocking the Heritage Language Treasure'. *Language Association Journal* 5 (2), 2–5.

Schleppegrell, M. and **Colombi, M.C.** (1997). 'Text Organization by Bilingual Writers'. *Written Communication* 14 (4), 418–503.

Schulman, L.S. (Summer 2005). 'Signature Pedagogies in the Professions'. *Deadalus* 134, 52–59.

Schwartz, A.M. (2001). 'Preparing Teachers to Work With Heritage Language Learners'. In J.K. Peyton, D.A. Ranard and S. McGinnis, eds, *Heritage Languages in America: Preserving a National Resource. Language in Education: Theory and Practice*. Washington, DC, and McHenry, IL: The Center for Applied Linguistics and Delta Systems.

Silva-Corvalán, C. (1994). *Language Contact and Change: Spanish in Los Angeles*. Oxford: Clarendon Press.

Thomsen, K. (2006). *Service-Learning in Grades K-8: Experiential Learning that Builds Character and Motivation*. Thousand Oaks, CA: Corwin Press.

Thompson, G. (2013). *Intersection of Service and Learning: Research and Practice in the Second Language Classroom*. Orlando, FL: University of Central Florida.

Tomlinson, C. (1999). *The Differentiated Classroom: Responding to the Needs of All Learners*. Alexandria, VA: Association for Supervision and Curriculum Development.

Trifonas, P.P., ed. (2003). *Pedagogies of Differences. Rethinking Education for Social Change*. New York: RoutledgeFalmer.

Trueba, T.E. and **Bartolomé, L.**, eds (2000). 'Immigrant Voices: In Search of Pedagogical Reform'. Lanham, MD: Rowman and Littlefield Publishers.

Trujillo, J.A. (2009). 'Con todos: Using Learning Communities to Promote Intellectual and Social Engagement in the Spanish Curriculum'. In M. Lacorte and J. Leeman, eds, *Español en Estados Unidos y Otros Contextos de Contacto: Sociolingüística, Ideología y Pedagogía*. Madrid: Iberoamericana.

Valdés, G. (1997). 'The Teaching of Spanish to Bilingual Spanish-Speaking Students: Outstanding Issues and Unanswered Questions'. In M.C. Colombi and F.X. Alarcón, eds, *La Enseñanza del Español a Hispanohablantes*. Boston, MA: Houghton Mifflin.

— (2005). 'Bilingualism, Heritage Language Learners, and SLA Research: Opportunities Lost or Seized?' *The Modern Language Journal* 89, 410–26.

Valdés, G. and **Geoffrion-Vinci, M.** (1998). 'Chicano Spanish: The Problem of the Underdeveloped Code in Bilingual Repertoires'. *Modern Language Journal* 82, 473–501.

Valdés, G., Lozano, A. and **García-Moya, R.**, eds (1981). *Teaching Spanish to the Hispanic Bilingual: Issues, Aims, and Methods*. New York, NY: Teachers College Press.

Varona, L. (1999). 'From Instrumental to Interactive to Critical Knowledge Through Service-Learning in Spanish'. In J. Hellebrandt, J. Varona and L. Varona, *Construyendo Puentes: Building bridges. Concepts and Models for Service Learning in Spanish*. Washington, DC: American Association for Higher Education.

Villa, J.D. (1996). 'Choosing a "Standard" Variety of Spanish for the Instruction of Native Spanish Speakers in the U.S.' *Foreign Language Annals* 29 (2), 191–200.

Webb, J.B. and **Miller, B.L.**, eds, (2000). *Teaching Heritage Language Learners: Voices from the Classroom.* New York: American Council on the Teaching of Foreign Languages.

Wurr, A.J. and **Hellebrandt, J.** (2007). *Learning the Language of Global Citizenship: Service-Learning in Applied Linguistics* 81. San Francisco: Jossey-Bass.

NOTES

1   Within these communities, family, social class and levels of education become an important factor. As Valdés (2001) and Valdés and Geoffrion-Vinci (1998) point out, the specific Spanish variant and range of registers spoken by a family will have features that encode the family's social class and education.

2   This is also what differentiates Spanish HL learners from foreign language learners (FLLs), who are usually English-speaking monolingual students with no previous family or cultural connection to the Spanish language.

3   Examples abound of teachers asking immigrant parents to stop speaking the home language so that their child does not get 'confused' in school while learning English. We also hear about teachers encouraging parents to enroll their children in bilingual programmes, and of parents refusing to do so out of fear that their child will suffer discrimination or lag behind academically.

11 CANADA'S 'OTHER' LANGUAGES: The Role of Non-Official Languages in Ethnic Persistence

Jack Jedwab (Association d'études Canadiennes)

Introduction

Considerable attention has been directed towards knowledge of English and/or French by Canadians whose mother tongue (the language they first learned) is not an official language. Knowledge and use of an official language on the part of newcomers to Canada is considered an important dimension in the process of newcomer adjustment. Far less attention has been directed at the use of non-official languages by immigrants and the degree to which such languages are transmitted across generations. More often, such analysis has been conducted by those engaged in the sociology of ethnicity. In effect, the retention of the language of origin on the part of the descendants of immigrants is not seen as an integration question despite the public debates around the preservation or perseverance of minority ethnic identities. Rarely have researchers that examine language shifts on the part of newcomers looked at what happens to the non-official language.

Language, as in many countries, is a fundamental marker of personal identity amongst Canadians. A 2010 survey conducted by the firm Leger Marketing for the Association for Canadian Studies reveals that 90% of Canadians are attached to 'their' language. Some 51% of allophone Canadians said they were very attached to 'their' language and another 40% said they were somewhat attached. Examining the retention of non-official languages in multi-ethnic societies offers insight into the expression and recognition of pluralism as well as the societal model employed in managing diversity. Since the late 1960s, the management of Canada's diversity cannot be fully understood without considering the federal government's promotion of knowledge of the country's two dominant languages, English and French.

Indeed the recognition of official languages in 1969 was an important precursor to the introduction of Canada's multicultural policy two years later.

Language learning is by no means zero-sum. Quite obviously, children of immigrants can retain or learn a non-official language while perfecting their knowledge of an official language(s). The relationship between the use of official and non-official languages is influenced by government language policies, the dominant language of one's residential area, the language(s) used at school or in the workplace and one's social network. In the attempt to properly evaluate the knowledge and use of official and non-official languages, analysts have been especially dependent on the type of information that is made available through the census of Canada. In general, those who design the census have made important efforts to permit measurement of ethnic identification and language knowledge and use. But some of the changes to the census have increasingly made for challenges across time in the effort to measure the ethnocultural characteristics of the population. Between 1991 and 2001, changes in the interpretation of ethnic origin on the part of census respondents contributed to an important increase in the percentage of respondents reporting 'Canadian' as a single answer or as part of a multiple reply to the question.

This chapter looks at the degree to which selected non-official languages are retained and transmitted by groups that have been selected on the basis of their demographic importance and the length of time they have been established in Canada. In 2001 a question on generational status was introduced into the census of Canada, thus providing analysts with the means to measure intergenerational transmission of non-official languages. Examining the relationship between ethnic identification, language acquisition and home use offers valuable insight into the evolution of language and identity over time. Does language loss occur along a straight line or are there bumps in the process of language transmission between the generations? Are there similar patterns in the rates of intergenerational transmission of non-official languages across various groups? What specific socio-demographic factors modify the retention process amongst speakers of non-official languages?

Generational status provides a broader lens than immigrant status (i.e. domestic versus foreign-born) through which to measure the evolution of non-official languages. In this chapter we use data from the 2001, 2006 and the 2011 census to examine acquisition and home use of non-official languages. We also employ data from the 2002 Ethnic Diversity Survey (conducted by Statistics Canada and the Department of Canadian Heritage) to determine whether heritage language (HL) retention has any bearing on the sense of belonging to Canada. Finally some observations are offered as to whether the rate of HL retention says anything about Canada's models of diversity.

The evolving non-official language landscape: heritage languages and immigration

When the policy of multiculturalism was introduced in 1971, the foreign-born population of Canada was predominantly of European origin. Since that time the composition of immigrants to the country has evolved significantly and the majority of newcomers are of non-European backgrounds. Consequently, over the past few decades the non-official language landscape has shifted considerably in Canada. There has been an increase in the numbers of non-official languages and their collective demographic importance. The debates over the adoption of the policies of official languages and multiculturalism saw some minority ethnic leaders advocate for the extension of official recognition of English and French to other languages. For example, they proposed government recognition of the Polish and Ukrainian languages in places where their numbers exceeded the local francophone population (Rudnyckyj, 1967). If one was to apply such logic to the contemporary language landscape, the demographics would clearly not work in the favour of extending recognition to those European languages. As revealed below, in 2011 the leading non-official mother tongue is Punjabi, followed by Spanish, which enjoyed a growth rate of 50% over a decade, rising from 500000 to 750000.

Table 1: Number of persons identified by non-official official languages as mother tongue, 1996–2011

Mother Tongue Canada	1996	2001	2006	2011
Panjabi (Punjabi)	214530	271720	367505	430705
Spanish	228580	245495	345350	410670
German	470505	438080	450570	409200
Italian	514410	469485	455040	407490
Cantonese	Under chinese langauges	322310	361450	372465

Mother Tongue Canada (continued from previous page)	1996	2001	2006	2011
Arabic	166150	199940	261640	327870
Tagalog			235620	327450
Mandarin	Under chinese langauges	101790	170950	248705
Portuguese	222870	213815	219275	211335
Polish	222355	208375	211175	191650
Ukrainian	174830	148085	134500	111540
Greek	N/A	120360	117285	108925

Source: Statistics Canada, Census of Canada, 1996–2011

As observed below, amongst those under the age of 15, the 2006 and the 2011 census together reveal that Punjabi is the country's leading non-official mother tongue. Between 2006 and 2011, Arabic closed the gap with Spanish, which nonetheless remained the second most important non-official mother tongue amongst the under-15 population. In that same age group, between 2006 and 2011 such European languages as Italian, Portuguese, Polish and Ukrainian declined as first languages amongst the youngest cohort. At the other end of the age spectrum, Italian and German remained by far the dominant mother tongues in 2011. It is worth noting that in 2011 there was a near 15 to 1 ratio in the number of mother tongue Italians over the age of 65 relative to those under the age of 15. In the case of the Ukrainian mother-tongue population there are more than 12 persons over the age of 65 for every one under the age of 15. In the case of the Arabic mother-tongue population in 2011 there are more than 3 persons under the age of 15 for every one over the age of 65.

Table 2: Number of persons identified by non-official official languages as mother tongue under the age of 15 and over the age of 65, 2006 and 2011

	15 years and under		65 years and over	
Mother tongue	2006	2011	2006	2011
Spanish	59 660	61 040	21025	26 210
German	44 005	46 135	165735	145 080
Italian	16 595	10 005	150135	148 350

	15 years and under		65 years and over	
Punjabi	77180	81170	36475	51125
Cantonese	42650	32105	47730	58940
Mandarin	28565	37265	9050	14655
Arabic	52570	60405	17105	22335
Portuguese	15420	9905	34935	38965
Polish	18675	11595	39170	34350
Ukrainian	5600	4375	66915	53910
Greek	8185	7085	29890	34630
Tagalog	22795	29300	18980	28075

Source: Statistics Canada, Census of Canada, 2006 and 2011

The source countries of immigration favour the continued growth of Punjabi, Arabic, Spanish, Mandarin and Tagalog amongst other non-European languages. Recent shifts in source countries of immigrants have seen increases in newcomers with English and French as a first language. As observed below, in 2012, the number of immigrants whose mother tongue was English surpassed those whose first language was Tagalog. Still, important numbers of newcomers whose first language was Mandarin, Arabic, Spanish or Punjabi migrated to Canada.

Table 3: Canada – Permanent residents by mother tongue for top sixteen languages per year, 2000–12

Mother tongue	2000	2003	2006	2009	2012
English	19560	18694	24884	27534	30245
Mandarin	31389	31715	28049	25137	21100
Arabic	15492	17218	20009	24351	17786
Spanish	8719	12489	17059	16306	14189
Tagalog	9612	11442	16099	25282	29954
Punjabi	14038	13845	17714	15682	14326
Urdu	13613	11960	11231	6456	8883
French	5343	5391	7430	9274	13052
Russian	9449	8392	7300	7268	5041
Korean	7661	7179	6295	5930	5291
Farsi	4502	5042	6117	5269	5430
Gujarati	5316	4731	5615	3562	3988
Hindi	4303	4395	5220	4984	4915

Mother tongue (continued from previous page)	2000	2003	2006	2009	2012
Romanian	4541	5559	4877	3096	2404
Tamil	6480	4915	5237	4443	3429
Cantonese	5322	5207	4677	2936	

Source: Facts and figures – Immigration overview, Citizenship and Immigration Canada, 2003 and 2012

The retention of HLs is rarely an issue for those immigrants whose mother tongue is neither English nor French, although there may be exceptions amongst immigrants that have arrived at a very young age as knowledge of the non-official language may erode over time. Three in four persons whose mother tongue is neither English nor French are immigrants. The share of immigrants amongst those whose mother tongue is Arabic or Spanish is even higher, rising to above 80%. It is only amongst those who first learned Ukrainian that the majority is born in the country.

Table 4: Numbers and ratio of immigrants and non-immigrants by selected non-official language by mother tongue, 2011

Canada 2011 mother tongue	Total	Non-immigrants	%	Immigrants	%
Total Population	32495935	25720170	79.1	6775765	20.9
Non-official languages	6308875	1531545	24.2	4777330	75.8
Cantonese	376485	83185	22.1	293300	77.9
Mandarin	236595	27025	11.4	209570	88.6
Arabic	304325	50780	16.6	253525	83.4
Polish	185770	44000	23.6	141770	76.4
Spanish	372095	65410	17.5	306685	82.5
Portuguese	202855	47535	23.4	155320	76.6
Panjabi (Punjabi)	425415	120020	28.2	305395	71.8
Italian	400960	153710	38.3	247260	61.7
Greek	110315	46930	42.5	63985	57.5
German	360475	159380	44.2	201095	55.8
Ukrainian	107705	73895	68.6	33810	31.4

Source: Statistics Canada, Census of Canada, 2011

Ethnic mixing and language retention

One of the factors associated with intergenerational retention or loss of non-official languages is the degree to which ethnic mixing arises from marriage outside one's ethnic community. Undoubtedly, the degree to which language and/or ethnic mixing occurs has an impact on language transmission. In effect, the non-official language has a better chance to survive across the generations when the partners share the same language. This is reflected in the table below which reveals that, when both marital partners identify with a non-official language, two in three children report that language as their mother tongue. However, when the partner with a non-official language mother tongue marries or lives in common law with someone whose mother tongue is either English or French, the mother tongue of the child is the non-official language in less than one case in ten.

Table 5: Mother tongue of children with mother tongue of married husband or living common-law partner where female wife/partner's mother tongue is the non-official language, Canada 2011

Canada 2011			
Mother Tongue Non-official language – wife	English	French	Non-official language
Total – Mother tongue of child	177895	33735	1250760
English	157460 (88.5%)	6380	353505
French	770	20460 (60.6)	40880
Non-official language	13240	3270	790795 (63.2%)
English and French	300	875	2215
English and non-official language	5935	150	53465
French and non-official language	35	2095	7230
English, French and non-official language	155	500	2675

Source: Statistics Canada, Census of Canada, 2011

This shift in the identification of children of mixed language parents also gives rise to a higher incidence of dual and multiple declarations of ethnic origin. Multiple declarations of ethnic background are increasingly common by the third generation and beyond, and are more common amongst groups of European origin than amongst those of non-European ethnic origin.

On the basis of generational status, at least seven out of ten persons reporting German or Ukrainian origins are third generation or more, as are a slight majority of the Polish-origin population (see Table 6 below). The largest share of persons of Italian origin are second-generation Canadians. The largest percentage of the population reporting Portuguese origin is first generation Canadian while the overwhelming majority of Chinese- and Latin-American-origin Canadians are first generation.

Table 6: Number and percentage by generational status for selected ethnic groups, Canada 2011

Canada 2011	Total Number	% First generation	% Second generation	% Third generation or more
Ethnic origins	32852320	22	17	61
German	3203330	11	19	70
Polish	1010705	21	26	53
Ukrainian	1251170	8	18	74
Greek	252960	33	40	27
Italian	1488425	23	35	42
Portuguese	429850	45	39	16
Spanish	368305	55	28	17
Latin, Central and South American origins	544380	62	33	5
Chinese	1487580	71	25	4

Source: Statistics Canada, Census of Canada, 2011

Declarations of single and multiple origins provide insight into the degree of ethnic mixing. Table 7 below illustrates the evolution of the ethnic mix across generations amongst several of the larger ethnic groups. Within the first generation it is only amongst those Canadians of German and Ukrainian background that multiple declarations constitute the majority. In effect the immigrants that declare such origin may already possess dual or multiple backgrounds prior to their arrival.

Table 7: Ratio of single to multiple origins for selected ethnic group by generational status, Canada 2011

Canada 2011	First Generation		Second Generation		Third Generation	
Ethnic Origin	Single	Multiple	Single	Multiple	Single	Multiple
German	46	54	25	75	13	87
Polish	66	34	30	70	7	93
Ukrainian	44	56	36	64	16	84
Greek	78	22	60	40	22	78
Italian	77	23	59	41	20	80
Portuguese	77	23	54	46	16	84
Latin American	67	33	31	69	8	92
Chinese	88	12	70	30	24	76

Source: Statistics Canada, Census of Canada, 2011

The percentage of those reporting a first language associated with their ethnic origin remains relatively important amongst the children of immigrants of Greek, Portuguese and Italian descent and less so amongst those of Ukrainian, German and Polish descent. However, by the third generation, in almost all ethnic groups examined here, the non-official language is rarely retained as the first language.

As observed in Table 8, the number of persons in the first, second and third generation with a non-official language as their mother tongue varies considerably on the basis of the length of time the group has been established in Canada. However, languages such as German will attract people that do not possess the language as their mother tongue, which in part explains their relatively higher numbers in the third generation.

Table 8: Numbers with non-official languages as mother tongue for selected ethnic group by generational status, Canada 2011

Canada 2011 Mother tongue	Total – Generation status	First generation	Second generation	Third generation or more
Non-official languages	6551520	5034965	1189180	327375
Italian	403425	250235	140280	12910
Portuguese	207980	160750	45625	1605
Spanish	399810	335465	61935	2410
German	366960	210720	94950	61290 ?
Polish	187450	143695	41475	2280
Ukrainian	108590	34800	50545	23255
Greek	111405	64705	40705	5995
Arabic	323125	273230	49165	730
Cantonese	381575	299400	81065	1105
Mandarin	252295	225970	26095	240

Source: Statistics Canada, Census of Canada, 2011

The relationship between ethnic identification and non-official language retention provides some insight into the degree of linearity in the erosion of ethnic salience. In Table 9 we examine this relationship amongst selected European origin groups that include a statistically significant group identifying as third generation. Persons of Italian and Greek ethnic origin have the highest overall retention of mother tongue as a result of possessing the greater share of persons in the first generation, but in the second generation it is the Greek and Ukrainian groups that have a higher share of persons whose first language is associated with their ethnic origin. Clearly when it comes to the relationship between ethnic identification and language retention, census data support the idea that the erosion of culture occurs along a relatively straight-line. By the third generation very few individuals that identify with the ethnic group speak the associated heritage language as their first language. The greater ethnic mix documented above amongst some of the groups likely explains the erosion in the initial acquisition of a HL amongst ethnic identifiers.

Table 9: Numbers by ethnic origin and mother tongue for selected groups and ratio of mother tongue to associated ethnic origin by generational status, 2011.

2011	First generation			Second generation			Third generation plus		
	Ethnic Origin	Mother Tongue	%	Ethnic Origin	Mother Tongue	%	Ethnic Origin	Mother Tongue	%
German	345805	210720	61	612200	94950	15	2245320	61290	3
Polish	211030	143695	68	263210	41475	16	536460	2280	0,4
Ukrainian	99810	34800	35	226875	50545	22	924485	23255	3
Greek	83240	64705	78	101695	40705	40	68025	5995	9
Italian	344030	250235	73	524480	140280	27	619915	12910	2
Portuguese	192860	160750	83	169460	45625	27	67540	1605	2

Source: Statistics Canada, Census of Canada, 2011

It might be argued that the measure of first language knowledge amongst ethnic groups by generation is insufficient to confirm its progressive erosion because the non-official language can persist as a second language amongst the relevant ethnic groups. Relying on data from the 2006 census, Table 10 tests the notion. It includes the total number of 'third generation plus' that report knowledge of non-official languages, alongside those for whom it was the first language learned and those identifying with the ethnic group associated with the language. While there are more individuals in the third generation that know the language than had first learned it, the overall percentage of the total 'third generation plus' with the relevant ethnic background seems rather modest. Hence the evidence presented here moderately supports the idea of an important intergenerational erosion in knowledge of non-official languages.

Table 10: Numbers of knowledge of non-official language, mother tongue to associated ethnic origin for third generation plus, 2006

Third Generation plus, Canada, 2006	Ethnic origin	Mother tongue	Knowledge of non-official language
German	1604225	80175	122905
Italian	311215	8840	40550
Ukrainian	642955	29475	37180
Cantonese	–	1985	2640
Portuguese	20665	2650	9225
Spanish	–	7045	197010
Polish	364975	5810	6915
Arabic	–	3070	4935
Greek	23915	2105	4600

Source: Statistics Canada, Census of Canada, 2006

Language used at home

As mentioned at the outset, there is much interest on the part of immigration policy-makers in the degree to which immigrants shift from the use of an official language in the home amongst those that first learned a non-official language. Referred to as language transfers, these shifts are viewed as an indicator of the pace of adaptation to society on the part of first- and second-generation Canadians. Indeed, such shifts tend to occur over time and are more common amongst the second generation, and hence the groups that are likely to speak a non-official language most often at home tend to reflect the source countries of more recent immigration. It is therefore not surprising that South Asian and Asian languages dominate the list of the top ten non-official languages spoken most often at home in Canada.

Table 11: Top twenty non-official languages spoken most often at home, Canada, 2011

Canada 2011			
Punjabi	317070	Russian	109735
Cantonese	288620	Vietnamese	104965
Spanish	252020	Korean	104900
Mandarin	203275	Tamil	98945
Arabic	181790	Portuguese	97210
Tagalog (Filipino)	161080	Polish	85210
Italian	139480	Gujarati	55720
German	126380	Romanian	54460
Persian (Farsi)	118830	Greek	47705
Urdu	113785	Hindi	47080

Source: Statistics Canada, Census of Canada, 2011

As observed in Table 12, those reporting mother tongue Mandarin, Cantonese and Punjabi have the highest rate of home language retention. Amongst the mother tongue German, Italian, Polish and Portuguese groups the rate of reported home language use is considerably lower.

Table 12: Numbers by mother tongue and home language for selected groups and ratio of home language to mother tongue, Canada 2011

Canada 2011	Mother tongue	Home language	% home language
Mandarin	248705	184270	74.1
Cantonese	372460	275600	74.0
Punjabi	430700	300325	69.7
Spanish	410670	232565	56.6
Arabic	327870	161400	49.2
Portuguese	211335	91695	43.3
Polish	191645	81560	42.5
Greek	108925	45255	41.5
Italian	407485	132695	32.5
German	409200	119755	29.2
Ukrainian	111540	23250	20.8

Source: Statistics Canada, Census of Canada, 2011

In the case of the population born in Canada that first learned a non-official language, its dominance in the home evolves with age. As observed in Table 13, amongst those below the age of 25 the majority of Canadian-born allophones report that the non-official language is either the only language spoken most often at home or spoken in combination with an official language. Beyond the age of 25, the Canadian-born allophones are less likely to use the non-official language most often at home.

Table 13: Numbers born in Canada by age cohort with mother tongue as non-official language that only speak the non-official language at home, by percentage, and speak the non-official language at home in combination with an official language, Canada, 2011

Born in Canada 2011	Mother tongue non-official language	Only non-official language is most often spoken at home	%	Combination of non-official language and official language spoken most often at home	%
Total	1531545	572300	37	100045	6
0–14 years	545100	344775	63	51015	9
15–24 years	238480	98935	42	23140	10
25–44 years	326005	74800	23	16560	5
45–54 years	175425	23035	13	4450	3
55–64 years	96220	14035	15	2040	2
65 years and over	150315	16720	11	2830	2

Source: Statistics Canada, Census of Canada, 2011

Heritage language, ethnic belonging and Canadian identification

Though the acquisition and use of one or both of Canada's non-official languages is widely regarded as essential for successful adjustment to Canadian society, it does not imply that the ability to comprehend or speak a non-official language weakens identification with Canada. What, if any, impact does the retention of a non-official language have on one's degree of belonging to Canada? In the 2001 and 2006 censuses, referring to 'Canadian' origin in their response to the census question on ethnicity is more prevalent amongst the third generation than the first or second generation. The greater identification as 'ethnically Canadian' amongst third generation non-British-non-French census respondents led some analysts to assume that the group was more attached to Canada (Hassman–Howard, 1999); however, no meaningful evidence has been offered in support of this assertion. Indeed, the 2002 survey of ethnic diversity (EDS) conducted by Statistics Canada revealed that persons reporting a strong sense of ethnic identification also reported a strong sense of belonging to Canada. Moreover, the 2002 EDS revealed that the use of a non-official language at home does not meaningfully undercut the sense of belonging to Canada. Indeed in the case of the Ukrainian, Portuguese and Punjabi groups those reporting the use of their mother tongue at home report a higher sense of belonging to Canada than those who do not. Only amongst the group that first learned Italian and continue to speak it most often at home is there a sizable gap when contrasting their sense of belonging to Canada with those who no longer speak the language at home.

Table 14: Percentage reporting a strong sense of belonging to Canada (4 and 5 combined where 5 represents 'strong' on a 5-point scale) by those who selected non-official Language as first language with same language or other language spoken most often at home, 2003

First language	Language spoken most often at home	Other language spoken at home
Ukrainian	90.1	85.1
Spanish	76.5	80.6
Punjabi	81.5	79.2
Portuguese	89.7	83.4
Polish	83.1	87.8
Italian	67.9	86.6
German	79.1	87.3
Chinese Languages	70.7	76.4
Arabic	84.9	90.9

Source: Statistics Canada and Department of Canadian Heritage, Ethnic Diversity Survey 2003

Non-official languages in the model of diversity: language retention in the Canadian mosaic

For several decades the debate within North America around models of diversity has been characterised by a distinction between the multiculturalism generally associated with the Canadian approach and the melting pot often assumed to be the 'American way'. The historic assumption about the melting pot is that newcomers and their descendants will melt into the national culture and drop much of their ancestral heritage. Conversely it is assumed that the retention of minority ethnic cultures across generations is an obstacle to the cultural meltdown that occurs in the US (Gordon 1964).

In the late 1930s, historian Marcus Lee Hansen (1938) questioned this thesis by countering with the idea that a reversal of the assimilative process arises as one moves from the second to the third generation. Subsequent research did not generate much evidence in support of this view. Nonetheless there was an acknowledgement that the third generation did frequently retain some element of the ancestral ethnic identity and culture (Isajiw 1990; Alba and Nee 1997).

Canada initially proposed a different course. Conceding that there was no official culture in the country, in 1971 the federal government introduced a policy of multiculturalism within the framework of establishing English and French as its two official languages. It conveyed a strong message to the effect that there was no contradiction between maintaining one's ethnic identity and being Canadian. Prime Minister Pierre Trudeau (1971) observed that the 'question of cultural and ethnic pluralism in this country and the status of our various cultures and languages [is] an area of study given all too little attention in the past by scholars.' He contended that: 'adherence to one's ethnic group is influenced not so much by one's origin or mother tongue as by one's sense of belonging to the group, and by the group's 'collective will to exist'. Canadian multiculturalism policies and programmes did not explicitly support the promotion of non-official languages. The introduction of the 1982 Canadian Charter of Rights and Freedoms included a provision to support the preservation and enhancement of the multicultural heritage of Canadians, yet Section 27 of the Canadian Charter of Rights and Freedoms does not offer much by way of elaboration with regard to the meaning of the stated commitment.

Legislation establishing a Department of Multiculturalism was adopted in 1991. A second related law provided for the establishment of a Heritage Languages Institute with the purpose of developing national standards for teacher training and curriculum content for ethnic minority languages classes in Canada. But in 1992 the creation of the Institute was deferred until further notice, and indeed it never emerged (Leman, 1999).

In the Canadian multicultural paradigm, knowledge of non-official languages hasn't been deemed essential to ethnic belonging. In effect, a strong sense of belonging to one's ethnic origins does not require knowledge of the associated language. That is not to say that Canadian government policy does not recognise the importance of language as an expression of culture. Policies directed at official language minority communities most certainly acknowledge the connection, as do some aspects of public policy towards aboriginal peoples. In these instances the government is bound by historic commitments to the cultural preservation of these groups and/or the demographic importance of English and French on a national scale. There is no similar commitment on the part of government to non-official languages. In 2009, Canadian Minister of Multiculturalism Jason Kenney captured this sentiment when he stated that 'I think it's really neat that a fifth-generation Ukrainian Canadian can speak Ukrainian – but pay for it yourself' (cited in National Post, March 27, 2009).

Conclusion

Based on the evidence presented here it would seem fair to argue that intergenerational language loss proceeds along a straight line with relatively few bumps. By the third generation and beyond, knowledge of non-official languages is relatively low and the degree to which they are used at home is quite marginal. This is the case for almost all the groups examined here including those with non-European backgrounds that are less likely to be ethnically mixed as they tend to exhibit lower rates of intergenerational exogamy. For the most part, in the second generation, the non-European groups tend to have higher degrees of non-official language persistence than those of European origin. Several critics of multiculturalism are convinced that government policies give rise to ethnic persistence beyond the first generation, yet they offer very little empirical evidence in support of this claim. If the retention of non-official languages is considered an important dimension of ethnic persistence then the evidence here clearly contradicts the view that cultural transmission is being encouraged via federal policies.

REFERENCES

Alba, R. and **Nee, V.** (1997) 'Rethinking Assimilation Theory for a New Era of Immigration'. *International Migration Review* 31 (4).

Gordon, Milton M. (1964). *Assimilation in American Life: The Role of Race, Religion and National Origins, United States*. Oxford: Oxford University Press.

Government of Canada (2013). 'Citizenship and Immigration Canada Facts and figures – Immigration Overview, 2000–2012'.

Hansen, M.L. (1938). 'The Problem of the Third Generation Immigrant'. Rock Island Illinois, Augustana Historical Society.

Howard-Hassman, R.E. (1999). '"Canadian" as an Ethnic Category: Implications for Multiculturalism and National Unity'. *Canadian Public Policy* xxv (4).

Isajiw, Wsevolod W. (1990). 'Ethnic-Identity Retention'. In R. Breton, et al., *Ethnic Identity and Equality: Varieties of Experience in a Canadian City*, Toronto: University of Toronto Press.

Jedwab, J. (2010). 'Canada's "Very Attached": Quebecers Push Language over Nation amongst Markers of Identity to which Canadians are Most Attached'. *Association for Canadian Studies*, June 2010. http://www.acs-aec.ca/en/social-research/identity-values/.

Kenney, J. (2009). Minister of Multiculturalism J. Kenney cited in *National Post*, March 27, 2009.

Leman, M. (1999). 'Canadian Multiculturalism'. *Political and Social Affairs Division*. Government of Canada, Ottawa. http://publications.gc.ca/Collection-R/LoPBdP/CIR/936-e.htm.

Rudnyckyj, J.B. (1967). 'Observations'. *Report of the Royal Commission on Bilingualism and Biculturalism* 1: *Official Languages*, Ottawa, Canada.

Statistics Canada (1996, 2001, 2006, 2011). Census of Canada.

Statistics Canada and Department of Canadian Heritage (2003). *Ethnic Diversity Survey*. Ottawa, Canada.

Trudeau, P.E. (1971). Speech in the House of Commons. Government of Canada, October 8, 1971.

RETHINKING HERITAGE LANGUAGE in a Critical Pedagogy Framework

Panayota Gounari (University of Massachusets)

Introduction

When I ask graduate students at the beginning of the semester 'what is language?' I usually get a mix of responses ranging from 'do you mean English?', 'a code for communication', to 'identity', 'culture', 'how we express ourselves in words', and so forth. These responses often point to general perceptions about the workings of language and they are important to the degree that they come from in-service or future educators of K-12 and adult students in the process of acquiring English. As I have argued elsewhere (Gounari 2003; 2006), the tendency is either to reduce language to a simple code of communication or, in the best case scenario, to connect it with culture and identity and tie it with struggles for social justice and equality. However, both perspectives do not even begin to capture the complicated net of geographical, social, cultural and political economy layers that language constitutes and articulates upon. As Paulo Freire would argue, 'the word is more than just an instrument which makes dialogue possible' (Freire 2000, 87). A simple question on the definition of language often serves as a point of departure for my graduate students and future language educators to re-contextualise the ways in which they think about language, and to understand and navigate the often confusing landscape of bilingualism and language policies in the US. I say confusing because of the following paradox: while there is an abundant production of solid, important, multidisciplinary research in the field of bilingualism and bilingual education, relevant language and educational policies seem to, at best, lag behind or, at worst, to rely on non-scientific data and dubious research in order to make decisions about bilingual students' lives. This dissonance between policy, research and reality (that which is actually happening on the ground, in schools and communities) is not coincidental, but it is the glue that holds together the reactionary agenda against bilingualism in the US. The ongoing 'misconception' about the workings of language and the silencing of the ways in which it connects with access to material and symbolic resources has become part of the mainstream discourse around educating 'minority children'. At this juncture, language becomes on occasion, a tool, a right, a resource, a handicap or a weapon.

Let us take the example of the term 'bilingual', which in the last decade has been slowly but systematically eliminated from the official educational discourse in the US. From the expiration of the historical Title VII in 2002, better known as the 'Bilingual Education Act', and its replacement with Title III under NCLB, to the renaming of the Federal Office of Bilingual Education and Minority Languages Affairs (OBEMLA) into Office of English Language Acquisition (OELA), with its focus on the development of English proficiency, we can identify a clear move to purge education from anything bilingual (Crawford 2004; Garcia 2009) and rename everything bilingual as 'language acquisition.' Different programmes for English Language Learners (ELLs) across the country these days rarely include the term 'bilingual' even when bilingualism is the goal (as is the case, for instance, with 'dual-language programmes'). This purging is taking place while, according to the US Census Bureau, the population speaking a language other than English at home has increased by 140% in the past three decades (US Census Report 2010). More than five million students speak a language other than English at home and are classified at school as having limited proficiency in English (NCELA 2011). At the same time, research suggests that 'within two or three generations, most non-English-speaking immigrants to the United States will have lost or almost lost their heritage languages' (Spolsky 2011, 3). Ironically, while the number of people speaking a language other than English at home radically increases, the shift to English is proceeding even faster.

In this context, there are two questions that critical researchers, educators, policymakers and other stakeholders must answer. First, how do we talk about students who negotiate more than one language in their lives in the current educational landscape? Throughout this chapter, the terms 'minority students', 'ELLs', 'heritage', 'bilingual students' and 'students who negotiate more than one language in their lives' will be used interchangeably in order to stress the problem with nomenclature. What are the referents and representations for the terms 'bilingual' and 'heritage' and how does language choice label the subjects of the educational process in particular ways? Second, how can we reconceptualise education for bilingual students through a critical pedagogy framework? This chapter builds on a critical discussion of how heritage languages (HLs) and speakers are talked about in the existing literature in North America. A review of the literature on HLs points to a widespread concern for the nomenclature and for the ways in which it positions subjects, objects and processes in the educational arena. As Wiley (2001) notes, 'the labels and definitions that we apply to HL learners are important, because they help to shape the status of the learners and the languages they are learning' (Wiley 2001, 35). There is much more in the name than the simple choice of words; these labels produce real or constructed subjectivities and inform material practices as well as pedagogies. As to the second question that arises – 'what kind of pedagogies for students who negotiate more than one language in their lives' – it is worth exploring concept of critical pedagogy as an emancipatory political theory of education. Critical educators need to take seriously the role of language in either enabling oppressed students to come to subjectivity and partake in the material resources and opportunities as the mainstream does, or shut them out of these. This is not to suggest that English is automatically a vehicle for social mobility without considering larger socioeconomic structural changes. It rather means to engage in rigorous analyses that would unveil the intimate relationship between language, power, political economy, and ideology and the ensuing pedagogical and social consequences.

The discourse of 'heritage language': what is in the name?

> Heritage (her·it·age): property that is or may be inherited; an inheritance/ valued objects and qualities such as cultural traditions, unspoiled countryside, and historic buildings that have been passed down from previous generations. *(Oxford Dictionary)*

'Heritage language' has been historically used in the official educational and language policy discourse in Canada to refer to the 'educational programmes that provincial governments of Canada set up within their elementary school systems, after the passage of its multicultural policy in the late 1960s' (Garcia 2009, 60). It was only in the late 1990s that 'heritage' became popular as a term in the bibliography in the US, in the constant process of naming, renaming and labeling those learners who negotiate more than one language or who are non-English speakers. The term 'heritage language' has been used in the US in the context of the 'study, maintenance, and revitalisation of non-English languages' (Valdés 2001) often spoken by ethnic communities.

It refers to 'languages other than the dominant language (or languages) in a given social context' – that is, languages other than English, that is the *de facto* dominant language in the US. While English has never been legislated as the official language of the nation, it has acquired, nevertheless, an official status as it is the primary language used in government, education, social services and public communication as well as in public business (voting). In addition, it should be noted that 28 states have enacted laws that declare English as the official language (Crawford 2005), while at least seven states prohibit instruction in languages other than English. This translates into the following picture: a core, strong, *de facto* official language and peripheral, often illegal 'heritage' languages. Therefore, 'any language other than English can be considered a "heritage language" for speakers of that language' (Keleher 2010). Interestingly though, if any language other than English spoken in the US is characterised as 'heritage', English is left out as heritage-less – that is, without a past (Cummins 2005). According to other definitions, the term applies to the non-English languages spoken by newcomers and indigenous, immigrant and refugees (Peyton, Ranard and McGinnis 2001; Cummins 2005). In an attempt to further define the term, Fishman (2001) talks about three different types of heritage language (HL): immigrant, indigenous (Amerindian) and colonial (non-indigenous languages that were already established before the US came into being). Guadalupe Valdés (2001) illuminates the issue further, noting that a 'heritage' speaker refers to 'a student who is raised in a home where a non-English language is spoken by one who speaks or merely understands the HL, and who is to some degree bilingual in English and the heritage language' (Valdés 2001, 1). Valdés correctly stresses that there is a degree of bilingualism that is not acknowledged. She insists that 'it is the historical and personal connection to the language that is salient and not the actual proficiency of individual speakers.' Therefore, in this view, 'heritage' has some emotional value since it alludes to provenance and origin and, in some ways, seems to be disconnected with the present. From all the nuanced definitions listed above, we can conclude that in the US context, any language other than English can be safely characterised a 'heritage' language; as such, it has a secondary status and is viewed as something inherited and passed down from one generation to the next. Its survival and maintenance is justified upon its historical and personal value, and not on real current societal needs. It follows then that the maintenance of HLs rests with the individuals and the communities and not with the State or the federal government. According to Fishman, 'for those individuals interested in strengthening endangered indigenous languages or maintaining immigrant languages that are not normally taught in school, *heritage language* refers to a language with which individuals have a personal connection' (Fishman 2001). Based on this statement, should we not be asking who puts languages in danger? For we are not looking here at a natural phenomenon. Language loss and language shift are complex processes and many factors can account for them, particularly those related to the power and status of the dominant language. These are a social phenomena and not linguistic when 'members of a less powerful and less prestigious group – who usually (thought not always) comprise a demographic minority – succumb to a variety of assimilative pressures and gradually adopt a dominant group's language as their own' (Crawford 2005, 9). Another cause of language shift is noted by Cummins: 'currently, there is massive loss of national language resources because young children are given few opportunities to use and become literate in their heritage languages' (2005, 590). Language shift becomes increasingly likely as a group becomes 'more integrated into the broader society, economy and political system; more urbanized and less isolated in rural enclaves; more exposed to mass culture in the dominant language; better educated, more affluent, and less dependent (socially and economically) on the ethnic community' (Crawford 2005, 59).

I made the case earlier that maintenance of the 'HL' has an emotional and social dimension. How then is the personal connected with the societal and in what ways does it shape a politics of representation and identity? Do English speakers not have a 'personal' connection with their language? Do they not also need to maintain it? Or do they preserve it so aggressively because they feel it is threatened?

What becomes clear from reviewing the HL bibliography is that there is a diversity of types of HL learners, multiple language situations/contexts/speakers fitting the definition, as well as a debate on whether to keep using the term. Why is this the case? Why do we have such difficulty talking about students who negotiate more than one language in their daily lives? If it is simply a matter of codification for the sake of scholarship, why can't we agree on the term? According to Hornberger,

> None of the terms for HL is in fact ever straightforward or neutral, even when it is originally intended to be so; rather these terms are contested and ever-shifting in meaning, even as the local heritage identities, knowledges, and purposes the languages convey are also inevitably contested and ever-shifting in their national contexts. That fluidity and negotiation is [...] the surest evidence of the adaptability and long-term survival of heritage languages in our ever-changing world. (Hornberger 2005, 608)

The shift in meaning resonates with the perceived status of languages other than English in the US, as well as with the hidden educational agenda for students who negotiate more than one language in their lives. The terms used also have an important historical dimension that reflects the perception of bilingual children and 'minority groups' in different historical periods as well as the attitudes towards societal bilingualism.

Consider, for instance, how in the official federal discourse in the US, second language learners are still referred to as Limited English Proficient (LEP). LEP is a term first used in 1975 in the Lau Remedies that told districts how to identify and evaluate children with limited English skills, after the investigation of 334 school districts by the Office of Civil Rights revealed that those districts failed to provide equal treatment to minority children. Currently, in order to identify a student as LEP (interchangeably used with ELL), s/he has to fall under some of the following categories: to be a student who was not born in the US or whose native language is a language other than English; who comes from an environment where a language other than English is dominant; who is migratory; who comes from an environment where a language other than English has had a significant impact on the individual's level of English language proficiency. However, these are very different student profiles. In addition, these ELLs are in the process of acquiring English, that is, in the process of becoming bilingual. For this reason, the term 'emergent bilingual' has also been used in the literature to mark the process of becoming bilingual, and to validate the home language of the student. The LEP labeling is highly problematic because it positions students in terms of what they lack, what they are short of. It names them on the basis of their limitations (*bilingualism minus* (-)) as opposed to their strengths and richness (*bilingualism plus* (+)). This discourse is built on the assumption that monolingualism is the norm, the default state of the brain and cognition, and that bilingualism or multilingualism are exceptions and are viewed as additions to the default (*monolingualism plus* (+)). This labeling is in line with a monoglossic framework where the two or more languages are autonomous codes developed separately, as additions to the first, and do not interact with each other (Garcia 2009). The labeling takes place always with reference to or in comparison with English, that is, with the dominant language.

The 'limited' perspective on bilingual or multilingual children ignores the well-documented fact that human beings shift between languages, but they also shift between discourses. Even monolingual speakers adapt their speech to the discursive needs of their contexts and the particular communicative conditions. One can only imagine the degree of the switching between discourses and languages amongst bilingual/multilingual speakers. I want to approach this language use as language practices through a translanguaging framework (Garcia 2009), that is, the use of language in action as in 'multiple discursive practices in which bilinguals engage in order to make sense of their bilingual worlds' (Garcia 2009). Bilingual or multilingual learners, families and communities translanguage all the time in order to produce meaning using their languages for different modalities. This seems to be the default state as opposed to monolingualism.

If different ways of naming shape to some degree the educational and language policy agenda, is 'heritage' language the term that we should be using in our scholarship, in our schools and with our students? If heritage resonates with preservation and/or maintenance of an ethnic group's heritage where language is used as a vehicle, what does this say about the politics behind it? Whose heritage is maintained and who decides on it? In this context, the use of 'heritage language' is positioned as a double-edged sword since on the one hand, its use does signal a retreat from all the gains of linguistic minorities during the civil rights era. On the other hand, as Garcia and Cummins (2005) argue, 'the use of the term "heritage languages" in education in speaking with teachers, parents, schools, administrators, and children provides a way to "crack" today's homogenous monolingual schooling of very different children in the United States, providing a space for the use of languages other than English in educating children' (Garcia and Cummins 2005, 602). I personally believe that Garcia is correct in pointing out that 'positioning languages other than English in the US as heritage languages clearly is rear-viewing. It speaks to what was left behind in remote lands, what is in one's past. By leaving the languages in the past, the term "heritage languages" connotes something that one holds onto vaguely as one's remembrances, but certainly not something that is used in the present or that can be projected into the future' (ibid., 601). If language is relegated to the past, if it is part of the historical background of an ethnic group, then it might be perceived as irrelevant in the current historical juncture. Or, to take it a step further, if it is made irrelevant to the present, it might also be less threatening to the dominant language. If it is irrelevant to the present, though, there is no imperative to maintain it and learn it. However, HL learners in the US are not only defined by their familial or ancestral ties to a particular language that is not English (Hornberger 2005). They are more importantly defined through the ways in which they position themselves in this heritage culture, the ways in which they shape their agency as they mediate 'heritage' in the 'here and now,' and the ways in which they negotiate dominant English in relation to their home languages. HL speakers are still bilingual people in the making, human beings who negotiate their identities by navigating multiple cultural, ethnic, linguistic and political referents. As agents of their lives, experiences and subjects in the educational process can be better understood within the framework of critical pedagogy theory. The next section attempts at drawing some preliminary connections between bilingual education and its main theoretical concepts.

Critical pedagogy and heritage language

Critical pedagogy as an educational theory and practice that is political at its core can offer a framework for rethinking language and education for students who negotiate more than one language in their lives. Critical pedagogy is grounded in scholarly work that emerged in the late 1970s and early 1980s in the US. Brazilian educator Paulo Freire's work laid the foundations for what became the American Critical Pedagogy School of the 1970s and onwards. Critical pedagogy has its theoretical roots in a long historical legacy of progressive and critical social thought in Europe, the US and Latin America, and it has capitalised on diverse theoretical traditions from both sides of the Atlantic ranging from Marxism, to critical theory, neomarxism, postcolonial studies and so forth. What follows are concepts drawn from critical pedagogy theory that could set and advance the agenda of educating bilingual students in the US. Language is fundamental in the critical pedagogy theoretical tradition in two ways. First, language inside or outside the educational process is never neutral; as an identity marker, it is part of cultural identification, it has an ideological layer and it can be a powerful weapon of oppressed groups who are trying to lay claims in cultural and material goods. Literacy in the critical pedagogy framework is not limited to learning to 'read and write', but rather to build consciousness and to be able to decode the word in relation to the larger sociopolitical picture. Language is not just strings of words but it is a tool for understanding and intervening in the world. Second, language is seen as an emancipatory tool in the forms of what has been called a 'language of critique and possibility,' that is, the articulation of an alternative discourse that originates in critiquing and thrives in producing new possibilities for human beings.

Political nature of education, curricula and language

One of the basic premises of critical pedagogy is that education is not neutral; it is inherently political. To see pedagogy as 'a transparent vehicle of truth' is to 'overlook important political issues regarding how canons are historically produced, whose interests they serve as well as whose they do not serve, and how they are sustained within specific forms of institutional power' (Giroux 1996). 'Political' implies that there are assymetrical power relations, conflicting interests and identities, and deliberate choices about what constitutes 'knowledge' and how it is produced, what experiences and languages it legitimises and/or marginalises. A political education is conducive to conscientisation, that is, critical awareness of the world, where students realise their subject position. As a political project, pedagogy 'should always function in part as a provocation that takes students beyond the world they know in order to expand the range of human possibilities and democratic values. Central to critical pedagogy is the recognition that the way we educate our youth is related to the future that we hope for and that such a future should offer students a life that leads to the deepening of freedom and social justice' (Giroux 2010). This kind of education could never function on the basis of excluding the basic means by which bilingual students become masters of their own thinking: their language. The way we educate bilingual students has to be connected with considerations of equal and full participation and access to symbolic, material and cultural resources. This means acknowledging that language is not a code of communication and that bilingual education is not just another model to educate 'minority' children. In the discussion of HL there are tensions between a dominant, official, legitimate, vibrant language and other 'subjugated,' old, irrelevant languages. Language is political to the degree that students from oppressed groups, in a monolingual framework, are denied their native language and are thus deprived from becoming 'masters of their own thinking' (Freire 2000). However, if allowed to become masters of their own thinking, students from subjugated groups can develop biliteracy in a pedagogically and socially sound way as part of a larger critical biliteracy.

Rethinking HL education in the context of political education would mean acknowledging that in the US, Americanisation and acculturation were fundamental goals of the curriculum as new waves of immigrants were reaching the American shores. Immigrants were perceived as a threat not only to the 'homogeneity' of the American fabric, but also to the sense of community, that has been constructed around the small American town as the guarantor of social order and stability (Aple 1979). In its genesis, one of the major roles of curriculum was to develop 'community'. However, in order to be part of this community, immigrant children or children with immigrant parents had to conform to the norms of Americanisation. An important element of this process was to learn English, the dominant language, at the expense of their native tongue. The nature of the curriculum field was defined in its early stage by white Anglo-Saxon protestant middle-class scholars and its social role was to develop a high degree of normative and cognitive consensus. Between 1870 and 1900, 'the school was pronounced as the fundamental institution that would solve the problems of the city, the impoverishment and moral decay of the masses and increasingly would adjust individuals to their respective places in an industrial economy' (Apple 1979, 67).

Critical language educators would benefit from looking at the institutions that have been producing and reproducing monolingualism and the ways in which they have functioned historically to legitimise some languages, forms of expression and knowledge at the expense of others. Schools are such sites of legitimisation/de-legitimisation. Let us not forget that from its genesis and in the first attempts at curricular theory, public schooling aimed at functioning as an instrument of homogenisation, social and cultural control, standardisation and elimination of diversity. The purpose of urban schooling was to work as a normalising agency, as well as a sifter for labour division and social stratification. Schools have historically functioned in parallel with the job demands of each historical period. However, currently there seems to be a 'creation of immigrant labour pools' in which 'growth poles in the global economy attract immigrant labour from their peripheries. The US economy has become increasingly dependent on immigrant labour.' (Robinson 2013). William Robinson talks about a 'Latinisation' of the US economy where Latino immigrants have massively swelled the lower rungs of the US workforce. [. . .] From the viewpoint of the dominant groups, the dilemma is how to super-exploit an immigrant labour force, such as Latinos in the US, yet how to simultaneously assure it is super controllable and supercontrolled' (ibid.). The state is then forced to strike a balance between a stable supply of cheap labour to employers, and at the same time, a viable system of state control over immigrants. Beyond criminalisation of immigrant communities, could schools also function towards that direction when they essentially fail immigrant students?

Schools have a central role in reproducing cultural capital and economic values. They exercise social and economic control not only materially (through routines, rules, etc.), but also through particular forms of meaning.

In this sense, schools play a role in preserving and even generating inequalities (Apple 1979), including linguistic inequalities. At the same time, 'they teach conformity to the social, cultural, and occupational hierarchy. In our contemporary world, they are not constituted to foster independent thought, let alone encourage independence of thought and action' (Aronowitz 2008). According to Aronowitz and Giroux (1993), knowledge becomes important not simply because it is legitimised by curriculum experts, but rather because of the degree to which it helps human beings understand not only the assumptions embedded in its form and content, but also the processes whereby knowledge is produced, appropriated and transformed within specific social and historical settings. Critical pedagogy claims that schools should teach a discourse of enquiry and analysis and that they should encourage students to explore the translation tools necessary for their developing agency that can be broadly understood as the negotiation between constraints and possibilities with the aim to act upon one's personal and social conditions. It assumes that the subjects of the educational process are free-thinking, independent human beings who should be able to make educated choices regarding knowledge and learning. This becomes all the more important when we talk about the education of students from marginalised and oppressed groups, since it talks to a degree of literacy that encompasses 'learning English'. Schools as sites of struggle and contestation that reproduce the dominant culture and ideology, as well as what is perceived as legitimate language/knowledge, make use of their institutional power to either affirm or deny a learner's language and knowledge, and thus his/her lived experiences and culture. In that sense, it is interesting to consider how 'monolingualism', as the norm, is constructed and spread within educational institutions through educational policies, curricula, textbooks, teacher attitudes and so forth. Learning English has less to do with learning the dominant language and much more to do with the sociopolitical and ideological 'story' behind it. Antonio Gramsci astutely understood this almsot a century ago when he noted: 'each time that in one way or another, the question of language comes to the fore, that signifies that a series of other problems is about to emerge, the formation and enlarging of the ruling class, the necessity to establish more 'intimate' and sure relations between the ruling groups and the popular masses, that is, the reorganisation of cultural hegemony' (Gramsci 1971, 52). As educators and researchers working in the field of language, we cannot separate questions of language from political economy. To expand further, 'the problematic of language and power is fundamentally a question of democracy' (Fairclough 1995, 221). In the case of English dominance, it is 'a problem to the extent that its role within the hegemonic bloc reinforces economic inequality, cultural suppression and political oppression'. According to Gramsci, 'language use is intimately tied to education, culture, ideology and politics'. It cannot be divorced from questions of subordination and domination but also contains possibilities for resistance and struggle in what Gramsci calls the 'war of position' in preparation for social change and a 'war of maneuver' (Ives 2010).

Critical pedagogy and the role of culture:

A nuanced understanding of culture is imperative for critical language educators. This understanding should go beyond a static touristic and folk perception of culture to include 'a dialectical instance of power and conflict, rooted in the struggle over both material conditions and the form and content of practical activity' (Giroux 1983, 1988). Culture incorporates social and institutional practices, social significations, language and forms of knowledge, amongst other things. In the terrain of culture, people understand who they are as agents; they name the world. For Critical pedagogy, culture is seen as a site of contestation and, at the same time, as an act of intervention. In this context, schooling represents an introduction to, a preparation for and a legitimation of, particular forms of social life (McLaren 2007). Along these lines, Freire has proposed an education that would enable people to reflect upon themselves, their responsibilities and their role in the given cultural climate, but mostly to reflect on or realise their own power of reflection. Such an education would help people to adopt an inquisitive attitude towards their problems, thus contributing to the establishment and operation of an authentic democracy. One of the basic elements of people's radicalisation was the emergence of literacy as an issue of primary political importance. Freire's focus on people's active participation was founded on his faith in humanisation, which portrayed people as creators of history and culture (Grollios 2009). A crucial element in Freire's pedagogy is the investigation of the students' thematic universe that refers to the thinking/language they use in order to access reality. Critical pedagogy gives great emphasis to Freire's concept of 'cultural power', which starts with the particular social and historical circumstances, problems, perspectives and actions that constitute a form of expression. The concept of cultural power can contribute to the need for teachers to make bilingual students' experiences an object of discussion and legitimise them (though using and legitimising their own language), with the goal of creating the conditions for active expression.

Conclusion

By reassigning language to a political and ideological context and by understanding the functions of schooling in general and for bilingual students,
in particular, we can reconceptualise 'heritage language'. In this framework
'heritage' should no longer be about something static, linear and revered.
Heritage is not a paradigm or a model, informed by specific cultural rules
about how to live one's life, nor a rigid guideline for identifying with a particular ethnic group. In using the term 'heritage' we must overcome the
assumption 'that there is nothing that people currently alive can do to change
the institutions they inherited, and that if oblivious to their impotence they
try to meddle with the legacy – then unimaginable disasters will follow,
whether brought about by divine punishment or by the laws of nature which
neither admit nor bear any violation' (Bauman 1999, 26). 'heritage language',
if this is the term we will be using, must be reinvented to include a more fluid
understanding of bilingualism/multilingualism, one that includes not just
home languages and translanguaging but also the ways in which this translanguaging breaks the continuity and tradition of existing cultural norms.
HLs are not tightly closed within ethnic communities. They are also the
bridges between these communities and the dominant language and culture.
The current challenge for critical language educators and progressive policy
makers is to reinvent 'heritage' as a living and relevant category that includes
multiple histories and experiences that reflect the lives, struggles, aspirations
and dreams of both dominant and subjugated groups. This will help move
these subjugated groups from the periphery of our school curricula into a
centre stage where they will be able to recount their own histories in their
own languages. Against a static and disarticulated view of the past, collective
ethnic memory could work as a pedagogical force that, according to Giroux,
'makes claim on certain histories, memories, narratives and representations'
(2001, 38). In this instance, history is not the predetermined sequence of the
determined, but 'the emergence of radical otherness, immanent creation,
[and] non-trivial novelty' (p. 39). 'Heritage' language must come alive in the
multiple translanguaging practices of bilingual and multilingual students
and their communities.

How then do we develop a radical pedagogy that makes languages other
than English not just relevant, but also necessary for all students? The basis
for a new radical pedagogy for all students must be drawn from a theoretically
sophisticated understanding of how language, power, resistance and human
agency can become central elements in the struggle for critical thinking and

learning. The struggle over language is a political struggle that will not be resolved in schools, but schools can, nevertheless, serve as sites where alternative discourses and educational practices can be articulated and where we will always be connecting language with material and symbolic possibilities.

REFERENCES

Apple, M. (1979). *Ideology and Curriculum*. New York, NY: Routledge.

Aronowitz, S. (2008). *Against Schooling*. Boulder, CO: Paradigm Publishers.

Bauman, Z. (1999). *In Search of Politics*. Stanford, CA: Stanford University Press, 136–7.

Crawford, J. (2005). *Educating English Learners*. Los Angeles, CA: Bilingual Education Services, Inc.

Cummins, J. (2005). 'A Proposal for Action: Strategies for Recognizing Heritage Language Competence as a Learning Resource within the Mainstream Classroom'. *The Modern Language Journal* 89 (4) (Winter), 585–92.

Fairclough, N. (1995). *Critical Discourse Analysis*. London: Longman.

Fishman, J. (2001). '300-plus Years of Heritage Language Education in the United States'. In Peyton, J.K., Ranard, D. and McGinnis, S., eds, *Heritage Languages in America*. Long Beach, CA: Center for Applied Linguistics.

Garcia, O. (2009). *Bilingual Education in the 21st Century: A Global Perspective*. Malden, MA: Wiley Blackwell.

— (2005). 'Positioning Heritage Languages in the United States'. *The Modern Languages Journal* 89 (4) (Winter), 601–5.

Giroux, H. (1996). *Fugitive Cultures: Race, Violence and Youth*. New York, NY: Routledge.

— (2001). *Public Spaces Private Lives: Beyond the Culture of Cynicism*. Boulder, CO: Rowman and Littlefield.

Gounari, P. (2003). *The Hegemony of English*. Boulder, CO: Paradigm Publishers.

Gounari, P. (2006). 'Language Policy In the United States: Uncommon Language and the Discourse of Common Sense'. *Belgian Journal of English Language and Literatures*, New Series 4, January, 39–50.

Gramsci, A. (1971). *Selections from Prison Notebooks*, ed. and trans. Quinten Hoare and Geoffrey Smith. New York: International Publishers.

Grollios, G. (2009). *Freire and the Curriculum*. Boulder, CO: Paradigm Publishers.

Hornberger, N. (2005). 'Opening and Filling Up Implementational and Ideological Spaces in Heritage Language Education'. In *The Modern Language Journal* 89 (4) (Winter), 605–9.

Hornberger, N. (2005). Heritage/Community Language Education: US and Australian Perspectives. *International Journal of Bilingual Education and Bilingualism* 8 (2 and 3), 101–8.

Ives, P. (2010). 'Global English, Hegemony and Education: Lessons from Gramsci'. In P. Mayo, ed., *Gramsci and Educational Thought*. Chichester: Wiley-Blackwell.

Keleher, A. (2010). 'What is a Heritage Language Programme?' Heritage Briefs CAL. www.cal.org/heritage.

McLaren, P. (2007). *Life in Schools. Boston.* MA: Allyn and Bacon.

NCELA (2011). *The Growing Numbers of English Learner Students 2009/10.* Washington, DC: National Clearinghouse for English Language Acquisition and Language Instruction Educational Programs.

Ricento, P. (2012). 'Political Economy and English as a Global Language' In *Critical Multicultural Studies.* 1 (1).

Robinson, W. (2013) 'The New Global Capitalism and the War on Immigrants'. *Truthout.* www.truth-out.org/news/item/18623-the-new-global-capitalism-and-the-war-on-immigrants.

Spolsky, B. (2010). 'Does the United States Need a Language Policy?' *CAL Digest.* San Francisco, CA: Center for Applied Linguistics.

Shin, Hyon B. and R.A. Kominski. (2010). *Language Use in the United States: 2007.* American Community Survey Reports, ACS-12. Washington, DC: US Census Bureau.

Valdés, G. (2001) 'Heritage Language Students Profiles and Possibilities'. In Peyton, J.K., Ranard, D., and McGinnis, S., eds, *Heritage Languages in America.* San Francisco, CA: Center for Applied Linguistics.

Wiley, T. (2001). 'On Defining Heritage Language and Their Speakers'. In Peyton, J. Ranard, D., and McGinnis, S., eds, *Heritage Languages in America.* McHenry, Il: The Center for Applied Linguistics and Delta Systems/CAL, 29–36.

INDEX

Acculturation 118

agency 8, 69, 83, 141, 183, 211, 216, 226, 246, 251, 262, 264, 265, 268

Arabic 28, 29, 41, 46, 47, 48, 49, 50, 60, 80, 94, 95, 103, 104, 153, 158, 163, 268, 269, 270, 274, 275, 277, 278, 279

Australia 3, 6, 8, 10, 13, 17, 25, 89, 91, 92, 93, 94, 95, 96, 97, 98, 99, 100, 102, 103, 104, 108, 110, 112, 139, 140, 141, 142, 143, 144, 145, 146, 147, 148, 151, 153, 154, 155, 156, 157, 159, 161, 162, 163, 165, 185, 189

bicultural identity 17, 118, 120, 121, 123, 127, 133

bilingual 29

biliteracy 29, 40, 70, 79, 241, 246, 248, 263

Canadian Studies 265

CEFR 4, 10, 13, 14, 19, 20, 209, 211, 213, 214, 215, 216, 222, 224, 227, 228, 229, 231, 232, 234, 235, 237, 238

Chinese 7, 16, 47, 48, 49, 53, 54, 58, 59, 62, 65, 66, 69, 70, 71, 72, 73, 74, 75, 76, 77, 78, 79, 80, 81, 82, 83, 84, 85, 86, 87, 88, 94, 95, 96, 97, 103, 104, 110, 111, 143, 153, 156, 157, 158, 163, 203, 272, 273, 279

Community-Based Research 18, 177, 178

community-based programmes, 18, 173, 179

Cosmopolitanism 219, 236

critical literacy 38, 39

critical pedagogy 4, 8, 21, 260, 254, 262, 263, 265, 266

cultural and linguistic maintenance 150

cultural competence 46

cultural identity 17, 118, 120, 121, 123, 126, 127, 128, 129, 133, 134, 190, 244, 246

cultural maintenance 17, 146, 147, 149, 151, 156, 164

cultural transition 118, 121, 134

curriculum design 45, 106

deconstruction 228

dialect 26

discrimination 32

educational policies 27

educational practices 31

Ekigusii 199, 202

English literacy 29

foreign languages 26

French 9, 20, 23, 25, 27, 28, 29, 30, 31, 38, 40, 48, 59, 70, 72, 93, 94, 95, 103, 143, 153, 158, 170, 172, 194, 199, 200, 211, 214, 225, 226, 234, 238, 239, 265, 267, 269, 270, 271, 279, 251, 252

German 9, 17, 28, 59, 94, 95, 103, 117, 122, 124, 136, 140, 143, 144, 153, 158, 225, 226, 236, 239, 267, 268, 270, 271, 272, 273, 274, 275, 277, 278, 279

Greek 6, 18, 48, 94, 95, 104, 110, 146, 153, 158, 159, 161, 163, 164, 166, 171, 172, 173, 178, 179, 180, 181, 182, 183, 184, 185, 186, 189, 190, 191, 268, 269, 270, 272, 273, 274, 275, 277, 278

heritage language 23

heteroglossia 83

Hindi 38, 48, 49, 62, 95, 104, 158, 269, 277

home language 15, 23, 30, 34, 35, 36, 40, 52, 80, 100, 167, 175, 198, 199, 201, 242, 245, 277, 278, 260

home languages 32

human capital 23, 54

identity 40

immigrant 9, 15, 16, 17, 18, 19, 20, 25, 26, 36, 43, 48, 54, 68, 69, 77, 92, 93, 113, 115, 116, 117, 118, 119, 120, 121, 122, 123, 124, 125, 126, 127, 128, 130, 131, 132, 133, 134, 139, 143, 166, 167, 170, 173, 174, 192, 194, 195, 196, 197, 198, 202, 203, 204, 208, 244, 249, 250, 264, 266, 258, 259, 264, 265

indigenous communities 26

instruction 7, 26, 27, 28, 29, 33, 34, 36, 39, 40, 44, 45, 46, 47, 48, 49, 50, 52, 53, 54, 57, 58, 59, 61, 63, 99, 144, 150, 158, 159, 168, 169, 171, 173, 180, 183, 196, 208, 240, 242, 243, 250, 256
international languages 25
Italian 9, 29, 48, 59, 92, 93, 94, 95, 96, 103, 110, 116, 126, 127, 131, 133, 143, 151, 153, 158, 163, 188, 225, 226, 267, 268, 270, 272, 273, 274, 275, 277, 278, 279

Japanese 47, 48, 54, 66, 94, 95, 96, 97, 103, 120, 138, 153, 156, 157, 158

Kiswahili 194, 199, 200, 202, 208
Korean 47, 48, 49, 53, 54, 57, 58, 66, 88, 94, 95, 96, 103, 156, 157, 158, 163, 269, 277

language loss 20, 77, 209, 266, 252
language shift 16, 19, 43, 69, 70, 77, 82, 173, 174, 176, 192, 195, 196, 202, 259
linguistic diversity 7, 12, 14, 16, 27, 32, 89, 155, 211, 212, 214, 215, 217, 229, 240
linguistic relativity 224, 225, 226

minority languages 18, 19, 68, 77, 79, 80, 82, 167, 192, 195, 196, 201, 204, 205, 208, 252
minority populations 83
multicompetence 101
multiculturalism 13, 27, 91, 92, 98, 112, 147, 148, 149, 153, 154, 155, 164, 171, 217, 267, 251, 252
multilingualism 13, 16, 17, 27, 65, 69, 82, 83, 85, 86, 91, 92, 98, 100, 136, 137, 147, 152, 163, 186, 187, 188, 194, 195, 206, 215, 217, 219, 221, 234, 235, 236, 237, 260, 267
multilinguality 16, 100, 101
multimodality 13, 101

neoliberalism 140, 141, 147
non-official languages 21, 30, 38, 168, 171, 184, 265, 266, 267, 274, 275, 277, 251, 252

official languages 19, 21, 25, 27, 29, 68, 69, 70, 82, 83, 170, 194, 211, 221, 231, 266, 267, 268, 270, 271, 274, 275, 277, 251
Ontario 30

Persian 57, 58, 95, 277
plurilingual competence 209, 216, 224
pluringualism 23

social competences 141
social justice 14, 147, 151, 154, 254, 263
Spanish 4, 6, 7, 9, 13, 20, 26, 28, 37, 44, 45, 47, 48, 49, 50, 53, 54, 57, 58, 59, 61, 62, 64, 65, 66, 94, 95, 104, 153, 158, 187, 188, 199, 200, 240, 241, 242, 243, 244, 245, 246, 247, 248, 249, 250, 251, 252, 253, 254, 255, 256, 257, 258, 259, 260, 261, 262, 263, 264, 267, 268, 269, 270, 272, 274, 275, 277, 278, 279
Switzerland 3, 9, 17, 113, 115, 116, 117, 120, 122, 124, 131, 133, 136, 137, 138, 139, 214

translanguaging 101, 223, 224, 232, 261, 267, 268
Turkish 158

UNESCO 167, 175, 189

Vietnamese 47, 48, 53, 54, 57, 58, 94, 95, 96, 104, 158, 277
vitality 18, 46, 53, 60, 61, 63, 79, 166, 174, 175, 182, 183